Contents

Contents

Name _____

Strategy Workshop

As you listen to the story "The Pumpkin Runner," by Marsha Diane Arnold, you will stop from time to time to do some activities on these practice pages. These activities will help you think about different strategies that can help you read better. After completing each activity, you will discuss what you've written with your classmates and talk about how to use these strategies.

Remember, strategies can help you become a better reader. Good readers

- use strategies whenever they read

- use different strategies before, during, and after reading

- think about how strategies will help them

Name _____

Strategy I: Predict/Infer

Use this strategy before and during reading to help make predictions about what happens next or what you're going to learn.

Here's how to use the Predict/Infer strategy:

1. Think about the title, the illustrations, and what you have read so far.
2. Tell what you think will happen next—or what you will learn. Thinking about what you already know about the topic may help.
3. Try to figure out things the author does not say directly.

Listen as your teacher begins "The Pumpkin Runner." When your teacher stops, complete the activity to show that you understand how to predict what you think might happen in the story.

Think about the story and respond to the question below.

What do you think might happen in the story?

_____

_____

_____

_____

As you continue listening to the story, think about whether your prediction was right. You might want to change your prediction or write a new one below.

_____

_____

_____

_____

_____

Name _____

Strategy 2: Phonics/Decoding

Use this strategy during reading when you come across a word
you don't know.

Here's how to use the Phonics/Decoding strategy:

1. Look carefully at the word.
2. Look for word parts that you know and think about the
   sounds for the letters.
3. Blend the sounds to read the word.
4. Ask yourself if this is a word you know and whether the
   word makes sense in the sentence.
5. If not, ask yourself what else you can try. Should you look
   in a dictionary?

Listen as your teacher continues to read the story. When your
teacher stops, use the Phonics/Decoding strategy.

Now write down the steps you used to decode the word *hundred*.

_____

_____

_____

_____

_____

_____

_____

_____

_____

_____

Remember to use this strategy whenever you are reading and come
across a word that you don't know.

Name _____

Strategy 3: Monitor/Clarify

Use this strategy during reading whenever you're confused about what you are reading.

Here's how to use the Monitor/Clarify strategy:
- Ask yourself if what you're reading makes sense—or if you are learning what you need to learn.
- If you don't understand something, reread, use the illustrations, or read ahead to see if that helps.

Listen as your teacher continues to read the story. When your teacher stops, complete the activity to show that you understand how to figure out why Joshua tells the man to give Aunt Millie a map of the course.

Think about the story and respond below.

1. What do you know about Joshua?

   _____

   _____

   _____

   _____

2. Can you tell from listening to the story why Joshua talks about checking his herd? Why or why not?

   _____

   _____

   _____

   _____

3. How can you find out why Joshua isn't talking about training?

   _____

   _____

   _____

Name _____

Strategy 4: Question

Use this strategy during and after reading to ask questions about important ideas in the story.

Here's how to use the Question strategy:
- Ask yourself questions about important ideas in the story.
- Ask yourself if you can answer these questions.
- If you can't answer the questions, reread and look for answers in the text. Thinking about what you already know and what you've read in the story may help you.

Listen as your teacher continues to read the story. When your teacher stops, complete the activity to show that you understand how to ask yourself questions about important ideas in the story.

Think about the story and respond below.

Write a question you might ask yourself at this point in the story.

_____

_____

_____

_____

_____

_____

_____

_____

_____

_____

If you can't answer your question now, think about it while you listen to the rest of the story.

Name _____

Strategy 5: Evaluate

Use this strategy during and after reading to help you form an opinion about what you read.

Here's how to use the Evaluate strategy:
- Think about how the author makes the story come alive and makes you want to read it.
- Think about what was entertaining, informative, or useful about the selection.
- Think about how you reacted to the story—how well you understood the selection and whether you enjoyed reading it.

Listen as your teacher continues to read the story. When your teacher stops, complete the activity to show that you are thinking of how you feel about what you are reading and why you feel that way.

Think about the story and respond below.

1. Tell whether or not you think this story is entertaining and why.

_____

_____

_____

2. Is the writing clear and easy to understand?

_____

_____

_____

3. This is an adventurous fiction story. Did the author make the characters believable and interesting?

_____

_____

Name _____

Strategy 6: Summarize

Use this strategy after reading to summarize what you read.

Here's how to use the Summarize strategy:
- Think about the characters.
- Think about where the story takes place.
- Think about the problem in the story and how the characters solve it.
- Think about what happens in the beginning, middle, and end of the story.

Think about the story you just listened to. Complete the activity to show that you understand how to identify important story parts that will help you summarize the story.

Think about the story and respond to the questions below:

1. Who is the main character?

_____

_____

_____

2. Where does the story take place?

_____

_____

_____

3. What is the problem and how is it resolved?

_____

_____

_____

_____

Now use this information to summarize the story for a partner.

Name _____

Think About Journeys

What kinds of journeys do you know about? Use the space below to jot down all kinds of journeys.

Journeys I've taken	Journeys taken by people I know	Journeys from books, the movies, or TV
Answers will vary. **(2 points)**	Answers will vary. **(2)**	Answers will vary. **(2)**

Choose one of the journeys above that was really important to the person who took it, and answer the following questions:

Who took the journey?

Answers will vary. **(1)** _____

Where did that person go and why?

Answers will vary. **(2)** _____

_____

How or why was that experience important?

Answers will vary. **(3)** _____

_____

_____

Assessment Tip: Total **12** Points

Name _____

Challenges Along the Way

As you read, complete the chart below for each story.

	What problems or challenges do the characters face on their journey?	**Why is the journey important to the characters?**
Akiak	injures paw; bad weather; gets disqualified; gets separated from team **(3 points)**	catches up to team on her own; saves the team from going the wrong way; first time that her team wins the race **(3)**
Grandfather's Journey	adjusting to different cultures; torn between two places **(3)**	saw many new places; learned another way of life **(3)**
Finding the Titanic	Ruth: ship sank, couldn't find her family; Ballard: deep water, no one knew exactly where *Titanic* was **(3)**	Ruth: survived a shipwreck; Ballard: first one to locate wreck of *Titanic*, fulfilled lifelong dream **(3)**
By the Shores of Silver Lake	nervous about leaving home and about train ride; noise and size of train scary; amazed at surroundings **(3)**	leave home to move to a new place they haven't seen; journey in a new kind of transportation **(3)**

Assessment Tip: Total **24** Points

Name _____

Cold Words

Match each word to its definition by writing the letter on the line beside the word. Then answer the questions that follow.

<u>c</u> ___ blizzard **(1 point)**

<u>d</u> ___ checkpoint **(1)**

<u>f</u> ___ courageous **(1)**

<u>e</u> ___ experienced **(1)**

<u>a</u> ___ musher **(1)**

<u>b</u> ___ rugged **(1)**

a. the driver of a dogsled team

b. having a rough, uneven surface

c. a very heavy snowstorm with strong winds

d. a place along a route where vehicles or travelers are counted

e. having skill or knowledge from doing something in the past

f. brave

1. How would a **blizzard** affect driving conditions? **(2)**

   Accept varied answers to the questions. _____

   _____

2. What have you done that is **courageous**? **(2)**

   _____

   _____

3. Why does a **musher** have to love animals? **(2)**

   _____

   _____

4. Why do **experienced** drivers make fewer mistakes? **(2)**

   _____

   _____

5. Why is a **checkpoint** a good thing to have in a long race? **(2)**

   _____

   _____

Name _____

Story Map

Main Characters

Akiak, Mick **(1 point)**

Setting

Iditarod race in Alaska **(1)**

Problem Facing Characters (page 37)

Akiak gets separated from Mick and the team by an injury. **(2)**

Step One (page 39)

Akiak escapes her handlers and runs away. **(2)**

Step Two (page 40)

Akiak follows the trail, looking for her team. **(2)**

Step Three (page 42)

Akiak is fed and cheered by onlookers. **(2)**

Solution (pages 49–50)

Akiak finds her team, guides them to victory. **(2)**

Assessment Tip: Total **12** Points

Name _____

Hero of the Trail

Complete the information for the TV special based on *Akiak*.

TV Sports Special

Title character: Akiak **(1 point)**

Brief description: an ambitious 10-year-old lead dog **(1)**

_____

Second main character: Mick **(1)**

Brief description: musher of the team led by Akiak **(1)**

_____

Background about the Iditarod: It's a dogsled race from Anchorage to Nome.

The race is dangerous, so mushers must follow many rules about rest periods and

care of their dogs. **(2)**

Organization of story: follows Akiak and Mick as they proceed day by day **(1)**

_____

Summary: For the first three days, Mick's team runs well. On the fourth day, Akiak

hurts her paw, and Mick tries to send her home. Akiak wants to stay in the race, so

she escapes before boarding the airplane. Mick replaces Akiak with a less

experienced lead dog and races on. Akiak runs alone without food to try to reach

her team. She digs in to wait out a blizzard. Along the trail, volunteers try to catch

Akiak, but she always escapes. By the eighth day, everyone wants her to catch

up with her team. On the ninth day, Mick tries to follow the first-place team, but her

dogs won't follow. Suddenly Akiak appears and shows them the right way to go.

The rules don't allow Akiak back into harness, so Mick takes her on the sled, and

they win the race. **(5)**

Name _____

Universal Knowledge

Read the story. Then complete the chart on the following page.

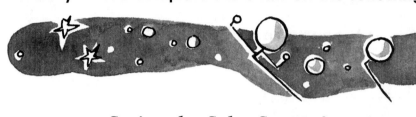

Saving the Solar System!

Justin stood back, turned on the switch, and watched the planets begin to move. He had worked for months creating a motorized model of the solar system to enter in the science fair. And today was the day. He carried the model out to the car, where his mother was waiting.

Jason tried to get the model into the car without damaging any parts. It didn't fit! "Mom!" Justin almost shouted. "Please! Let's ask Mrs. Kravitz from next door if she'll help with her minivan."

Justin explained his problem to Mrs. Kravitz, who smiled and said, "I'd be honored to help save the universe!"

When they finally reached school, Justin removed the model from the minivan, thanked Mrs. Kravitz, and carried in his project. He took his assigned place and then realized that there was no electrical outlet close enough to plug in his model. And the judging was about to start!

Justin spotted the janitor, Mr. Jackson. Justin asked if he might borrow an extension cord. Mr. Jackson smiled as he handed the cord to Justin and said, "I'm happy to do anything to help the universe."

Justin thanked Mr. Jackson, quickly attached the extension cord, and finally plugged in his model. Just as the judges were stepping up to his area, Justin flipped the switch. The planets slowly began to move, just as they should. Justin sighed with relief. The solar system had been saved.

Name _____

Universal Knowledge

**Complete this Problem-Solution Frame for the story
"Saving the Solar System."**

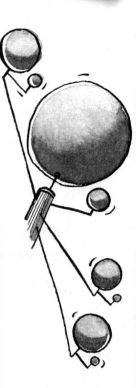

The Problems That Justin Faces and the Solutions He Finds
Problem 1: The model won't fit in his mother's car. **(2 points)**
Solution 1: Mrs. Kravitz drives Justin and his project to school in her minivan. **(2)**
Problem 2: There's no electrical outlet to plug in the model near Justin's assigned place at the science fair. **(2)**
Solution 2: Justin borrows an extension cord from the janitor. **(2)**

If you had been Justin, what would you have done in advance to
avoid the problems he faced on the day of the science fair?
Answers will vary. **(2)**

_____

What might Justin have done if Mrs. Kravitz and her minivan were
unable to transport his project?
Answers will vary. **(2)**

_____

Name _____

Adding -*er* and -*est* to Adjectives

Add -*er* to an adjective to compare two people, places, or things:

Willy's team of dogs is fast**er** than the other team.

Add -*est* to an adjective to compare three or more people, places, or things:

Mick's team is fast**est** of all.

Read each sentence. Change the adjective in parentheses to the correct form as you write it in the puzzle. Remember the spelling rules! (2 points each)

Across

1. People believed Akiak was the (brave) sled dog of all.
3. After the race, Mick was the (happy) musher in Alaska.
4. A dog's undercoat is (fine) than its outer coat.
7. Huskies are not the (friendly) breed of dogs.

Down

2. The ice is (thin) at the edge of the lake than in the middle.
3. The snowfall is (heavy) today than yesterday.
4. Isn't that the (fat) Husky puppy you've ever seen?
5. The cocoa is (hot) than the tea.
6. The sky on the first day was (blue) than a robin's egg.

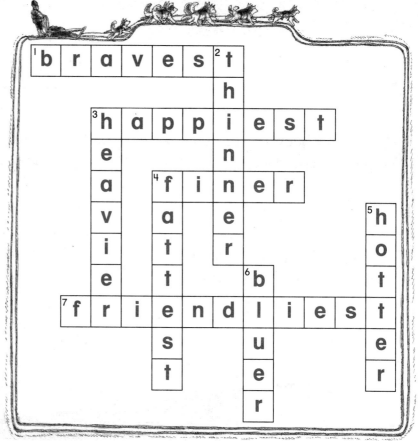

Assessment Tip: Total **18** Points

The /ă/, /ā/, /ĕ/, and /ē/ Sounds

Remember that the /ă/ sound is usually spelled *a* followed by a consonant sound. When you hear the /ā/ sound, think of the patterns *a*-consonant-*e*, *ai*, and *ay*.

/ă/ p**a**st   /ā/ s**a**f**e**, g**ai**n, gr**ay**

Remember that the /ĕ/ sound is usually spelled *e* followed by a consonant sound. When you hear the /ē/ sound, think of the patterns *ea* and *ee*.

/ĕ/ k**e**pt   /ē/ cr**ea**m, sw**ee**t

► In the starred words *break* and *steak*, *ea* spells the /ā/ sound, not the /ē/ sound.

► In the starred words *field* and *chief*, the /ē/ sound is spelled *ie*.

Write each Spelling Word under its vowel sound.

Order of answers for each category may vary.

/ă/ Sound
past **(1 point)**

glass **(1)**

/ā/ Sound
gain **(1)**

safe **(1)**

gray **(1)**

break **(1)**

shape **(1)**

pray **(1)**

pain **(1)**

steak **(1)**

/ĕ/ Sound
kept **(1)**

west **(1)**

/ē/ Sound
cream **(1)**

sweet **(1)**

reach **(1)**

field **(1)**

east **(1)**

steep **(1)**

cheap **(1)**

chief **(1)**

Spelling Words

1. gain
2. cream
3. sweet
4. safe
5. past
6. reach
7. kept
8. gray
9. field*
10. break*
11. east
12. shape
13. steep
14. pray
15. pain
16. glass
17. west
18. cheap
19. steak*
20. chief*

Assessment Tip: Total **20** Points

Name _____

Spelling Spree

Finding Words Write the Spelling Word hidden in each word below.

1. painting   pain **(1 point)**

2. reshapes   shape **(1)**

3. cheapest   cheap **(1)**

4. screams   cream **(1)**

5. again   gain **(1)**

6. preacher   reach **(1)**

7. sprayer   pray **(1)**

8. pasture   past **(1)**

POSTAGE

Familiar Phrases Write the Spelling Word that completes each phrase.

9. grill a steak **(1)**

10. found safe **(1)** and sound

11. tastes as sweet **(1)** as honey

12. a big glass **(1)** of milk

13. the chief **(1)** of police

14. kept **(1)** a secret

15. a field **(1)** of wheat

Spelling Words

1. gain
2. cream
3. sweet
4. safe
5. past
6. reach
7. kept
8. gray
9. field*
10. break*
11. east
12. shape
13. steep
14. pray
15. pain
16. glass
17. west
18. cheap
19. steak*
20. chief*

Assessment Tip: Total **15** Points

Name _____

Proofreading and Writing

Proofreading Circle the five misspelled Spelling Words in this weather report. Then write each word correctly.

The weather for this week's Iditarod will start off cold and (grae.) Then a storm front from the (wast) will bring snow to the area. The snow will be very heavy to the (est,) up in the mountains. If you're traveling in that area, play it safe! Watch out for ice on the (steap) hills. We should get a (braek) in the weather later in the week. The clouds will move away, the sun will return, and the temperature will warm up to just below freezing!

Spelling Words

1. gain
2. cream
3. sweet
4. safe
5. past
6. reach
7. kept
8. gray
9. field*
10. break*
11. east
12. shape
13. steep
14. pray
15. pain
16. glass
17. west
18. cheap
19. steak*
20. chief*

1. gray **(1 point)**
2. west **(1)**
3. east **(1)**
4. steep **(1)**
5. break **(1)**

✏️➤ **Write an Explanation** The Iditarod is a difficult race that requires skill, courage, and lots of training. Do you like snowstorms and sledding? Have you ever trained a dog? Would you like to race in the Iditarod? Why or why not?

On a separate piece of paper, write a paragraph explaining why you would or would not like to take part in the race. Use Spelling Words from the list. Responses will vary. **(5 points)**

Name _____

Multiple-Meaning Words

> **de•scent** (di sent´) *noun* **1.** Movement from a higher place to a lower one: *the descent of an elevator.* **2.** Downward slope or inclination: *a staircase with a steep descent.* **3.** Ancestry or birth: *That family is of Russian descent.* **4.** A sudden attack: *The bird's descent on the worm was swift.*

For each sentence, choose the correct definition of the underlined word and write its number on the line.

1. The hill's <u>descent</u> was not very steep, so we reached the bottom easily. <u>2 **(1 point)**</u>

2. Many people of Inuit <u>descent</u> live in Alaska. <u>3 **(1)**</u>

3. The explorers had a difficult <u>descent</u> down the rocky mountain. <u>1 **(1)**</u>

4. The hungry dogs made a quick <u>descent</u> on the food. <u>4 **(1)**</u>

> **ref•uge** (ref´ ūj) *noun* **1.** Shelter or protection from danger: *The frightened cat took refuge under the bed.* **2.** A place providing shelter or protection: *There are many animals in the wildlife refuge.* **3.** A source of comfort or relief: *Listening to music is her refuge when she's feeling sad.*

For each underlined word, choose the correct definition and write its number on the line at the end of the sentence.

5. The injured elephant was sent to a <u>refuge</u> for sick animals. <u>2 **(1)**</u>

6. During the blizzard, the lost dog found <u>refuge</u> behind a snowdrift. <u>1 **(1)**</u>

7. After losing the game, the team took <u>refuge</u> in knowing that they played their best. <u>3 **(1)**</u>

8. The huge tree provided a <u>refuge</u> for the bird's nest. <u>2 **(1)**</u>

Assessment Tip: Total **8** Points

Finding Kinds of Sentences

Rewrite each sentence on the lines below, adding the correct end mark. Then write what type of sentence it is.

1. The trail is very long and difficult

   The trail is very long and difficult. statement **(2 points)**

   _____

2. Did Akiak ever win a race before

   Did Akiak ever win a race before? question **(2)**

   _____

3. How many teams began the race

   How many teams began the race? question **(2)**

   _____

4. What a smart lead dog she is

   What a smart lead dog she is! exclamation **(2)**

   _____

5. Hold on to the dog, please

   Hold on to the dog, please. command **(2)**

   _____

Name _____

Sentences About Alaska

Read the facts below about Alaska, and use the facts to write five sentences. Write at least one command, one question, one statement, and one exclamation.

Facts

- became 49th state in 1959
- largest state of all
- Mt. McKinley: highest mountain in North America
- Yukon River: 2,000 miles long
- many active volcanoes
- midsummer sun shines all night
- capital is Juneau
- Iditarod race in March each year

1. Responses may vary. **(2 points)** _____

_____

2. **(2)** _____

_____

3. **(2)** _____

_____

4. **(2)** _____

_____

5. **(2)** _____

_____

Assessment Tip: Total **10** Points

Akiak

Grammar Skill Improving
Your Writing

Capitalizing and Punctuating Sentences

Careful writers capitalize the first word of every sentence and make sure that each sentence has the right end mark. Read the sentences below. Rewrite each sentence, adding capital letters and end marks where needed. Then write what kind of sentence each is.

1. this race was the first one for some dogs

   This race was the first one for some dogs. statement **(2 points)**

2. did you ever see the Iditarod race

   Did you ever see the Iditarod race? question **(2)**

3. how fast the sled dogs run

   How fast the sled dogs run! exclamation **(2)**

4. watch the lead dog of the sled team

   Watch the lead dog of the sled team. command **(2)**

5. which team won the race

   Which team won the race? question **(2)**

Name _____

Planning Chart

Use this chart to help you plan your news article.

Topic of news article: _____

Who?	What?
(2 points)	(2)
When?	**Where?**
(2)	(2)
Why?	**How?**
(2)	(2)

Assessment Tip: Total **12** Points

Name _____

Adding Details

From the details given below, choose the detail that you think adds the right information to each sentence and write it in the blank provided.

> Through icy water and confusing trails   fifty-eight
>
> a maze of   deep, wet
>
> wait out the storm   From Anchorage to Nome,

1. From Anchorage to Nome **(2 points)** _____,
   the sled dog teams battled wind, snow, and steep, rugged trails.

2. The race began and one by one, the <u>fifty-eight</u> **(2)** _____
   teams took off.

3. Through icy water and confusing trails **(2)** _____,
   Akiak never got lost, but always found the safest and fastest way.

4. Akiak was limping because the
   deep, wet **(2)** _____

   snow had made one of her paws sore.

5. Akiak burrowed into a snowdrift to <u>wait out the storm</u> **(2)** _____

   _____.

6. Halfway to the checkpoint, Mick's team came upon
   a maze of **(2)** _____ snowmobile tracks.

Name _____

Evaluating Your Personal Narrative

Reread your story. What do you need to make it better? Use this page to help you decide. Put a checkmark in the box for each sentence that describes your personal narrative.

Rings the Bell!

☐ The beginning catches the reader's interest.

☐ The story is told in sequence and is easy to follow.

☐ Everything in my story is important to the topic.

☐ The sentences flow smoothly and don't repeat unnecessary information.

☐ There are almost no mistakes.

Getting Stronger

☐ The beginning could be more interesting.

☐ The sequence of events isn't always clear.

☐ There are some things that I could take out that don't relate to the story topic.

☐ I could combine some sentences to make this flow more smoothly.

☐ There are a few mistakes.

Try Harder

☐ The beginning is boring.

☐ Events are out of order and confusing to the reader.

☐ A lot of the story doesn't relate to the main topic.

☐ There are a lot of mistakes.

Name _____

Varying Sentences

Change these paragraphs in the spaces provided. Each paragraph should have at least one example of each type of sentence: declarative, interrogative, command, and exclamatory.
Answers may vary.

Balloon Bread
No Sentence Variation

My mom and I made bread. We mixed warm water and flour. We added yeast. We let the dough rise. The dough kept rising and rising. We baked the bread. It came out way too light and fluffy — like a balloon. We put in too much yeast. Better luck next time.

Balloon Bread
Sentence Variation

(5 points) _____

_____

_____

Junk Food
No Sentence Variation

Am I unusual? Why don't I like junk food? Why do I lose my appetite at fast food places? Do you like junk food? Does it make you sick? Do you think it's unhealthy? If so, then why do you eat it? And why does everyone else like it so much? Why am I so confused?

Junk Food
Sentence Variation

(5) _____

_____

_____

Name _____

Spelling Words

Words Often Misspelled Look for familiar spelling patterns to help you remember how to spell the Spelling Words on this page. Think carefully about the parts that you find hard to spell in each word.

Write the missing letters and apostrophes in the Spelling Words below.

1. ca n___ n___ ot **(1 point)**
2. ca n___ '___ t___ **(1)**
3. do n___ '___ t___ **(1)**
4. hav e___ n___ '___ t___ **(1)**
5. w o___ n___ 't **(1)**
6. w o___ u___ l___ dn't **(1)**
7. I '___ d___ **(1)**
8. I' l___ l___ **(1)**
9. let '___ s___ **(1)**
10. we '___ r___ e___ **(1)**
11. I '___ m___ **(1)**
12. did n___ '___ t___ **(1)**
13. o___ '___ c___ lock **(1)**
14. that '___ s___ **(1)**
15. ther e___ '___ s___ **(1)**

1. cannot
2. can't
3. don't
4. haven't
5. won't
6. wouldn't
7. I'd
8. I'll
9. let's
10. we're
11. I'm
12. didn't
13. o'clock
14. that's
15. there's

Study List On a separate piece of paper, write each Spelling Word. Check your spelling against the words on the list. Order of words may vary.

Spelling Spree

Write the Spelling Word that fits each clue.

1. If you're talking about your future, you might use this contraction. I'll **(1 point)**

2-3. This contraction and this word both say you're not able to do something. can't, cannot **(1)**

4. A group of people talking about themselves might use this contraction. we're **(1)**

5. This contraction tells you things not to do. don't **(1)**

6. This contraction can tell time. o'clock **(1)**

7. This contraction is the past tense of *doesn't.* didn't **(1)**

8. This contraction is a quick way to say you don't have something. haven't **(1)**

9. "I will not" can also be said "I won't **(1)** ."

Find a Rhyme Write a Spelling Word that rhymes with the underlined word. Be sure it makes sense.

10. I'm **(1)** trying to find words that <u>rhyme</u>.

11. Ina <u>couldn't</u> pay attention to the movie because Ben wouldn't **(1)** leave her alone.

12. If my ankle wasn't hurting me, I'd **(1)** try to <u>ride</u> that horse.

13. My sister said there's **(1)** a kid in her class who eats four <u>pears</u> for lunch every day.

14. Well, let's **(1)** see who <u>gets</u> to the end of the block the quickest.

15. I think that's **(1)** the girl who <u>bats</u> from both sides of the plate.

Spelling Words

1. cannot
2. can't
3. don't
4. haven't
5. won't
6. wouldn't
7. I'd
8. I'll
9. let's
10. we're
11. I'm
12. didn't
13. o'clock
14. that's
15. there's

did not = didn't

I will = I'll

of the clock = o'clock

Theme 1: **Journeys** 21

Assessment Tip: Total **15** Points

Proofreading and Writing

Proofreading Circle the five misspelled Spelling Words in this advertisement. Then write each word correctly.

1. cannot
2. can't
3. don't
4. haven't
5. won't
6. wouldn't
7. I'd
8. I'll
9. let's
10. we're
11. I'm
12. didn't
13. o'clock
14. that's
15. there's

Think you (dont) have enough money to take a journey? Think again! With Express Airlines' new sale fares, you (ca'nt) afford not to travel! We've got flights going all over the country, at prices you won't believe. You can leave any time between six (oclock) in the morning and midnight. And (we'ere) proud to offer the best service of any airline out there. So you see, (theres) no reason not to fly with us!

1. don't **(1 point)**

2. can't **(1)**

3. o'clock **(1)**

4. we're **(1)**

5. there's **(1)**

Journey Sentences Suppose you were going on a journey to a place where they spoke a foreign language. What are some things you might want to know how to say once you got there?

On a separate piece of paper, write five sentences you would want to know for your journey. Use Spelling Words from the list. Responses will vary. **(5 points)**

Name _____

Traveling Words

Write the words next to their definitions. Unscramble the circled letters to answer the question that follows.

Vocabulary

bewildered	homeland	longed
marveled	reminded	surrounded

1. country you were born in **(1)**

h	o	m	e	l	(a)	n	d

2. wanted very much **(1)**

l	o	(n)	g	e	d

3. filled with wonder **(1)**

m	(a)	r	(v)	e	l	e	d

4. puzzled greatly **(1)**

b	(e)	w	i	l	d	e	(r)	e	d

5. made someone remember **(1)**

r	e	m	(i)	n	d	e	d

6. put all around **(1)**

s	u	r	r	(o)	u	n	d	e	d

What is a word for someone who takes a trip?

v	a	c	a	t	i	o	n	e	r

(2)

Assessment Tip: Total **8** Points

Name _____

Word Web

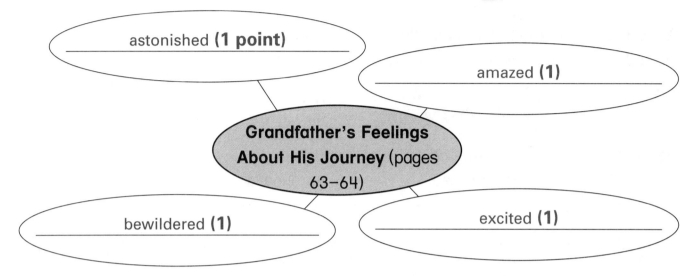

astonished **(1 point)**

amazed **(1)**

Grandfather's Feelings About His Journey (pages 63–64)

bewildered **(1)**

excited **(1)**

Author's Viewpoint

I can infer that the author thinks America is a wonderful place. **(2)**

_____

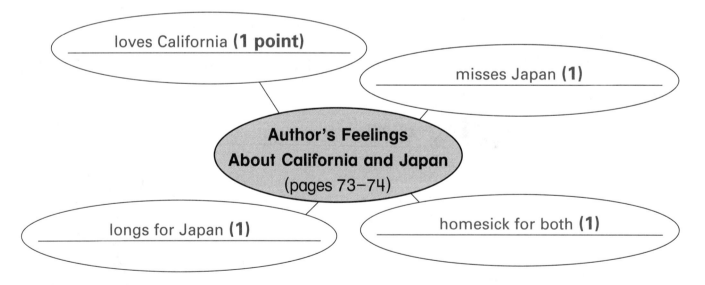

loves California **(1 point)**

misses Japan **(1)**

Author's Feelings About California and Japan (pages 73–74)

longs for Japan **(1)**

homesick for both **(1)**

Author's Viewpoint

I can infer that the author feels that both countries are very important to him. **(2)**

_____

Assessment Tip: Total **12** Points

Name _____

Grandfather's Diary

Help grandfather write his diary by filling in the blanks.

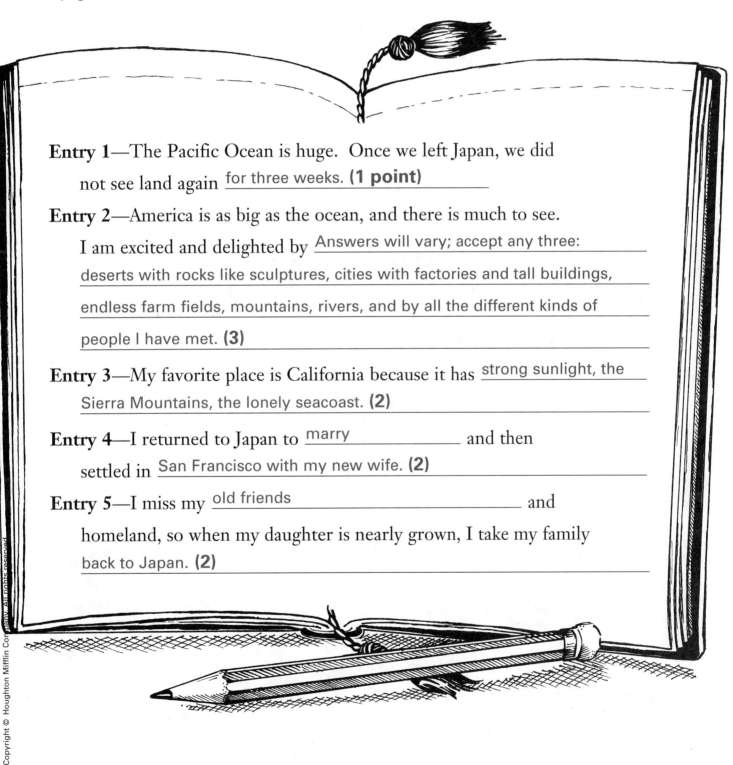

Entry 1—The Pacific Ocean is huge. Once we left Japan, we did not see land again <u>for three weeks.</u> **(1 point)**

Entry 2—America is as big as the ocean, and there is much to see. I am excited and delighted by <u>Answers will vary; accept any three:</u> <u>deserts with rocks like sculptures, cities with factories and tall buildings,</u> <u>endless farm fields, mountains, rivers, and by all the different kinds of</u> <u>people I have met.</u> **(3)**

Entry 3—My favorite place is California because it has <u>strong sunlight, the</u> <u>Sierra Mountains, the lonely seacoast.</u> **(2)**

Entry 4—I returned to Japan to <u>marry</u> and then settled in <u>San Francisco with my new wife.</u> **(2)**

Entry 5—I miss my <u>old friends</u> and homeland, so when my daughter is nearly grown, I take my family <u>back to Japan.</u> **(2)**

Name _____

A Moving View

Read the story. Then answer the questions on the following page.

Saying Good-bye, Saying Hello

"Hurry up, Anna! We've got a long drive ahead of us! We've got to get started now!" Recently, all my father seemed to do was shout. All I did was mope and complain. It only seemed fair because we were moving away from our home and from the friends I loved. As our car pulled away from the curb, I waved weakly at Andrea and Kelly. They were my very best friends in the whole world. And even though they promised to write every day, I knew our friendship might never be the same.

On the long drive from Indiana to New Mexico, my father talked and talked and talked about how happy we were going to be in our new home near my grandparents. But I didn't care. All I could think of was losing my whole life.

When I opened my eyes, the gentle desert sunlight smiled hello to me. We turned down a dirt road and out of a sand-colored house came running my grandparents and many other smiling relatives. My cousin Sunita pulled me away from the crowd and told me that we would be going to the same school and might even be in the same class. She also told me her favorite jokes, and I started laughing really hard.

I thought to myself, "Maybe I only left a part of my life behind. Maybe this next part will also be wonderful."

Name _____

A Moving View continued

Answer these questions that refer to the story "Saying Good-bye, Saying Hello." Accept reasonably varied answers.

What phrases does the narrator use to describe moving from Indiana?

mope and complain, waved weakly, losing my whole life **(3 points)**

What can you infer about the narrator's feelings toward Indiana?

She loves it there. She can't imagine living in a better place. **(3)**

What phrases describe the narrator's experience in New Mexico?

gentle sun smiled, smiling relatives, she laughs **(3)**

How does the narrator feel about New Mexico?

She likes it there because everyone is nice and she is surrounded

by family. **(3)**

What is the author's purpose in writing this story?

To tell readers that one bad experience in life won't ruin everything **(3)**

Name _____

Suffixes -*ly* and -*y*

Add -*ly* or -*y* to a base word to mean "in the manner of."

high/high**ly**   rain/rain**y**

When a base word ends in a consonant and *y*, change the *y* to *i* before adding -*ly*.

speed**y**/speed**ily**   easy/eas**ily**

When a base word ends in a short vowel and a consonant, double the consonant before adding -*y*.

fog/fog**gy**   tin/tin**ny**

**Choose one of the pictures to write about in a short paragraph.
Add -*y* or -*ly* to at least four of the words under the picture. Use
them in your paragraph.**

| chill | happy | haste | salt | | sad | merry | luck | sun |
| final | fog | sudden | weary | | silk | lone | hungry | soft |

Accept all reasonable paragraphs. **(10 points)**

_____

_____

_____

_____

       Assessment Tip: Total **10** Points

Name _____

The /ĭ/, /ī/, /ŏ/, and /ō/ Sounds

Remember that the /ĭ/ sound is often spelled *i* followed by a consonant sound. When you hear the /ī/ sound, think of the patterns *i-consonant-e*, *igh*, and *i*.

/ĭ/ st**i**ll   /ī/ cr**ime**, fl**igh**t, gr**i**nd

► In the starred words *build* and *built*, the /ĭ/ sound is spelled *ui*.

Remember that the /ŏ/ sound is usually spelled *o* followed by a consonant sound. When you hear the /ō/ sound, think of the patterns *o-consonant-e*, *oa*, *ow*, and *o*.

/ŏ/ **o**dd   /ō/ wr**ote**, c**oa**st, sn**ow**, g**o**ld

Write each Spelling Word under its vowel sound.
Order of answers for each category may vary.

/ĭ/ Sound
still **(1 point)**

build **(1)**

inch **(1)**

built **(1)**

/ī/ Sound
grind **(1)**

crime **(1)**

flight **(1)**

blind **(1)**

ripe **(1)**

sigh **(1)**

/ŏ/ Sound
odd **(1)**

shock **(1)**

/ō/ Sound
snow **(1)**

coast **(1)**

gold **(1)**

wrote **(1)**

broke **(1)**

folk **(1)**

grown **(1)**

coal **(1)**

Name _____

Spelling Spree

Letter Math Write a Spelling Word by adding and subtracting letters from the words below.

Example: sm + poke – p = *smoke*

1. s + high – h = <u>sigh **(1 point)**</u>

2. b + quilt – q = <u>built **(1)**</u>

3. c + goal – g = <u>coal **(1)**</u>

4. gr + blown – bl = <u>grown **(1)**</u>

5. r + swipe – sw = <u>ripe **(1)**</u>

6. f + yolk – y = <u>folk **(1)**</u>

7. cr + slime – sl = <u>crime **(1)**</u>

Inside Switch Change one letter on the inside of each word to make a Spelling Word. Write the words.

Example: drip *drop*

8. grand   <u>grind **(1)**</u>

9. shack   <u>shock **(1)**</u>

10. blond   <u>blind **(1)**</u>

11. itch   <u>inch **(1)**</u>

12. old   <u>odd **(1)**</u>

13. brake   <u>broke **(1)**</u>

14. stall   <u>still **(1)**</u>

15. write   <u>wrote **(1)**</u>

Spelling Words

1. snow
2. grind
3. still
4. coast
5. odd
6. crime
7. gold
8. wrote
9. flight
10. build*
11. broke
12. blind
13. folk
14. grown
15. shock
16. ripe
17. coal
18. inch
19. sigh
20. built*

Assessment Tip: Total **15** Points

Name _____

Proofreading and Writing

Proofreading Circle the five misspelled Spelling Words in the tour schedule. Then write each word correctly.

California Dream Tour!

Day 1: Your plane lands in Los Angeles. Tour this famous city. Then ride along the area's beautiful (cost.)

Day 2: Spend a relaxing day on the beach at Santa Monica. Sun, surf, or (bild) your own sandcastle.

Day 3: Ride by bus to Yosemite National Park. Play in the (sno) on the mountains, then rest up at the lodge.

Day 4: Visit Sacramento. Explore the spot where (golde) was discovered in 1848. Pan for any of the precious metal that might still be left in the mountain streams.

Day 5: Take a bus to beautiful San Francisco and catch your (flite) home.

1. coast **(1 point)**   4. gold **(1)**

2. build **(1)**   5. flight **(1)**

3. snow **(1)**

Spelling Words

1. snow
2. grind
3. still
4. coast
5. odd
6. crime
7. gold
8. wrote
9. flight
10. build*
11. broke
12. blind
13. folk
14. grown
15. shock
16. ripe
17. coal
18. inch
19. sigh
20. built*

Write a Contest Entry A local travel agency is having a contest. First prize is a trip to anywhere in the United States. Where would you go if you had the opportunity? Would it be San Francisco? The Rocky Mountains? The Florida Everglades?

On a separate piece of paper, write a paragraph telling where you would go if you won the contest and why you want to go there. Use Spelling Words from the list. Responses will vary. **(5 points)**

Name _____

What's the Order?

**Put each group of words in alphabetical order. Write the words
on the lines provided.**

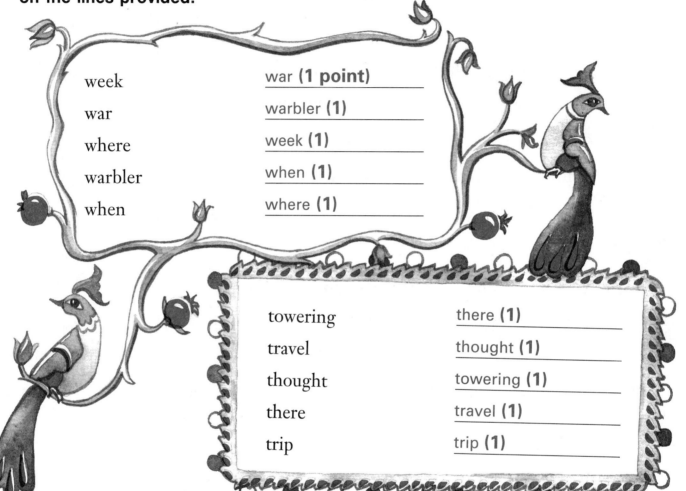

week	war **(1 point)**
war	warbler **(1)**
where	week **(1)**
warbler	when **(1)**
when	where **(1)**

towering	there **(1)**
travel	thought **(1)**
thought	towering **(1)**
there	travel **(1)**
trip	trip **(1)**

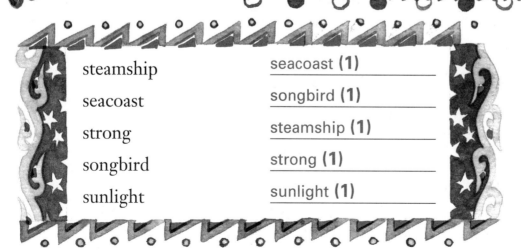

steamship	seacoast **(1)**
seacoast	songbird **(1)**
strong	steamship **(1)**
songbird	strong **(1)**
sunlight	sunlight **(1)**

Assessment Tip: Total **15** Points

Name _____

Identifying Subjects and Predicates

Rewrite each sentence and draw a vertical line between the complete subject and the complete predicate of each sentence. Then circle the simple subject and underline the simple predicate.

1. (Grandfather) <u>met</u> many different people in his travels.

   Grandfather | met many different people in his travels. **(4 points)**

2. The (seacoast) of California <u>appealed</u> to him.

   The seacoast of California | appealed to him. **(4)**

3. The young (man) <u>found</u> a bride in Japan.

   The young man | found a bride in Japan. **(4)**

4. The two (people) <u>made</u> their home in San Francisco.

   The two people | made their home in San Francisco. **(4)**

5. (Memories) of Japan <u>filled</u> Grandfather's mind.

   Memories of Japan | filled Grandfather's mind. **(4)**

Name _____

Connecting Subjects and Predicates

Draw a line connecting each subject in Column 1 with the predicate in Column 2 that makes the most sense. Put the two sentence parts together and write the whole sentence on the lines below. Then circle the simple subject and underline the simple predicate of each sentence you wrote.

Column 1	Column 2
1. The old man	a. went back home with him.
2. Songbirds	b. laughed with him.
3. The man's family	c. reminded him of Japan.
4. His old friends	d. married a man in Japan.
5. The couple's daughter	e. remembered his homeland fondly.

1. The old (man) remembered his homeland fondly. **(4 points)**

2. (Songbirds) reminded him of Japan. **(4)**

3. The man's (family) went back home with him. **(4)**

4. His old (friends) laughed with him. **(4)**

5. The couple's (daughter) married a man in Japan. **(4)**

Name _____

Sentence Combining

Use the joining word in parentheses to combine each pair of sentences below with a compound subject or a compound predicate. Write the new sentence. Then circle the compound part in your new sentence and write whether it is a compound subject or a compound predicate.

1. The grandfather talked with his grandson.

   The grandfather told stories about California. (and)

   The grandfather (talked with his grandson and told stories about California.) compound predicate **(4)**

2. Grandfather raised songbirds.

   Grandfather loved their songs. (and)

   Grandfather (raised songbirds and loved their songs.) compound predicate **(4)**

3. Warblers were his favorite birds.

   Silvereyes were his favorite birds. (and)

   (Warblers and silvereyes) were his favorite birds. compound subject **(4)**

4. Bombs fell.

   Bombs ruined many homes. (and)

   (Bombs fell and ruined many homes.) compound predicate. **(4)**

5. The old man lost a home.

   His family lost a home. (and)

   (The old man and his family) lost a home. compound subject **(4)**

Name _____

What Are My Thoughts?

Title of Story Responses will vary. **(2 points)** _____

Response Journal

Use the questions below to write your responses to the story.
Responses will vary.

How do I feel about the events of the story?

(1) _____

How do I feel about the main character?

(1) _____

What do I like best about the story? What do I like least?

(1) _____

What do I think will happen next in the story?

(1) _____

What puzzles me about the story?

(1) _____

Which character in the story is most like me? Why?

(1) _____

What else would I like to say about the story?

(2) _____

_____

Name _____

Giving Examples

Improve each of the following response journal entries by adding examples based on *Grandfather's Journey*. Write your examples on the lines provided.

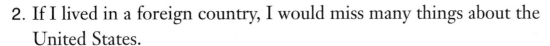

1. If I were to travel in a foreign country, I would like to do and see many things.

   Examples will vary. **(2 points)**

   _____

   _____

2. If I lived in a foreign country, I would miss many things about the United States.

   Examples will vary. **(2)**

   _____

   _____

3. When I was the age of the small boy in the story, I too had a favorite thing to do on a weekend with my family.

   Examples will vary. **(2)**

   _____

   _____

4. Some things puzzle me about the people in the story.

   Examples will vary. **(2)**

   _____

   _____

5. I have some class project ideas related to Japan.

   Examples will vary. **(2)**

   _____

Name _____

Seaworthy Words

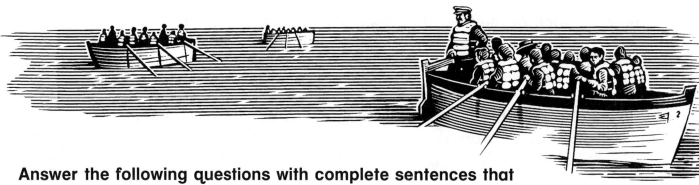

Answer the following questions with complete sentences that show you understand the boldfaced vocabulary words. Accept varied answers.

1. Where would you find a **shipwreck** and what pieces of **wreckage** might you find there?
   (6 points)

   _____

   _____

2. Can an **unsinkable** ship be made? Why or why not?
   (3) _____

   _____

3. Where would you like to take a **voyage**? What would you do on the trip?
   (3) _____

   _____

4. Where might you find **plaques**? Why would they be there?
   (3) _____

   _____

5. What would rescued **survivors** look like?
   (3) _____

   _____

Name _____

Organizational Outline

I. Chapter One

A. Main Idea: _____
   Underwater sled searches for shipwrecked Titanic. **(1 point)**

B. What the pictures show: _____
   the search team watching the pictures the sled is taking **(1)**

II. Chapter Two

A. Main Idea: _____
   Ruth Becker and family begin their voyage. **(1)**

B. What the pictures show: _____
   parts of the ship **(1)**

III. Chapter Three

A. Main Idea: _____
   Titanic hits an iceberg and sinks. **(1)**

B. What the pictures show: _____
   lifeboats being lowered and ship sinking **(1)**

IV. Chapter Four

A. Main Idea: _____
   Survivors are rescued. **(1)**

B. What the pictures show: _____
   survivors in lifeboats and survivors boarding rescue ship **(1)**

V. Chapter Five

A. Main Idea: _____
   Three-man submarine explores the wreck. **(1)**

B. What the pictures show: views seen from sub and robot; a
   newspaper headline about the tragedy **(1)**

Name _____

Time Goes On

Complete the sentences about the time line. Then answer the question below.

1910

April 10, 1912 The *Titanic*, a brand new luxury liner as tall as an <u>eleven-story building</u>, set sail from Southampton, England. **(1 point)**

April 15, 1912 The *Titanic* crashed into an <u>iceberg</u>. Many people were still on board when the giant ship <u>sank **(2)**</u>.

1950

August 25, 1985 The *Titanic* lay <u>two and a half miles down</u> on the ocean floor, too deep for any diver, but the *Argo*, an <u>underwater sled</u> equipped with a video camera, searched and found the *Titanic*. **(2)**

August 31, 1985 The first piece of the *Titanic* found by the cameras was a <u>huge coal boiler</u> used to drive the ship's engines. **(1)**

1980

1985

July 13, 1986 The robot, <u>Jason Junior</u>, photographed the shiny chandelier that hung over the Grand Staircase. **(1)**

1990

How is it possible that the *Titanic* could not be found for seventy-five years but can now be seen and photographed?

<u>New inventions and new advances in technology make all kinds of exploration possible today. **(1)**</u>

Assessment Tip: Total **8** Points

Name _____

Organizing the Wreckage

Read the story. Then answer the questions on the following page.

Why Did the *Lusitania* Sink?

1. Exploring the Wreck

Dr. Robert Ballard, the explorer who discovered the *Titanic*, decided to look for the *Lusitania*. He wanted to find out what caused the huge explosion onboard the ship. He also wanted to know why it sank so quickly. Using high-technology submarines and robots, his crew explored the wreck. What they found was a huge hole in the ship's bow. The hole was right where there were compartments used to store coal, which fueled the ship. And to their amazement, the hole looked like it was blasted from the inside out!

2. Setting Sail

On May 7, 1915, the British ocean liner *Lusitania* was sailing off the coast of Ireland. It was on its way from New York to England. In Europe, World War I was being fought, but no one thought that a submarine would sink an ocean liner filled with passengers. On that day, however, a submarine launched a torpedo toward the *Lusitania*. When the torpedo struck the ship, there was a huge explosion. The ship sank in less than 20 minutes, and many passengers and crew lost their lives.

Time Line: The Wreck of the *Lusitania*

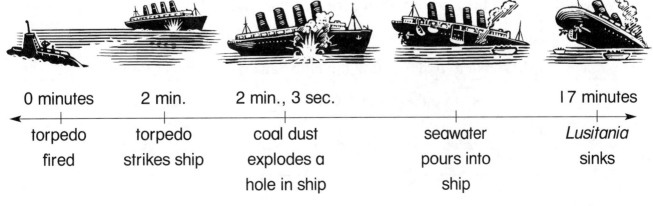

0 minutes	2 min.	2 min., 3 sec.		17 minutes
torpedo fired	torpedo strikes ship	coal dust explodes a hole in ship	seawater pours into ship	*Lusitania* sinks

Name _____

Organizing the Wreckage

continued

Answer the following questions about the sinking of the *Lusitania*.

1. What are this story's special features?

   a story title, chapter titles, a time line **(3 points)**

2. What is the purpose of the visual aid?

   It gives information from the text in a way that is easy to understand. **(3)**

3. How well does this visual aid work? Explain your answer.

   (accept reasonable answers) It works very well. It gives specific information

   about why the ship sank and shows how long it actually took to sink. **(3)**

4. What would you do to better organize this story? Explain
   your answer.

   I would change the story's title. It's too specific. Something like "The Sinking of

   the *Lusitania*" would be better. I would change the order of the paragraphs. It

   makes more sense to explain how the ship sank before talking about exploring

   it. Also, I would rename the second paragraph. It's about the ship sinking, not

   sailing. **(6)**

Name _____

Syllabication

All words contain **syllables**, which are smaller parts you hear when you say a word out loud. For example, the name *Titanic* contains three syllables: /tī - TAN - ĭlkl/. Some long words such as *thought* have only one syllable.

dreamed	largest	passenger
dreamed (one)	larg-est (two)	pas-sen-ger (three)

Use what you've learned about syllabication to break each word into syllables. Rewrite the word to show the syllables. (The first one is done for you.) Then arrange the words with three syllables to make an exciting newspaper headline from 1985.

OCEAN DAILY TIMES

Titanic _____   discovered _____

underneath _____   Atlantic **(4 points)** _____ !

1. cabin	**cab-in**	7. Atlantic	At-lan-tic **(1)**
2. explore	ex-plore **(1)**	8. iceberg	ice-berg **(1)**
3. signals	sig-nals **(1)**	9. discovered	dis-cov-ered **(1)**
4. underneath	un-der-neath **(1)**	10. sinking	sink-ing **(1)**
5. huge	huge **(1)**	11. straight	straight **(1)**
6. bigger	big-ger **(1)**	12. Titanic	Ti-tan-ic **(1)**

Name _____

The /ŭ/, /yo͞o/, and /o͞o/ Sounds

Spelling Words

Remember that the /ŭ/ sound is usually spelled *u* followed by a consonant sound. When you hear the /yo͞o/ or the /o͞o/ sound, think of the patterns *u*-consonant-*e*, *ew*, *ue*, and *ui*.

| /ŭ/ br**u**sh | /yo͞o/ and /o͞o/ t**u**be, f**ew**, tr**ue**, j**ui**ce |

▶ In the starred word *done*, the /ŭ/ sound is spelled *o*. In the starred word *truth*, the /o͞o/ sound is spelled *u*.

Write each Spelling Word under its vowel sound.
Order of answers for each category may vary.

/ŭ/ Sound	/yo͞o/ or /o͞o/ Sound
brush **(1 point)**	juice **(1)**
lunch **(1)**	fruit **(1)**
crumb **(1)**	tube **(1)**
done **(1)**	few **(1)**
pump **(1)**	true **(1)**
dull **(1)**	truth **(1)**
trunk **(1)**	suit **(1)**
sum **(1)**	due **(1)**
	tune **(1)**
	blew **(1)**
	glue **(1)**
	threw **(1)**

1. brush
2. juice
3. fruit
4. tube
5. lunch
6. crumb
7. few
8. true
9. truth*
10. done*
11. suit
12. pump
13. due
14. dull
15. tune
16. blew
17. trunk
18. sum
19. glue
20. threw

Assessment Tip: Total **20** Points

Name _____

Spelling Spree

Word Search **Write the Spelling Word that is hidden in each sentence.**

Example: We found shelter in a small gras<u>s hut</u>. *shut*

1. Don't trip over the cable wire.
2. The two sisters sang a duet.
3. Beth reworded her opening paragraph.
4. You can fill that tub easily with a garden hose.
5. The snowstorm was not unexpected.
6. The frisky lamb rushed to the pasture.
7. The explorers found a small uncharted island.
8. That ruthless villain must be punished!

1. blew **(1 point)**
2. due **(1)**
3. threw **(1)**
4. tube **(1)**
5. tune **(1)**
6. brush **(1)**
7. lunch **(1)**
8. truth **(1)**

Alphabet Puzzler **Write the Spelling Word that would appear alphabetically between each pair of words below.**

9. forest, fruit **(1)** , gate
10. castle, crumb **(1)** , cute
11. trumpet, trunk **(1)** , trust
12. garden, glue **(1)** , hard
13. duke, dull **(1)** , dusty
14. jam, juice **(1)** , justice
15. robot, suit **(1)** , suitcase

Spelling Words

1. brush
2. juice
3. fruit
4. tube
5. lunch
6. crumb
7. few
8. true
9. truth*
10. done*
11. suit
12. pump
13. due
14. dull
15. tune
16. blew
17. trunk
18. sum
19. glue
20. threw

Name _____

Proofreading and Writing

Proofreading Circle the five misspelled Spelling Words in this interview. Then write each word correctly on the lines below.

Reporter: I'm writing a story about the
Titanic. Can you answer a (fue) questions?

Scientist: I'll try. Do you mind if I eat lunch while
we talk?

Reporter: No, I don't mind at all. Tell me, is it (troo)
that the ship broke in two before it sank?

Scientist: Yes, that is correct. After the impact the crew
tried to (pomp) the water out, but it was no use. The
iceberg had (dun) too much damage.

Reporter: Can you (som) up for us what you've learned
from the Titanic?

Scientist: There's no such thing as an unsinkable ship.

Spelling Words

1. brush
2. juice
3. fruit
4. tube
5. lunch
6. crumb
7. few
8. true
9. truth*
10. done*
11. suit
12. pump
13. due
14. dull
15. tune
16. blew
17. trunk
18. sum
19. glue
20. threw

1. few **(1 point)**   4. done **(1)**

2. true **(1)**   5. sum **(1)**

3. pump **(1)**

✏️▸ **Write a Story** Have you ever wondered what you would do in an unfamiliar or dangerous situation? Write the beginning of an adventure story. The setting could be anywhere—an underwater cave or a galaxy far, far away.

On a separate sheet of paper, write the opening paragraph for your story. Use Spelling Words from the list. Responses will vary. **(5)**

Name _____

Find a Better Word

In each sentence, replace the underlined word with a better word or words. Choose your word or words from the thesaurus entries below and write them on the line. Remember that more than one word may be correct in some cases.

1. **bottom:** base, floor, depths, foot, ground
   Many ships have sunk to the <u>bottom</u> of the ocean as a result of accidents or storms at sea.
   floor, depths **(2 points)**
   _____

2. **group:** band, body, crew, crowd, gang, heap
   There was a large <u>group</u> of people on the dock waving good-bye to the passengers.
   band, crowd, gang **(2)**
   _____

3. **recovery:** bailout, release, rescue, salvage
   In the distance the survivors could see the <u>recovery</u> ship.
   rescue **(2)**
   _____

4. **hard:** stable, solid, sound, stout, sturdy, tough
   The <u>hard</u> deck of the ship felt good beneath her feet.
   solid, sturdy **(2)**
   _____

5. **dangerous:** adventurous, bad, perilous, risky, serious
   Alvin's first trip to video the wreckage was <u>dangerous</u>.
   perilous, risky **(2)**
   _____

Name _____

Connecting Compound Sentences

Underline the two sentences that have been combined in the compound sentences below. Then circle the conjunction that joins them.

1. The *Titanic* had nine decks, (and) it was as tall as an eleven-story building. **(2 points)**

2. The Becker family boarded the ship, (and) a steward helped them to find their room. **(2)**

3. Ruth took the elevator to the lowest level, (and) she found a swimming pool there. **(2)**

4. Ruth wanted to go on deck, (but) the weather was too cold. **(2)**

5. The ship was traveling fast, (but) ice could slow it down. **(2)**

Name _____

Compound Sentences in a Letter

Read this student's letter to a friend. On the lines below, write compound sentences.

Dear Sylvia,

I just read about the sinking of the *Titanic*. The author of the piece is a scientist. His name is Robert Ballard, and he explores the oceans. Ballard has found undersea mountains, but he is also interested in sunken ships. He searched the Atlantic Ocean for the *Titanic*, and his crew finally found it. The ship was on its first trip to the United States in 1912. It was supposed to be unsinkable, but it hit an iceberg. The iceberg tore a hole in the hull of the ship, and the ship sank.

　　Your friend,

　　Janice

His name is Robert Ballard, and he explores the oceans. **(2 points)**

Ballard has found undersea mountains, but he is also interested in sunken ships. **(2)**

He searched the Atlantic Ocean for the *Titanic*, and his crew finally found it. **(2)**

It was supposed to be unsinkable, but it hit an iceberg. **(2)**

The iceberg tore a hole in the hull of the ship, and the ship sank. **(2)**

_____

_____

_____

Name _____

Writing Compound Sentences

Good writers often combine two sentences with related ideas into a compound sentence. Read the following pairs of sentences. Then rewrite each pair by combining the sentences into a single compound sentence, adding one of the joining words *and* or *but*. Punctuate the sentences correctly.

1. The three-man crew climbed into the tiny submarine. It slowly went down to the ocean floor.

   The three-man crew climbed into the tiny submarine, and

   it slowly went down to the ocean floor. **(2 points)**

2. The captain looked out the window. A black wall of steel appeared.

   The captain looked out the window, and a black wall of steel appeared. **(2)**

   _____

3. He looked for the yellow letters "Titanic." They were covered over with rust.

   He looked for the yellow letters "Titanic," but they were covered over

   with rust. **(2)**

4. The little robot was steered into a hole in the deck. Soon its camera was taking pictures of the wreck.

   The little robot was steered into a hole in the deck, and soon its camera was

   taking pictures of the wreck. **(2)**

Assessment Tip: Total **8** Points

Writing an Answer to a Question

For each question, write the answer on the lines provided. Write the start of the answer on the first answer line. Write the rest of the answer on the other answer lines. The first one is done for you.

Question: Would you enjoy a camping trip?

Start of answer: Turn question into statement

I would enjoy a camping trip because

Rest of answer: Facts that complete the statement and answer the question asked.

I enjoy outdoor activities such as hiking, rafting, and walking in the forest.

Question: Would you enjoy a train trip?

Start of answer: Turn question into statement

I would/would not enjoy a train trip **(1 point)** _____ because

Rest of answer: Facts that complete the statement and answer the question asked.

Responses will vary. **(3)** _____

_____

_____

Question: Would you enjoy a trip on an ocean liner?

Start of answer: Turn question into statement

I would/would not enjoy a trip on an ocean liner **(1)** _____ because

Rest of answer: Facts that complete the statement and answer the question asked.

Responses will vary. **(3)** _____

_____

_____

Name _____

Writing Complete Sentences

Incomplete sentences can sink your writing, so make sure you know them when you see them! Mark each of these items as follows: If it is an incomplete sentence because it is missing a subject or a predicate, write an X in the "Sink" column. If it is complete write an X in the "Swim" column.

	Sink	Swim
Example: The *Titanic*, the largest ship afloat.	X	
1. Sailed from Southampton, England, to New York.	X **(1)**	
2. Ruth Becker was excited about traveling on the beautiful ship.		X **(1)**
3. Ruth peeked inside an open door to a first-class cabin.		X **(1)**
4. The Beckers and other passengers in the lounge.	X **(1)**	
5. Forgot their life belts.	X **(1)**	
6. The *Titanic*'s twenty lifeboats.	X **(1)**	
7. She asked to get into the lifeboat.		X **(1)**
8. Ruth Becker stood in the lifeboat.		X **(1)**
9. Many survivors' hands.	X **(1)**	
10. Was unwilling to speak about the disaster.	X **(1)**	

Assessment Tip: Total **10** Points

Name _____

Railroad Words

Write an original story using the vocabulary words. The words may be used in any order. Be sure to give your story a title.

(15 points)

_____

_____

_____

_____

_____

_____

_____

_____

_____

_____

_____

_____

_____

_____

_____

_____

_____

Vocabulary

conductor

depot

jolting

lurching

platform

satchels

Name _____

Detail Map

	Details Accept varied answers.
Waiting for the train 	It's a nice sunny day. Ma counts money out of her pocketbook. Laura's hair is braided. Carrie is fidgeting. Carrie worries if Pa will meet them when they arrive. Laura holds onto Mary. Black smoke rolls up from the train's smokestack. train roars and shakes everything **(5 points)**
Riding the train 	The depot slides backward. conductor punches round holes in tickets strips of wood shine like glass two men with hats read a big, white map Laura sways while walking in the train. There's a hole under the tin cup. A boy sells candy for ten cents. train stops with jolting crash **(5 points)**

Assessment Tip: Total **10** Points

Name _____

The Train Ride

Look at the summary of the Ingalls family's train ride. Draw a line through each mistake you find and correct it on the line to the right.

Laura and her family are traveling by train to meet their ~~grandmother~~ in a place far from Plum Creek called ~~Golden~~ Lake. The family has quite a distance to go, so they had to take a train. Travel by train is ~~slower~~ than traveling by horse and buggy, so everyone ~~knows~~ it will be a safe ride. Ma gets the family to the station ~~10 minutes~~ early. The train arrives at the station, and everyone climbs on board.

Because of Mary's blindness, Laura describes the car and passengers for her. The ~~brakeman~~ comes by and punches little holes in everyone's ticket. Laura watches a man go down the aisle to get water. He turns a handle and water flows into a ~~paper~~ cup. Laura went to get some water ~~without~~ Ma's permission and has a hard time walking in the moving train. Laura brought back drinks of water for Carrie and ~~Mary~~. After a while a boy appears in the aisle selling ~~popcorn~~ from a basket. Ma buys some as a special treat on their first train ride. Suddenly it's noon and the train ride is over. (**1 point** for each correction)

father _____

Silver _____

faster _____

hopes _____

one hour _____

conductor _____

tin _____

with _____

Grace _____

candy _____

Theme 1: **Journeys**   55
Assessment Tip: Total **10** Points

Name _____

A Hospital Chart

Read the story. Then complete the Detail Chart on the following page.

"Please, Mom, Tell Me We're Not There Yet!"

When I was little and we were on a car trip, I would ask, "Mom, are we there, yet?" every five minutes. But just last week we went on a car trip and I kept saying, "Please, Mom, tell me we're not there yet!" Why? Mom was driving me to the hospital's emergency room!

It all started on the soccer field. After two minutes of play I fell, grabbing at my stomach. Coach Toth immediately stopped the game. Somehow I made it over to the bench on the sidelines where my mother anxiously waited. My mother and Coach Toth carried me to the car.

I remember looking out the car window on the way to the hospital trying to keep my mind off the pain in my stomach. I saw that someone had painted a house we used to live in a sickening shade of green. I saw the tree that I once fell out of and broke my arm. Then I started to sweat like crazy.

At the emergency room, they kept us waiting only a short time, but it seemed like forever as the pain grew worse. Suddenly a doctor appeared. He seemed to be about eight feet tall. He asked me some questions and felt the sore place on my stomach. I yelled. He asked my mom if I still had my appendix. She told him yes. He said, "Well, she won't for long," and smiled at me. A nurse gave me a shot. The next thing I knew I was wide awake in a hospital room—minus one appendix!

Name _____

A Hospital Chart continued

Complete these Detail Charts for the story "Please, Mom, Tell Me We're Not There Yet!" Answers may vary.

Before the Hospital 	**More Important Details** I had a terrible pain in my stomach. **(1 point)** Then I remember starting to sweat like crazy. **(1)** **Less Important Details** I saw that someone had painted a house we used to live in a sickening shade of green. **(1)** I saw the tree that I once fell out of and broke my arm. **(1)**
At the Hospital 	**More Important Details** The pain in my stomach grew worse. **(1)** Doctor says she won't have an appendix for long. **(1)** **Less Important Details** He seemed to be about eight feet tall. **(1)** A nurse gave me a shot. **(1)**

By the Shores of
Silver Lake
___
Structural Analysis Word
Roots *tele* and *rupt*

Name _____

Word Roots *tele* and *rupt*

Tele and *rupt* are word roots. They have meaning but cannot stand alone. *Tele* means "distance" or "over a distance." *Rupt* means "break."

telescope   television   interrupt   abrupt

Complete each sentence with a word from the box. Use a dictionary to check word meanings if you are not sure which word to choose.

televise	telescope	telegraph	telephone
interrupt	abrupt	disruptive	bankrupt

1. Please don't __interrupt **(1 point)**__ the conductor when he's taking tickets.

2. One of the astronomers carried her __telescope **(1)**__ on the train.

3. Is the noise from the dining car __disruptive **(1)**__?

4. Many railroads went __bankrupt **(1)**__ when the automobile became popular.

5. Will they __televise **(1)**__ the first run of the new high-speed train?

6. Before the invention of the __telegraph **(1)**__, Pony Express was one way to send messages quickly.

7. The train came to an __abrupt **(1)**__ stop when someone pulled the emergency brake.

8. Call me on the __telephone **(1)**__ when you reach the station.

Name _____

Homophones

Homophones are words that sound alike but have different meanings and spellings. When you write a homophone, be sure to spell the word that has the meaning you want.

/stēl/   st**ee**l   a metal made from iron and carbon
/stēl/   st**ea**l   to take without having permission

Write each Spelling Word under the matching sound.
Order of answers for each category may vary.

TICKETS

/ē/ Sound

steel **(1 point)**

steal **(1)**

creak **(1)**

creek **(1)**

beet **(1)**

beat **(1)**

meet **(1)**

meat **(1)**

peek **(1)**

peak **(1)**

/ĕ/ Sound

lead **(1)**

led **(1)**

/ā/ Sound

wait **(1)**

weight **(1)**

Rhymes with *sing*

ring **(1)**

wring **(1)**

Vowel Sound + *r*

wear **(1)**

ware **(1)**

deer **(1)**

dear **(1)**

Spelling Words

1. steel
2. steal
3. lead
4. led
5. wait
6. weight
7. wear
8. ware
9. creak
10. creek
11. beet
12. beat
13. meet
14. meat
15. peek
16. peak
17. deer
18. dear
19. ring
20. wring

Name _____

Spelling Spree

Double Trouble Circle the correct Spelling Word.
Write the words on the lines.

1. Please (ring/**wring**) the clothes dry.

2. I heard the bell (**ring**/wring).

3. In winter I (**wear**/ware) a scarf.

4. Those cabinets hold cooking (wear/**ware**).

5. I write with a (led/**lead**) pencil.

6. She (**led**/lead) the hikers along the trail.

7. A (**beet**/beat) is a red-colored vegetable.

8. She can usually (beet/**beat**) me at chess.

9. A pound is not a lot of (wait/**weight**).

10. It was a long (**wait**/weight) for the bus.

SALE!

HUGE SALE!
on stuffed animals!
PRICES slashed

Spelling Words

1. steel
2. steal
3. lead
4. led
5. wait
6. weight
7. wear
8. ware
9. creak
10. creek
11. beet
12. beat
13. meet
14. meat
15. peek
16. peak
17. deer
18. dear
19. ring
20. wring

1. wring **(1 point)**
2. ring **(1)**
3. wear **(1)**
4. ware **(1)**
5. lead **(1)**

6. led **(1)**
7. beet **(1)**
8. beat **(1)**
9. weight **(1)**
10. wait **(1)**

Hint and Hunt Write the Spelling Word that answers
each question.

11. What is a forest animal with four legs?

12. What do old bones sometimes do?

13. What is a bargain sometimes called?

14. What do you buy from a butcher?

15. What do you write to start a letter?

16. What is part of a game that babies love?

11. deer **(1)**
12. creak **(1)**
13. steal **(1)**
14. meat **(1)**
15. dear **(1)**
16. peek **(1)**

Assessment Tip: Total **16** Points

Proofreading and Writing

Proofreading Circle the five misspelled Spelling Words in this poster. Then write each word correctly.

See the West the Easy Way!

All aboard! Come to the untamed West, where deer, elk, and buffalo still roam the range. Travel on to San Francisco, where the mountains (meat) the sea. Ride the (stel) rails from St. Louis all the way to the Pacific Ocean. Cross every valley, river, and (creak) with ease. See every canyon and snowy (peek) from the comfort of your passenger seat. Don't wait another minute—get your train tickets today!

Spelling Words

1. steel
2. steal
3. lead
4. led
5. wait
6. weight
7. wear
8. ware
9. creak
10. creek
11. beet
12. beat
13. meet
14. meat
15. peek
16. peak
17. deer
18. dear
19. ring
20. wring

1. meet **(1 point)**
2. steel **(1)**
3. creek **(1)**
4. peak **(1)**

✏️ **Write a List of Rules** Laura and her sisters were very careful to behave properly on the train. Have you ever been on a bus, a train, or in any public place where people have behaved in a rude or improper way? How did it make you feel? Think of some rules to remember when sharing a public place with other people.

On a separate sheet of paper, write five rules of good behavior to follow in public places. Use Spelling Words from the list. Responses will vary. **(10 points)**

Name _____

Find the Guide Words

Match each word with the correct guide words. In the first column, write each word under the correct guide words. Then write each word in alphabetical order between the guide words.

bond	boil	immediate
boggle	immense	imagine
bold	imitate	

(Accept words in any order.)

bog/bone

1. bond **(1 point)**
2. boggle **(1)**
3. bold **(1)**
4. boil **(1)**

bog

boggle **(1)**

boil **(1)**

bold **(1)**

bond **(1)**

bone

(Accept words in any order.)

image/immobile

1. immense **(1)**
2. imitate **(1)**
3. immediate **(1)**
4. imagine **(1)**

image

imagine **(1)**

imitate **(1)**

immediate **(1)**

immense **(1)**

immobile

Assessment Tip: Total **16** Points

Name _____

Finding Common Nouns

Read each sentence, and look for common nouns. Then write each common noun on the lines provided.

1. People waited on the platform for the train.
   People   platform   train **(2 points)**

2. A traveler rode along at a speed of twenty miles an hour.
   traveler   speed   miles   hour **(2)**

3. The conductor punched holes in the tickets.
   conductor   holes   tickets **(2)**

4. Many weeks and months had gone by.
   weeks   months **(2)**

5. The family sat on a bench in the station.
   family   bench   station **(2)**

6. The woman bought the tickets with money from her pocketbook.
   woman   tickets   money   pocketbook **(2)**

7. Her dress had a collar and a cuff on each sleeve.
   dress   collar   cuff   sleeve **(2)**

8. One daughter had long hair with braids and a bow.
   daughter   hair   braids   bow **(2)**

9. Black smoke and white steam came out of the smokestack.
   smoke   steam   smokestack **(2)**

10. The passengers gathered up their bags and packages.
    passengers   bags   packages **(2)**

Name _____

Choosing Common Nouns

In each sentence, fill in the blank with a noun from the box. Then, on the following line, write whether the noun you chose names a person, a place, or a thing.

| weeks | holes | conductor | windows |

1. The <u>conductor</u> _____ smiled.

   <u>person</u> **(1 point)**

2. The <u>windows</u> _____ on the train were clear.

   <u>thing</u> **(1)**

3. He punched <u>holes</u> _____ in the tickets.

   <u>thing</u> **(1)**

4. Many <u>weeks</u> _____ had gone by before the trip.

   <u>thing</u> **(1)**

Write two examples of each type of common noun.

Person	Place	Thing
5. <u>Answers will vary.</u>	7. _____	9. _____
6. <u>**(1 point each)**</u>	8. _____	10. _____

Use one of the common nouns you wrote for each category to write your own sentence.

<u>Responses will vary. **(2 points)**</u>

_____

_____

Name _____

Writing Nouns in a Series

Using Commas in a Series Good writers often combine ideas. Sometimes a sentence will have three or more words of the same kind that follow one another in a series. When three or more words are written in a series, a joining word comes before the last word, and the words are separated by commas.

Read each group of sentences. Then combine the sentences into one sentence with words in a series. Add commas where they are needed. Write your sentences on the lines below.

1. a. People carried satchels.
   b. People carried handbags.
   c. People carried packages.

   People carried satchels, handbags, and packages. **(2 points)**

   _____

2. a. Out the train window, Laura could see houses.
   b. Out the train window, Laura could see barns.
   c. Out the train window, Laura could see haystacks.

   Out the train window, Laura could see houses, barns, and haystacks. **(2)**

   _____

3. a. The candy was red.
   b. The candy was yellow.
   c. The candy was striped.

   The candy was red, yellow, and striped. **(2)**

   _____

4. a. Ma gave the boy a nickel.
   b. Ma gave the boy three pennies.
   c. Ma gave the boy two pennies more.

   Ma gave the boy a nickel, three pennies, and two pennies more. **(2)**

   _____

Name _____

Writing a Friendly Letter

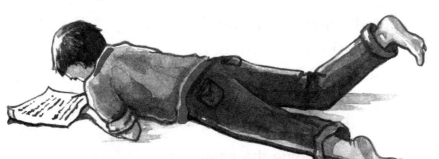

The Person I Am Writing To: **(1 point)**

My Address: **(1)**

The Date: **(1)**

My Greeting: **(1)**

My Purpose in Writing: **(1)**

The Most Important Thing I Want to Say: **(3)**

Important Details I Want to Include: **(3)**

My Closing: **(1)**

Assessment Tip: Total **12** Points

Name _____

Using Commas in Dates and Places

In the following letter, add commas as necessary in dates and place names. Each comma is worth **1 point**.

Paducah, Kentucky
September 14, 1878

Dear Cousin Ethan,

    I am so happy to hear that you are doing well at your new homestead. The town of Tracy, South Dakota, is very lucky to have someone as hardworking as you!

    In your letter of April 23, 1878, you described a family on the train you took to Tracy. There were several daughters. Did you ever meet them?

    Now that you are settled, I would like to come visit you. I can take a train from Cincinnati, Ohio, all the way to Tracy If I arrive on May 4, 1879, will you meet me at the station?

            Your cousin,
            Elizabeth

Name _____

Choosing the Best Answer

Use the test-taking strategies and tips you have learned to help you answer these multiple-choice questions. You may go back to *Akiak* if you need to. This practice will help you when you take this kind of test.

Read each question. Fill in the circle for the best answer in the answer row at the bottom of the page.

1   Where does the story take place?

    A   Alaska   **C**   Greenland

    B   Canada   **D**   Siberia

2   What happened when Mick caught up with Willy?

    F   Willy blocked Mick from passing.

    G   Mick forced Willy off the trail.

    H   Willy pulled over to let Mick pass.

    J   Mick took a different trail to get around Willy.

3   Why did Roscoe take Akiak's place to lead the dog team?

    A   It was Roscoe's turn to lead the team.

    B   Akiak was too old and tired to continue the trip.

    C   Mick thought Roscoe would do a better job than Akiak.

    D   Akiak had a sore pawpad.

4   What happened when the volunteer took Akiak to the airplane?

    F   The dog tipped the plane over.

    G   The dog ran off.

    H   Mick came back for the dog.

    J   The pilot had taken off because of a storm.

ANSWER ROWS   1 Ⓐ Ⓑ Ⓒ Ⓓ **(5 points)**   3 Ⓐ Ⓑ Ⓒ Ⓓ **(5)**

2 Ⓕ Ⓖ Ⓗ Ⓙ **(5)**   4 Ⓕ Ⓖ Ⓗ Ⓙ **(5)**

Name _____

Choosing the Best Answer continued

5 How did Akiak survive the whiteout during the blizzard?

  A She took refuge in Galena.

  B She kept running along the trail.

  C She stayed in a cabin with some volunteers.

  D She burrowed in a snowdrift.

6 What did Akiak find when she reached Elim?

  F The people had put food out for her.

  G The trail volunteers were waiting to catch her.

  H Mick was waiting for her.

  J The mushers were ready to chase her into the community hall.

7 Why doesn't Mick put Akiak back in her usual spot at the harness?

  A Mick thought Akiak was too tired to lead the dog team.

  B Mick was afraid Akiak would get lost.

  C Mick knew it was against the rules.

  D Mick wanted Akiak to stay off her injured pawpad.

8 What was the noise that Mick heard as she approached Nome?

  F It was the sound of another blizzard.

  G It was a crowd of people cheering.

  H It was the dog teams that were ahead of her.

  J It was the roar of snowmobile engines.

ANSWER ROWS 5 Ⓐ Ⓑ Ⓒ ⬤**D** **(5 points)** 7 Ⓐ Ⓑ ⬤**C** Ⓓ **(5)**

  6 ⬤**F** Ⓖ Ⓗ Ⓙ **(5)** 8 Ⓕ ⬤**G** Ⓗ Ⓙ **(5)**

Assessment Tip: Total **40** Points

Name _____

Spelling Review

Write Spelling Words from the list on this page to answer the questions.

Order of answers in each category may vary.

1–15. Which fifteen words have the /ă/ or /ā/ sound or
the /ĕ/ or /ē/ sound?

1. safe **(1 point)**
2. steep **(1)**
3. past **(1)**
4. steel **(1)**
5. kept **(1)**
6. gain **(1)**
7. steal **(1)**
8. reach **(1)**
9. wait **(1)**
10. gray **(1)**
11. weight **(1)**
12. creek **(1)**
13. meat **(1)**
14. creak **(1)**
15. meet **(1)**

16–24. Which nine words have the /ĭ/ or /ī/ sound or the
/ŏ/ or /ō/ sound?

16. sigh **(1)**
17. still **(1)**
18. coast **(1)**
19. grown **(1)**
20. gold **(1)**
21. odd **(1)**
22. wrote **(1)**
23. crime **(1)**
24. blind **(1)**

25–30. Which six words have the /ŭ/, /yo͞o/, or /o͞o/ sound?

25. few **(1)**
26. tube **(1)**
27. suit **(1)**
28. trunk **(1)**
29. true **(1)**
30. crumb **(1)**

Spelling Words

1. safe
2. few
3. tube
4. steep
5. past
6. steel
7. kept
8. gain
9. suit
10. steal
11. reach
12. sigh
13. wait
14. trunk
15. gray
16. still
17. coast
18. weight
19. grown
20. gold
21. odd
22. creek
23. wrote
24. crime
25. meat
26. blind
27. true
28. crumb
29. creak
30. meet

Assessment Tip: Total **30** Points

Name _____

Spelling Spree

Puzzle Play Write the Spelling Word that fits each clue.
Then use the letters in the boxes to write the secret word.
Begin the secret word with a capital letter.

Spelling Words

1. past
2. weight
3. kept
4. steel
5. creek
6. still
7. meat
8. blind
9. creak
10. steal
11. trunk
12. tube
13. crumb
14. wait
15. meet

1. did not throw out   k e p [t] **(1 point)**

2. unable to see   b l [i] n d **(1)**

3. what toothpaste comes in   [t] u b e **(1)**

4. opposite of future   p [a] s t **(1)**

5. a large box for storage or travel   t r u [n] k **(1)**

6. not moving   s t [i] l l **(1)**

7. a tiny piece of food   [c] r u m b **(1)**

Secret Word: _Titanic_

Hint: This famous ship struck an iceberg and sank on its first journey.

Homophone Hunt Write two Spelling Words that sound the same in each sentence.

8. We always _meet **(1 point)**_ in the butcher shop to buy _meat **(1)**_.

9. I can't _wait **(1)**_ to find out my _weight **(1)**_!

10. In the breeze, the trees _creak **(1)**_ near the shallow _creek **(1)**_.

11. The robber tried to _steal **(1)**_ the old _steel **(1)**_ safe.

Assessment Tip: Total **15** Points

Name _____

Proofreading and Writing

In the News Write the Spelling Word that completes each headline. Begin each word with a capital letter.

1. Woman Rescues Cat Breathes _Sigh_ **(1 point)**
2. Many Leave Town But _Few_ **(1)** Return
3. Miners Look for _Gold_ **(1)** Nearby
4. Dry Cleaner Loses Man's New _Suit_ **(1)**
5. Two Climbers Lost on _Steep_ **(1)** Mountain
6. Schools _Gain_ **(1)** a Lot with New Plan
7. Lost Hiker Is Found _Safe_ **(1)** But Hungry
8. _Odd_ **(1)** Behavior in Skunks Signals Rabies
9. Two Arrested During _Crime_ **(1)** Spree

Spelling Words

1. reach
2. steep
3. gain
4. gold
5. gray
6. crime
7. coast
8. grown
9. odd
10. wrote
11. few
12. true
13. safe
14. suit
15. sigh

Proofreading Circle the six misspelled Spelling Words in this travel story. Then write each word correctly.

We left early and sailed along the (coste.) We hoped to (reech) the island in a few weeks, but it took a year. Some may think it strange that I never (wroat) about this journey before. Now my hair is (graye), and my children are (grone). At last, I can tell the (trewe) story.

10. _coast_ **(1)**
11. _reach_ **(1)**
12. _wrote_ **(1)**
13. _gray_ **(1)**
14. _grown_ **(1)**
15. _true_ **(1)**

Continue the Story On a separate sheet of paper, write the rest of the story about the sailor's strange journey. Use the **Spelling Review Words.** Responses will vary. **(5)**

Name _____

The Perfect Detective

Think about the two detectives you have read about in *Focus on Mysteries*. Use the chart below to describe their characteristics. Then list which characteristics you think the perfect detective would have. How do Encyclopedia Brown and the Judge compare to your perfect detective?

Encyclopedia Brown	The Judge
1. smart	1. smart
2. Possible answers may include:	2.
3. curious, confident, observant,	3.
4. clever, stern, fair. **(1 point each)**	4.

The Perfect Detective

1. Answers will vary. **(4)**

2.

3.

4.

How the Detectives Compare

1. Answers will vary. **(4)**

2.

3.

4.

Assessment Tip: Total **14** Points

Name _____

The Interview

Imagine that you are interviewing Encyclopedia Brown for your school newspaper. You want to show that someone Encyclopedia Brown's age can be a good detective. List the questions you would ask him. Then act out your interview with a friend.

I. Answers will vary. **(4 points each)** _____

_____

_____

2. _____

_____

_____

3. _____

_____

_____

4. _____

_____

Name _____

Tell About America

**You are visiting another country and meet someone your age.
Your new friend wants to know about the United States,
and asks you the questions below. Help your friend learn about
the United States by answering these questions.**

1. What kind of food do people in the United States like to eat?

   Answers will vary. **(2 points)** _____

2. What is an American school like?

   Answers will vary. **(3)** _____

3. What do you and your friends like to do on weekends?

   Answers will vary. **(3)** _____

**Think of another question your friend might ask. Write an
answer to it.**

Questions and answers will vary. **(4)** _____

_____

_____

_____

Theme 2: **American Stories** 77
Assessment Tip: Total **12** Points

Name _____

New Places

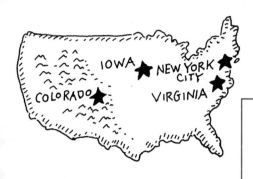

	Who is the story about? Where do they go in the story?	How are the characters' lives changed by going to the new place?
Tomás and the Library Lady	Tomás; Iowa, the library **(2 points)**	developed a love of reading; he became the storyteller in the family **(4)**
Tanya's Reunion	Tanya; Virginia, the family farm **(2)**	learns about her family's history; grows up/matures. **(4)**
Boss of the Plains	John Stetson; the Old West **(2)**	improved health; got inspiration to create a popular new hat; became a success **(4)**
A Very Important Day	various immigrants to United States; New York, the courthouse **(2)**	became citizens of the United States; America is now their home **(4)**

Assessment Tip: Total **24** Points

Name _____

Let's Read

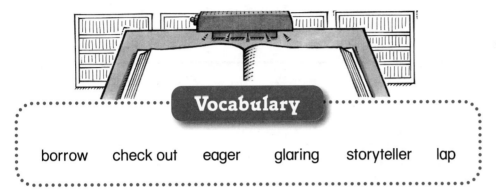

Vocabulary

borrow   check out   eager   glaring   storyteller   lap

Choose the best meaning for the underlined word.
Write the letter of your answer on the line provided.

1. Many people <u>borrow</u> books and records from libraries. _A_ **(2 points)**

   A. use for a short time   B. lend   C. dig a hole for   D. steal

2. I would like to <u>check out</u> that book for two weeks. _B_ **(2)**

   A. pay the bill for   B. borrow   C. prove true   D. add up

3. I am very <u>eager</u> to read the book you gave me for my birthday. _D_ **(2)**

   A. careful   B. uninterested   C. demanding   D. interested

4. The old house near the bus stop, with its broken windows
   <u>glaring</u> down at us, can be scary. _D_ **(2)**

   A. obvious   B. dark   C. sharp   D. to stare in an angry way

5. Stories always seem better when read aloud by a good <u>storyteller</u>. _A_ **(2)**

   A. person who tells stories   B. liar   C. actor   D. speaker

6. After school I will read, and my cat will quietly <u>lap</u> up her milk. _B_ **(2)**

   A. spill   B. lick up   C. pour   D. share

Assessment Tip: Total **12** Points

Name _____

Event Map

Pages 160–161

At midnight, the family was headed by car _____
toward Iowa to work on a farm picking corn. **(1 point)**

Pages 162–165

The boys carried water to the field, and when they got hot, they _____
sat under a tree with Papá Grande. **(1)**

Pages 166–167

First the library lady brought Tomás some water. Then she _____
brought books to his table. **(1)**

Pages 168–170

All summer, whenever he could, Tomás _____
went to the library. **(1)**

Pages 171–174

In the evenings, Tomás _____
read stories to Mamá, Papá, Papá Grande, and Enrique. **(1)**

Assessment Tip: Total **5** Points

Name _____

Check Your Memory

Think about the selection. Then complete the sentences.

1. The Rivera family traveled to Iowa each summer because Tomás's parents worked there. **(2 points)**

2. Tomás wanted to learn new stories so he could teach his family stories they didn't know. **(2)**

3. Tomás was able to forget about both Iowa and Texas when he got lost in the books he was reading. **(2)**

4. Tomás got a small sample of what it's like to be a teacher when he taught the library lady some words in Spanish. **(2)**

5. Tomás was sad to say the word *adiós* because it meant he was leaving the library lady and going back to Texas. **(2)**

Name _____

A Summer Sequence

Read the story below and answer the questions on the following page.

Audrey's Dream

It was a late summer afternoon. Sitting in the shade not far from her friend Sharon, Audrey looked through the book her father had loaned her. The book was all about the world of dinosaurs. In the heat, Audrey felt sleepy.

As she read, Audrey seemed to see real dinosaurs standing by a pond and drinking cool water. Even though her eyes were closing, Audrey seemed to hear the cry of the wild snakebird. A minute later, she was on the back of a dinosaur. She felt its warm neck as she held on tight.

The dinosaur carried Audrey across fields and swamps and into forests. Together they traveled many miles toward the setting sun. At last they ended up on a grassy plain. All was still. Audrey could hear nothing, but the dinosaur was listening for something that only it could hear.

Then in the distance, Audrey saw a shadow. A moment later, she saw a huge, fierce dinosaur she recognized from the book. The dinosaur she was riding began to run.

Faster and faster it ran across the plain. Looking behind her, Audrey saw huge teeth and claws getting closer and closer. Just then she heard a loud thud.

"Audrey, wake up!" she heard Sharon say. "You fell asleep. What would your father say if he knew you let his book fall in the dirt?"

Name _____

A Summer Sequence continued

Answer the following questions.

1. What first happens to Audrey as she falls asleep?

   She seems to see real dinosaurs standing by a pond. **(2 points)**

   _____

2. What happens next, after the dinosaur carries Audrey away?

   They end up on a grassy plain. **(2)**

   _____

3. What causes the *loud thud*?

   the book falling onto the ground **(2)**

   _____

4. What takes place once Audrey recognizes the fierce dinosaur in the distance?

   The dinosaur she's riding begins to run. **(2)**

   _____

5. Which two of these questions are out of sequence?

   three and four **(2)**

   _____

Name _____

A Contraction Conversation

Read Marisa's conversation with her father and circle all the contractions. There are five contractions in each speech balloon.

Dad, (I'm) ready. (Let's) go to the library. (I've) got two books to return, and (I'd) like to get a good mystery. (Wouldn't) you like to get a book too?

(That's) a great idea! (We'll) walk there. It (won't) take long. (It's) only three blocks away. (Don't) forget your scarf.

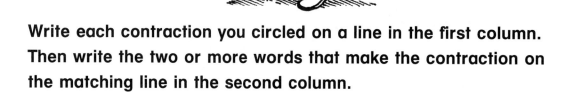

Write each contraction you circled on a line in the first column. Then write the two or more words that make the contraction on the matching line in the second column.

1.	I'm _____	I am **(1 point)**
2.	Let's _____	Let us **(1)**
3.	I've _____	I have **(1)**
4.	I'd _____	I would **(1)**
5.	Wouldn't _____	Would not **(1)**
6.	That's _____	That is **(1)**
7.	We'll _____	We will **(1)**
8.	won't _____	will not **(1)**
9.	It's _____	It is **(1)**
10.	Don't _____	Do not **(1)**

Assessment Tip: Total **10** Points

Name _____

The /ou/ and /ô/ Sounds

When you hear the /ou/ or the /ô/ sound, think of these patterns:

　　　/ou/ *ou* or *ow*　　　/ô/ *aw, au,* or *a* before *l*

Remember that a consonant sound usually follows the *ou* or the *au* pattern.

　　　/ou/ p**ou**nd, h**ow**l　　　/ô/ j**aw**, c**au**se, **a**lways

▶ In the starred word, *couple, ou* spells the /ŭ/ sound, not the /ou/ sound.

Write each Spelling Word under its vowel sound.

1. pound
2. howl
3. jaw
4. bounce
5. cause
6. always
7. shout
8. aloud
9. south
10. couple*
11. drawn
12. scout
13. false
14. proud
15. frown
16. sauce
17. gown
18. couch
19. dawn
20. mount

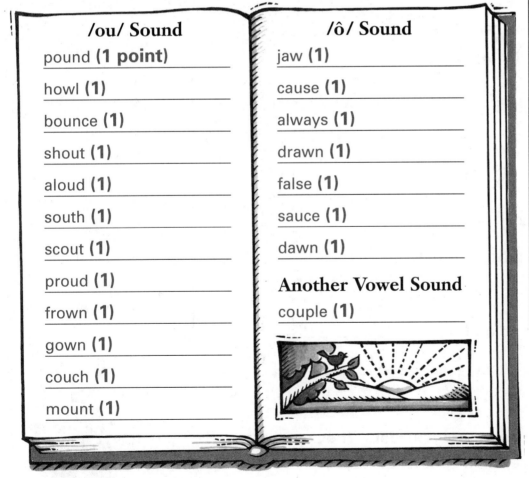

/ou/ Sound

pound **(1 point)**

howl **(1)**

bounce **(1)**

shout **(1)**

aloud **(1)**

south **(1)**

scout **(1)**

proud **(1)**

frown **(1)**

gown **(1)**

couch **(1)**

mount **(1)**

/ô/ Sound

jaw **(1)**

cause **(1)**

always **(1)**

drawn **(1)**

false **(1)**

sauce **(1)**

dawn **(1)**

Another Vowel Sound

couple **(1)**

Order of answers for each category may vary.

Theme 2: **American Stories**　　85
Assessment Tip: Total **20** Points

Name _____

Spelling Spree

Letter Swap **Change the first letter of each word to make a Spelling Word. Write the word.**

Example: talk   *walk*

1. sound   <u>pound **(1 point)**</u>

2. down   <u>gown **(1)**</u>

3. brown   <u>frown **(1)**</u>

4. law   <u>jaw **(1)**</u>

Puzzle Play **Write a Spelling Word to fit each clue.**

Example: a joking performer who does tricks

c l o (w) n

5. filled with pride **(1)**

6. a pair **(1)**

7. a liquid topping for food **(1)**

8. attracted; sketched **(1)**

9. to explore for information **(1)**

10. to cry out **(1)**

11. to climb or get up on **(1)**

12. to move with a bobbing motion **(1)**

p (r) o u d
c o u p l (e)
s (a) u c e
(d) r a w n
s c o u (t)
s h (o) u t
(m) o u n t
b o u n c (e)

Spelling Words

1. pound
2. howl
3. jaw
4. bounce
5. cause
6. always
7. shout
8. aloud
9. south
10. couple*
11. drawn
12. scout
13. false
14. proud
15. frown
16. sauce
17. gown
18. couch
19. dawn
20. mount

Now write the circled letters in order. They spell three words Papá Grande often said to Tomás.

R e a d   t o   m e . **(3)**

Assessment Tip: Total **15** Points

Name _____

Proofreading and Writing

Proofreading Circle the five misspelled Spelling Words in this postcard. Then write each word correctly.

Dear Antonio,

After a couple of (fallse) starts, we finally got on the road last Friday. It is sure a long way from the (sowth) up to Iowa! We hope to arrive by (daun) tomorrow. Papá Grande's stories have been making us (houl) with laughter. He (allways) makes the trips go faster!

Your friend,
Tomás

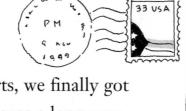
PM
9 NOV
1999
33 USA

Spelling Words

1. pound
2. howl
3. jaw
4. bounce
5. cause
6. always
7. shout
8. aloud
9. south
10. couple*
11. drawn
12. scout
13. false
14. proud
15. frown
16. sauce
17. gown
18. couch
19. dawn
20. mount

1. false **(2 points)**

2. south **(2)**

3. dawn **(2)**

4. howl **(2)**

5. always **(2)**

✏ **Write a Description** Tomás and his family often made the trip between Texas and Iowa. Have you taken an interesting trip? Did you travel by car, bus, train, or plane? What did you see and do?

On a separate sheet of paper, write a description of a trip you have taken. Use Spelling Words from the list.

Responses will vary. **(5 points)**

Name _____

Antonym Puzzle

Complete the crossword puzzle by writing the correct antonym for each clue. Choose your answers from the words in the box. Remember, an antonym is a word that means the opposite or nearly the opposite of another word.

Vocabulary

above	asleep	lost	start	true
after	least	push	sunny	winter
appear	loose	raise	top	return

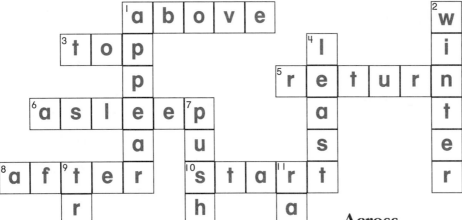

Across
1. below
3. bottom
5. leave
6. awake
8. before
10. finish
12. tight
13. cloudy

Down
1. vanish
2. summer
4. most
7. pull
9. false
11. lower
12. found

Assessment Tip: Total **15** Points

Name _____

Finding Proper Nouns

Underline the proper nouns in each sentence.

1. As a boy, <u>Tomás Rivera</u> traveled with his parents. **(1 point)**
2. The <u>Rivera</u> family came to the <u>United States</u> from <u>Mexico</u>. **(1)**
3. The family picked crops in <u>Texas</u> and in <u>Iowa</u>. **(1)**
4. The young boy called his parents <u>Mamá</u> and <u>Papá</u>. **(1)**
5. The boy's grandfather told stories to him and his brother, <u>Enrique</u>, in <u>Spanish</u>. **(1)**
6. The boy sometimes told stories to <u>Papá Grande</u> in <u>English</u>. **(1)**
7. The boy grew up to become a famous <u>Mexican American</u>. **(1)**
8. A beautiful library in <u>Riverside, California</u>, is named for him. **(1)**

Write each underlined proper noun in the correct space below. (2 points)

Person	Place	Thing
Tomás Rivera	United States	Spanish
Rivera	Mexico	English
Mamá	Texas	
Papá	Iowa	
Enrique	Riverside, California	
Papá Grande		
Mexican American		

Name _____

Completing with Proper Nouns

Complete each sentence with a proper noun from
Tomás and the Library Lady.

(1 point)

1. Tomás's family is driving to the state of <u>Iowa</u>.

2. Tomás calls his grandfather <u>Papá Grande **(1)**</u>.

3. Tomás's brother's name is <u>Enrique **(1)**</u>.

4. Their grandfather tells stories in <u>Spanish **(1)**</u>.

5. The <u>Tomás Rivera Elementary School **(1)**</u>

   is in Denton, Texas.

**Write a proper noun for each person, place, or thing
described.** Answers will vary.

6. the first and last name of a friend or relative **(1)** _____

   _____

7. the state where you live **(1)** _____

   _____

8. a language you speak **(1)** _____

   _____

9. your favorite book or movie **(1)** _____

   _____

10. the name of your school or library **(1)** _____

   _____

Name _____

Writing Proper Nouns

**Proofread the paragraph below. Find common nouns that have
capital letters. Find proper nouns that need capital letters. Use
the proofreading marks to show the corrections. Then write the
corrected common and proper nouns in the columns below.** (1 point
for each)

Proofreading Marks

Make a small letter   Story

Make a capital letter   mexico

> The Woman who wrote the story is pat mora. She was born in
> El Paso, texas. The Illustrator is Raul colón. He is an Artist from
> puerto rico. The story is about a young Boy named tomás rivera.
> He learns to love Books from the kind library lady. He grew up to
> become a famous mexican american.

Common Nouns	**Proper Nouns**
woman	Pat Mora
illustrator	Texas
artist	Colón
boy	Puerto Rico
books	Tomás Rivera
	Mexican American

Name _____

Writing an Essay

Use this page to help you plan your essay. Write your focus idea first. Then write two reasons or facts about your topic in the boxes below. Finally, think of some examples you could use to make each reason or fact clear.

My Focus Idea

_____

_____

_____

_____

_____

Reason/Fact	**Reason/Fact**
(2 points)	(2)

Example	**Example**
(2)	(2)

Assessment Tip: Total **8** Points

Name _____

Improving Your Writing

Read the following essay. Then add reasons to the main idea of paragraphs 2, 3 and 4 that support that idea. Write your reasons on the lines provided.

Afternoons at the Library

One afternoon a week, I usually stop by our local public library. Each time I go, I try to find at least one book that I want to read. Sometimes I find a new book of stories. Sometimes I discover an exciting mystery novel. Sometimes I find a nonfiction book about science or history.

Stories always appeal to me.
Add two or three sentences that give possible reasons why stories are appealing.
(4 points)

_____

_____

_____

I have to admit that mystery novels get my attention, too.
Add two or three sentences that give possible reasons why mystery novels might be interesting to read.
(4 points)

_____

_____

_____

Books about science and history are my favorite kinds of nonfiction.
Add two or three sentences that give reasons why science or history might be appealing choices for a reader.
(4 points)

_____

_____

_____

Evaluating Your Description

Reread your description. What do you need to make it better? Use this page to help you decide. Put a checkmark in the box for each sentence that describes what you have written.

Rings the Bell!

☐ The beginning clearly tells what the description is about.

☐ I use exact and vivid words to bring the story to life.

☐ The details are well organized.

☐ My ending is interesting.

☐ There are almost no mistakes.

Getting Stronger

☐ The beginning could be more clear.

☐ I could choose more vivid words to bring the story to life.

☐ I could organize the details in a better way.

☐ The ending could be more interesting.

☐ There are a few mistakes.

Try Harder

☐ The beginning is not clear.

☐ I haven't chosen words that bring the story to life.

☐ The details are poorly organized.

☐ There are a lot of mistakes.

Name _____

Sentence Combining

Combine each pair of sentences into one sentence. Write a new sentence that has a compound subject or compound predicate, or write a compound sentence. Use the joining word in parentheses. Add commas where they are needed.

1. Mary fed the cat.
2. Ben fed the cat. (or)

   Mary or Ben fed the cat. **(2 points)**

3. The cat sat on my favorite chair.
4. The cat took a nap. (and)

   The cat sat on my favorite chair and took a nap. **(2)**

5. The dog held a bone in its paws.
6. The dog chewed on it. (and)

   The dog held a bone in its paws and chewed on it. **(2)**

7. The kitten knocked over the lamp.
8. The puppy knocked over the lamp. (or)

   The kitten or the puppy knocked over the lamp. **(2)**

9. The kitten watched the raindrops through the window.
10. The puppy barked at the thunder. (but)

    The kitten watched the raindrops through the window, but the puppy barked

    at the thunder. **(2)**

11. The kitten snuggled up next to the puppy.
12. Soon both animals were fast asleep. (and)

    The kitten snuggled up next to the puppy, and soon both animals were fast

    asleep. **(2)**

Spelling Words

Words Often Misspelled Look for familiar spelling to help you remember how to spell the Spelling Words on this page. Think carefully about the parts that you find hard to spell in each word.

Write the missing letters in the Spelling Words below.

1. a l o t **(1 point)**
2. oth e r **(1)**
3. a n other **(1)**
4. a nyone **(1)**
5. ev e ry **(1)**
6. som e one **(1)**
7. mys e l f **(1)**
8. fam i ly **(1)**
9. fr i e nd **(1)**
10. p e o ple **(1)**
11. a g a i n **(1)**
12. a nything **(1)**
13. a nyway **(1)**
14. ev e r yone **(1)**
15. f i rst **(1)**

Spelling Words

1. a lot
2. other
3. another
4. anyone
5. every
6. someone
7. myself
8. family
9. friend
10. people
11. again
12. anything
13. anyway
14. everyone
15. first

Study List On a separate piece of paper, write each Spelling Word. Check your spelling against the words on the list. Order of words may vary.

96   Theme 2: **American Stories**
Assessment Tip: Total **5** Points

Name _____

Spelling Spree

Sentence Fillers **Write the Spelling Word that best completes each sentence.**

1. Did you ever find your __other **(1 point)**__ glove?
2. I'd like you to meet my best __friend **(1)**__ , Philip.
3. My sister got __every **(1)**__ question on her math test right.
4. Can we get you __anything **(1)**__ from the store?
5. It was hard to get __everyone **(1)**__ to agree on a movie.
6. Next summer, we're visiting my mom's __family **(1)**__ out west.
7. I'm getting __another **(1)**__ piece of pizza.
8. I think that __someone **(1)**__ called our house late last night.

Word Clues **Write a Spelling Word to fit each clue.**

9. a word meaning "just the same" __anyway **(1)**__
10. one more time __again **(1)**__
11. a synonym for anybody __anyone **(1)**__
12. a crowd of human beings __people **(1)**__
13. coming before anything else __first **(1)**__
14. the opposite of a little __a lot **(1)**__
15. a word you use when talking about you __myself **(1)**__

I'll do it myself!

Name _____

Proofreading and Writing

Proofreading Circle the five misspelled Spelling Words in this speech. Then write each word correctly.

If (somone) were to ask you, "What is an American?" what would you say? I think that (evryone) has his or her own answer. But when I ask (myslef) this question, my first answer is "a person who believes in democracy." It is democracy that lets each one of the American (peple) have a say in the direction of our country. If there is (anythin) more important to being an American, I can't think of it.

Spelling Words

1. a lot
2. other
3. another
4. anyone
5. every
6. someone
7. myself
8. family
9. friend
10. people
11. again
12. anything
13. anyway
14. everyone
15. first

1. someone **(1 point)**
2. everyone **(1)**
3. myself **(1)**
4. people **(1)**
5. anything **(1)**

✏️➤ **Tag-Team Poetry** **Pair up with a classmate. Then create a poem about America by taking turns writing lines. Use Spelling Words from the list.**

Responses will vary. **(5 points)**

Name _____

A Family Get-Together

Aunt Sally had to miss the big family party. Kara writes to tell her all about it. Complete Kara's letter by filling in the blank with the correct word from the list.

Dear Aunt Sally,

I am sorry that you missed the family
<u>reunion **(1 point)**</u>. We all had great fun, and
saw many relatives from both near and far away. Nearly
sixty people came for the party. It was the largest family
<u>gathering **(1)**</u> in years. There were
many familiar faces, and a few I didn't know at all. Two
great-aunts and one <u>great-uncle **(1)**</u> came
all the way from Oregon. My dad made the travel
<u>arrangements **(1)**</u> for them. They had not
seen our house for twenty years. They called our house and
the surrounding land the <u>homestead **(1)**</u>.

One of the things that I like is that everyone
<u>pitches in **(1)**</u> to prepare food. It's too
much work for just a few people. I got a great deal of
<u>satisfaction **(1)**</u> from seeing how many of
the relatives liked my potato salad. The only thing wrong
with the day was that the bees <u>persisted **(1)**</u>
in buzzing around the desserts.

I hope you can come visit soon.

Yours truly,
Your niece Sarah

Name _____

Character Development Flow Chart

Story Event or Character Detail	+	My Own Experience	=	Inference About Character
page 189 When Grandma says she's leaving for the reunion without Tanya and the family, silence falls across the dinner table.	+	I know that I have felt worried before when someone made a shocking announcement. **(1 point)**	=	I can infer that Tanya is feeling worried about Grandma traveling alone. **(1)**
page 196 When Tanya gets to the farm, she doesn't find what she expects.	+	I know that I sometimes get disappointed when things aren't what I expect. **(1)**	=	I can infer that Tanya is probably feeling disappointed when she first sees the farm. **(1)**
page 196 When Aunt Kay hugs Tanya, the warm, soft hug reminds Tanya of Grandma.	+	I know that if someone or something reminds me of someone I love, I feel good. **(1)**	=	I can infer that Aunt Kay's hug is helping Tanya feel a little better about being at the farm. **(1)**
page 200 Tanya stops and looks closely at the family "memories" in the sitting parlor.	+	I know that when I look closely at something it means I am interested in it or want to learn about it. **(1)**	=	I can infer that Tanya is interested in her family's history and wants to learn about it. **(1)**

Assessment Tip: Total **8** Points

Name _____

Just the Facts

Complete the following to show the setting, major events, and the ending for *Tanya's Reunion*.

Setting:

Aunt Kay and Uncle

John's farm in Virginia

(2 points)

_____

Events:

Sample: Tanya's family is having a

big reunion. Her Grandma announces that she

will go to her sister's farm before the family arrives

to help with the arrangements. Tanya is excited to be

allowed to make the trip with Grandma. But Tanya finds

that she is disappointed once she arrives at the farm. There

are no horses, the house is faded, and everything is dusty.

Also, Tanya is homesick for her family and her own

room. But she talks more with her Grandma and

learns things that she didn't know. Tanya finds

out how much Grandma loves the farm

and why she left it. **(6)**

Ending:

Tanya thinks about what

Grandma has told her and

begins to love the family farm

as Grandma does. **(2)**

_____

Name _____

What Characters!

Read the story below. Then complete the chart on the following page.

Family Tree

"Let's make a family tree!" said Meghan. "We can look for family records on the Internet."

"We could never do that," said her brother Brian, shaking his head. "The Internet is too huge."

"Nonsense," said Meghan. "We know that some of our great-grandparents lived in Lowell, Massachusetts. Using the Internet, we can scan the Lowell city records for other information."

A few computer clicks later, Meghan and Brian found the city's records. "Look, there they are!" said Meghan, her hands trembling. "Bridget and James O'Toole were married in Lowell on June 11, 1896. It says her parents were Sean and Maeve Boyle. His parents were James and Rose O'Toole."

"Can we tell where they were born?" asked Brian.

"Maybe," said Meghan. "Here are passenger lists for ships arriving in Boston in the 1880s and 1890s. Let's check to see if we can find their names."

"Look!" said Brian, staring wide-eyed at the computer screen. "Here are James and Rose O'Toole listed as passengers on the *Adelaide* that sailed in 1888 from Ireland."

Meghan sighed. "That means that if we want more information, we'll have to look for records in Ireland!"

Name _____

What Characters! continued

Use the story and your own experiences to complete the following chart.

Story Event	+	My Own Experience	=	Inference About Character
Brian shakes his head when Meghan suggests searching the Internet.	+	I may shake my head when I disagree with someone. **(1 point)**	=	I can infer that Brian disagrees with Meghan's idea. **(2)**
Meghan's hands tremble when she finds the family records.	+	My hands may tremble when I am excited. **(1)**	=	I can infer that Meghan is excited to find out about her family. **(2)**
Brian stares wide-eyed at the computer screen.	+	I may stare wide-eyed when something amazes me. **(1)**	=	I can infer that Brian is amazed to find his family's passenger records. **(2)**
Meghan sighs when she learns that their search must extend to Ireland.	+	I may sigh when I am disappointed. **(1)**	=	I can infer that Meghan is disappointed that she must continue the search. **(2)**

Name _____

Root It Out

The word root *sign* means "a sign or mark."
The word root *spect* means "to look at."

Example: The spectators cheered loudly.

The runners waited for the **signal** to start the race.

**Use the words in the box to complete the story. If you
need help, use a dictionary.**

signaled	suspected	inspect	signified	spectacular
respect	signature	spectacles	designs	expected

When Jenna woke up, she knew the raindrops hitting her
window <u>signaled **(1 point)**</u> another day inside. Jenna
decided to <u>inspect **(1)**</u> the dusty attic. A lot
of the items she found looked like junk, but Jenna knew each item
<u>signified **(1)**</u> an important part of her family's
history and deserved <u>respect **(1)**</u>. Jenna loved
the colorful <u>designs **(1)**</u> on the old quilts.
They were <u>spectacular **(1)**</u>! Next she tried
looking through <u>spectacles **(1)**</u> that she
<u>suspected **(1)**</u> belonged to her grandmother long
ago. Then Tanya read some letters that had her great-grandfather's
<u>signature **(1)**</u>. She hadn't
<u>expected **(1)**</u> to find that!

Assessment Tip: Total **10** Points

Name _____

The /o͞o/ and /o͝o/ Sounds

When you hear the /o͞o/ sound, think of the pattern *oo*. Remember that the /o͞o/ sound is often spelled *oo* or *u* followed by a consonant or a cluster.

　　　/o͞o/ **too**l　　　/o͝o/ **woo**d, **pu**t

► The starred words *group*, *prove*, *soup*, and *move* use different spelling patterns for the /o͞o/ sound.

Write each Spelling Word under its vowel sound. Include *roof* **with the** /o͞o/ **sound.** Order of answers for each category may vary.

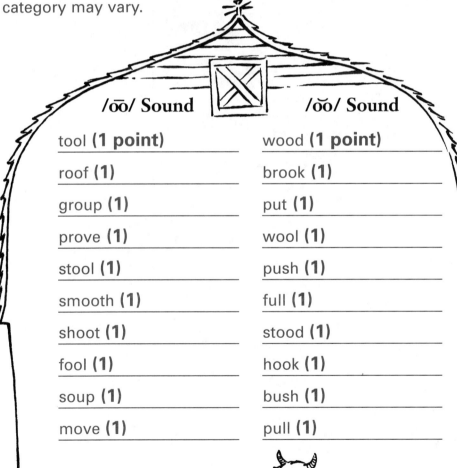

/o͞o/ Sound

tool **(1 point)**

roof **(1)**

group **(1)**

prove **(1)**

stool **(1)**

smooth **(1)**

shoot **(1)**

fool **(1)**

soup **(1)**

move **(1)**

/o͝o/ Sound

wood **(1 point)**

brook **(1)**

put **(1)**

wool **(1)**

push **(1)**

full **(1)**

stood **(1)**

hook **(1)**

bush **(1)**

pull **(1)**

Spelling Words

1. wood
2. brook
3. tool
4. put
5. wool
6. push
7. full
8. roof
9. group*
10. prove*
11. stood
12. stool
13. hook
14. smooth
15. shoot
16. bush
17. fool
18. pull
19. soup*
20. move*

Name _____

Spelling Spree

Hink Pinks Write a Spelling Word that answers the
question and rhymes with the given word.

Spelling Words

1. wood
2. brook
3. tool
4. put
5. wool
6. push
7. full
8. roof
9. group*
10. prove*
11. stood
12. stool
13. hook
14. smooth
15. shoot
16. bush
17. fool
18. pull
19. soup*
20. move*

Example: What do you call a stand that sells teeth?

_____tooth_____ booth

1. What do you call a silly person on a cold day?
   cool __fool **(1 point)**__

2. What makes the best fires?
   good __wood **(1)**__

3. What is a large farm animal after a
   meal? __full **(1)**__ bull

4. What would you use to "fish" at the
   library? book __hook **(1)**__

5. What do you call a mean hammer?
   cruel __tool **(1)**__

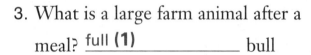

Letter Math Write a Spelling Word by solving
each word problem.

Example: spot − t + on = spoon

6. p + rob − b + ve = __prove **(1)**__

7. room − m + f = __roof **(1)**__

8. smoke − ke + oth = __smooth **(1)**__

9. won + old − n − d = __wool **(1)**__

10. stop − p + od = __stood **(1)**__

11. bus + fish − fis = __bush **(1)**__

12. s + hop − p + ot = __shoot **(1)**__

       Assessment Tip: Total **12** Points

Name _____

Proofreading and Writing

Proofreading Circle the five misspelled Spelling Words in this diary entry. Then write each word correctly on the lines below.

> Today a groop of us made taffy for the reunion. After cooking it, we putt it on a counter. One person's job was to poush the blob of taffy down. Then two others picked it up. Their job was to pul the blob to stretch it. This helped to make the taffy smooth. We did this over and over. It was hard work! Tonight I am so sore I can hardly mouve.

Spelling Words

1. wood
2. brook
3. tool
4. put
5. wool
6. push
7. full
8. roof
9. group*
10. prove*
11. stood
12. stool
13. hook
14. smooth
15. shoot
16. bush
17. fool
18. pull
19. soup*
20. move*

group **(2 points)** _____

put **(2)** _____

push **(2)** _____

pull **(2)** _____

move **(2)** _____

Write a Recipe What food dish would you like to take to a family reunion?

On a separate piece of paper, write a recipe for a dish that you might make. List what is in the dish and explain how to make it. Use Spelling Words from the list. Responses will vary. **(5 points)**

Theme 2: **American Stories** 107
Assessment Tip: Total **15** Points

Name _____

Identify Parts of a Definition

Choose the correct label for each part of the definition of
family **from the list. Write the labels in the spaces provided.**

entry word	third meaning	syllable break
part of speech	fourth meaning	pronunciation
first meaning	fifth meaning	sample sentence
second meaning	sixth meaning	word form with a
part of speech	sample sentence	different ending

entry word **(1 point)**

part of speech **(1)**

sample sentence **(1)**

first meaning **(1)**

second meaning **(1)**

family *noun* **1.** A group consisting of parents and
their children. **2.** The children of a father and a
mother; offspring: *We are a large family.* **3.** A group
of persons related by blood; relatives. **4.** All the
members of a household who live under one roof.
5. A group of things that share certain features or
properties: *English is a member of a larger family of
languages.* **6.** A group of related plants or animals.
fam•i•ly (făm′ ə lē) noun, plural, **families**

third meaning **(1)**

fourth meaning **(1)**

fifth meaning **(1)**

sample sentence **(1)**

sixth meaning **(1)**

syllable break **(1)**

part of speech **(1)**

pronunciation **(1)**

word form with a different ending **(1)**

Assessment Tip: Total **14** Points

Name _____

Finding Singular and Plural Nouns

**In each sentence, circle each singular common noun.
Underline each plural common noun.**

1. Tanya didn't like traveling on buses. **(1 point)**

2. In the (barnyard,) Tanya couldn't see any horses. **(1)**

3. From inside the (house,) Tanya saw raindrops on the (window.) **(1)**

4. The (girl) and her cousins played games. **(1)**

5. Lights far away seemed like torches through the sheets of (rain.) **(1)**

6. Patches of (ground) were soaked. **(1)**

7. In the (kitchen,) boxes were scattered all over. **(1)**

8. The trees in the (orchard) were full of ripe apples. **(1)**

Write each plural noun in the correct column below. (2 points)

Adds *s* to form the plural	**Adds *es* to form the plural**
horses	buses
raindrops	torches
cousins	Patches
games	boxes
Lights	
sheets	
trees	
apples	

Name _____

Puzzle with Plurals

Complete the crossword puzzle about things that Tanya saw on her trip to the family reunion in Virginia. Use the general clues to write the plural forms of these exact nouns from the story.

ACROSS

3. fields for growing fruit trees
5. rooms for cooking
7. soft, gentle winds
9. daytimes before noon
10. farm buildings

DOWN

1. containers made of cardboard or wood
2. farm birds that lay eggs
4. fees paid to governments
6. body parts for seeing
8. tools for sweeping

Create a Puzzle Use the plural forms of these nouns to create your own crossword on a separate sheet of paper. Trade puzzles with a classmate and complete one another's puzzles.

porch	horse	pocket
glass	bus	farm

Assessment Tip: Total **10** Points

Name _____

Using Exact Nouns

Read each sentence below. Then rewrite the sentence on the lines below it, substituting an exact noun for the general noun or words in parentheses.

1. Everyone was going to a family (get-together). **(2 points)**

   Everyone was going to a family reunion. _____

   _____

2. Tanya had been on the bus for nine (periods of 60 minutes). **(2)**

   Tanya had been on the bus for nine hours. _____

   _____

3. Tanya grew hungry when she smelled delicious (smells). **(2)**

   Tanya grew hungry when she smelled delicious aromas. _____

   _____

4. From the porch, Tanya could see the (place where fruit trees grow). **(2)**

   From the porch, Tanya could see the orchard. _____

   _____

5. Before she went to the barn, Tanya put on a pair of (heavy shoes). **(2)**

   Before she went to the barn, Tanya put on a pair of boots. ___

   _____

Name _____

A Character Sketch

Use this page to help you plan a character sketch. Write at least two specific details about what the person looks like, what the person says and does, and how you feel about the person.

Introduction

Whom is my character sketch about?

_____

What the Person Looks Like

Details: 1. **(1 point)** _____

2. **(1)** _____

3. **(1)** _____

What the Person Says

Details: 1. **(1 point)** _____

2. **(1)** _____

3. **(1)** _____

What the Person Does

Details: 1. **(1 point)** _____

2. **(1)** _____

3. **(1)** _____

Conclusion: How I Feel About the Person

(3) _____

_____

On a separate sheet of paper, write your character sketch.

Name _____

Improving Your Writing

► Two or more sentences that run together make a **run-on sentence**.
► Correct run-on sentences by making separate sentences. Add
sentence end marks and capital letters where they are needed.

**Read the character sketch. Find all the run-on sentences. Then
rewrite the character sketch, including corrections you made.**

My Grandmother

I think my grandmother is my favorite relative, she
knows more than anyone I know. I sometimes wonder if I'll
ever know all that she knows.

She can cook anything you can name, and it always tastes delicious.
You should see her spice cabinet, it's full of all kinds of herbs and spices
for cooking. She says she learned how to use them from her mother and
grandmother.

Sometimes I wonder how she remembers all the things she does.
Maybe I can learn a part of what she knows. Then I'll know a lot about
many things, that's why my grandmother is my favorite relative.

I think my grandmother is my favorite relative. She knows more than anyone

I know. I sometimes wonder if I'll ever know all that she knows.

She can cook anything you can name, and it always tastes delicious. You should

see her spice cabinet. It's full of all kinds of herbs and spices for cooking. She

says she learned how to use them from her mother and grandmother.

Sometimes I wonder how she remembers all the things she does.

Maybe I can learn a part of what she knows. Then I'll know a lot about many

things. That's why my grandmother is my favorite relative.

(2 points each)

Name _____

Go West!

Like John Stetson, many people traveled west in the 1800s to seek their fortunes. Complete the story by filling in each blank with the correct word from the list. Then answer the question.

Vocabulary

adventurers
determined
frontier
gear
opportunity
pioneers
settlers
tanned
wranglers

Many _adventurers **(1 point)**_ came from the East to live out West. They were seeking _opportunities **(1)**_ to make their fortunes. A great number of them were _determined **(1)**_ to find gold.

New people were arriving at the _frontier **(1)**_ almost daily. These people were true _pioneers **(1)**_ who had traveled across the prairie to the Colorado territory. They stayed to become _settlers **(1)**_ of the new area. Those who drove cattle were called _wranglers **(1)**_. The hide of the cattle was often _tanned **(1)**_ to make useful items like hats, boots, and belts. In addition, cowboys needed other special _gear **(1)**_ for their outdoor work. What piece of equipment might a cowboy need for outdoor work? _possible answers: horse, rope, tent **(1)**_

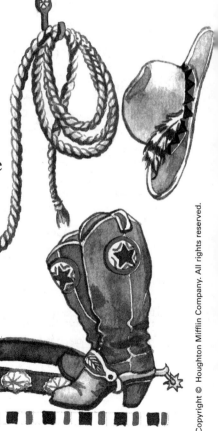

Name _____

Generalization Chart

Question: What was St. Joseph, Missouri, like in 1859? (page 224)

Details: Streets were bustling. **(1 point)** Streets were crowded with people bound for the frontier. **(1)** Travelers were talking about going west to find gold. **(1)**

Generalization: St. Joseph, Missouri, was a busy, exciting place. **(1)**

Question: What was the reaction to the hat samples John sent out west? (pages 233–234)

Details: The first two weeks were quiet, then orders began pouring in. **(1)** People sent cash in the mail to try to get a hat faster. **(1)** Out west, cowboys tossed away their old hats. **(1)**

Generalization: Almost all the cowboys wanted to own a Boss of the Plains. **(1)**

Question: What does the story show about the process of inventing something?

Details: John worked in his family's hat shop for many years. **(1)** John knew how to make felt. **(1)** John kept making different styles of hats to sell. **(1)**

Generalization: Inventing something takes perseverance, knowledge, and experience. **(1)**

Question: Look at the reasons why the Boss of the Plains became successful. What things are needed for an invention to be a success?

Details: A hat was needed for protection from the weather. **(1)** According to John, felt was thick, warm, and stronger than a piece of cloth. **(1)** You can smell it across a room, but you can't wear it out. **(1)**

Generalization: An item will almost always be successful if there is a need for the item and it's durable. **(1)**

Name _____

What's It About?

Complete the description for each part of a three-part documentary about the life of John Stetson.

Television—What's On TV This Week

Monday, 8:00 P.M., Part 1

Twelve-year-old John Batterson Stetson is hard at work in the family's hat-making shop in New Jersey. Young John first hears about the West. <u>from customers and neighbors **(1 point)**</u> .

In 1859, John B. Stetson, now a young man, decides to head west <u>after he becomes sick **(1)**</u> .

Wednesday, 8:00 P.M., Part 2

John mines for gold and realizes the hat he is wearing offers very little protection from the weather. John decides to make <u>a hat that</u> <u>is suited for weather in the West **(1)**</u> .

One day a horseman rides into camp and <u>offers John a five-</u> <u>dollar gold piece for his hat **(1)**</u> .

Thursday, 8:00 P.M., Part 3

John decides to move to Philadelphia and <u>set up a hat-making</u> <u>shop **(1)**</u> .

The shop is not successful until one day John remembers the horseman who bought his hat. John spends all his money making samples of the hat and sends them <u>to clothing stores out west **(1)**</u> .

For weeks, John hears nothing. Then suddenly the orders roll in. In no time, John Stetson's Boss of the Plains <u>is the most popular hat</u> <u>west of the Mississippi **(1)**</u> .

116   Theme 2: **American Stories**
       Assessment Tip: Total **10** Points

Name _____

General Statements

Read the article below and complete the chart on the following page.

Settling Colorado

Before Colorado became a state in 1876, some Native Americans lived in the mountain valleys and on the plains. A few people wandered through the mountains looking for gold and other valuable minerals. Only a few farming families lived anywhere in the region.

In 1858, people found gold near what is now Denver. Soon, thousands of people had settled in the region. Tiny settlements became large towns. Farmers and ranchers settled in the mountain valleys.

Today, residents of Colorado no longer live in the wide-open spaces of the Old West. Instead, four out of every five people in the region live in one of six large cities. Many people move to these cities every year. Also, many of the mountain areas still have no residents.

Name _____

General Statements continued

In the chart below write the details that answer the questions. Then form the generalizations.

What was the population like in Colorado before the 1850s?

Details: Some Native Americans lived in valleys and on the plains. A few people looking for gold wandered through the mountains. A few farming families lived in the area. **(2 points)**

Generalization: Almost nobody lived in Colorado before the 1850s. **(2 points)**

How did Colorado change after the 1850s?

Details: Thousands of people settled in the region. Tiny settlements became large towns. Farmers and ranchers settled in the valleys. **(2)**

Generalization: Many people came to Colorado hoping to find gold. **(2)**

What is the population of Colorado like today?

Details: Four out of five people live in one of six cities. More people move to these cities every year. Many of the mountain areas still have no residents. **(2)**

Generalization: Few people in Colorado today live in the mountains. Most people live in cities. **(2)**

Assessment Tip: Total **12** Points

Name _____

Super Suffixes

Write the word from the box that matches each clue. Write only one letter on each line. Remember, the endings -*er, -or,* and *-ist* each mean "someone who." If you need help, use a dictionary. To solve the riddle, write the numbered letter from each answer on the line with the matching number.

composer	sailor	teacher
conductor	traveler	settler

1. Someone who sails (**1 point**)   s a i l o r
                                                          6

2. Someone who takes a trip (**1**)   t r a v e l e r
                                                              1

3. Someone who settles
   a new place (**1**)   s e t t l e r
                                    5

4. Someone who is in
   charge of a train (**1**)   c o n d u c t o r
                                                4

5. Someone who teaches (**1**)   t e a c h e r
                                                      3

6. Someone who writes music (**1**)   c o m p o s e r
                                                                2

Riddle: What did the alien say to the book?

Take me to your r e a d e r !
                          1   2   3   4   5   6

Name _____

The /îr/, /är/, and /âr/ Sounds

When you hear the /îr/, /är/, and /âr/ sounds, think of these patterns and examples:

Patterns	Examples
/îr/ ear, eer	g**ear**, ch**eer**
/är/ ar	sh**ar**p
/âr/ are, air	st**are**, h**airy**

► The spelling patterns for the vowel + r sounds in the starred words are different. In *heart*, the /är/ sound is spelled *ear*. In *weird*, the /îr/ sound is spelled *eir*. In *scarce*, the /âr/ sound is spelled *ar*.

Spelling Words

1. gear
2. spear
3. sharp
4. stare
5. alarm
6. cheer
7. square
8. hairy
9. heart*
10. weird*
11. starve
12. charm
13. beard
14. hardly
15. spare
16. stairs
17. year
18. charge
19. dairy
20. scarce*

Write each Spelling Word under its vowel + r sound.
Order of answers for each category may vary.

/îr/ Sound

gear **(1 point)**   weird **(1)**

spear **(1)**   beard **(1)**

cheer **(1)**   year **(1)**

/är/ Sound

sharp **(1)**   charm **(1)**

alarm **(1)**   hardly **(1)**

heart **(1)**   charge **(1)**

starve **(1)**

/âr/ Sound

stare **(1)**   stairs **(1)**

square **(1)**   dairy **(1)**

hairy **(1)**   scarce **(1)**

spare **(1)**

120   Theme 2: **American Stories**
        Assessment Tip: Total **20** Points

Name _____

Spelling Spree

Word Search **Write the Spelling Word that is hidden in each sentence.**

Example: Ea<u>ch air</u>plane was on time. *chair*

1. Does the diver need air yet? <u>dairy **(1 point)**</u>

2. This harp has a broken string. <u>sharp **(1)**</u>

3. How often does the spa replace the mud? <u>spare **(1)**</u>

4. The royal armada sailed the seas. <u>alarm **(1)**</u>

5. Children of that age are cute. <u>gear **(1)**</u>

6. The show will star very famous people. <u>starve **(1)**</u>

7. How much armor did knights wear? <u>charm **(1)**</u>

8. His pea rolled off his fork. <u>spear **(1)**</u>

Book Titles **Write the Spelling Word that best completes each funny book title. Remember to use capital letters.**

Example: *Something's in the* __Air__
by Lotta Smoke

9. *Getting by When Money Is* _____ by B. A. Tightwad

10. *Ways to* _____ *Up a Gloomy Pal* by May Kem Laff

11. *Climb the* _____ *to Success* by Rich N. Famous

12. *Taking* _____ *of Your Life* by U. Ken Dewitt

9. <u>Scarce **(1 point)**</u>   11. <u>Stairs **(1)**</u>

10. <u>Cheer **(1)**</u>   12. <u>Charge **(1)**</u>

Spelling Words

1. gear
2. spear
3. sharp
4. stare
5. alarm
6. cheer
7. square
8. hairy
9. heart*
10. weird*
11. starve
12. charm
13. beard
14. hardly
15. spare
16. stairs
17. year
18. charge
19. dairy
20. scarce*

Theme 2: **American Stories** 121
Assessment Tip: Total **12** Points

Name _____

Proofreading and Writing

Proofreading Circle the five misspelled Spelling Words in this paragraph from a story. Then write each word correctly.

Suddenly, a hush came over the room. I could (hardely) hear a sound. I turned, and there in the doorway stood a huge cowpoke with a long (beerd.) I couldn't help but (stayre) at him because he looked so odd. A Stetson hat sat on his head. His (weard) hands were as hairy as bear paws. He was covered with dust too. Then he grinned and said shyly, "Howdy, folks!" Someone yelled, "It's Big John, home from a (yier) on the trail!" The crowd broke into a cheer, and everyone ran up to shake John's hand.

Spelling Words

1. gear
2. spear
3. sharp
4. stare
5. alarm
6. cheer
7. square
8. hairy
9. heart*
10. weird*
11. starve
12. charm
13. beard
14. hardly
15. spare
16. stairs
17. year
18. charge
19. dairy
20. scarce*

1. hardly **(2 points)**
2. beard **(2)**
3. stare **(2)**
4. weird **(2)**
5. year **(2)**

✏️ **Write an Ad** If you were to create a new style of hat, what would it look like? Why would people want to buy one of your hats?

On a separate piece of paper, write an ad that tells about your hat. Make the hat seem so great that everyone will want to buy one. Use Spelling Words from the list. Responses will vary. **(5 points)**

Name _____

It's All in the Context

Choose the correct definition from the list below for each underlined word in the paragraph. Write the letter after the number matching the word. Use context clues to help choose the right definition.

a. to protect or cover
b. small in amount
c. explore for valuable metals
d. one-of-a-kind
e. the flat, broad lower edge of a hat
f. beautiful; scenic
g. setting a person or thing apart from others
h. a rock containing gold or silver
i. strike out; make a new path
j. a remote area with few people

John Stetson and the Pikes Peakers headed away from the cities and into the <u>frontier</u>. Along the way, they passed
₁

<u>picturesque</u> landscapes that seemed to be painted in red
₂

and gold. John's <u>distinctive</u> hat made him stand out from
₃

the rest. It was <u>unique</u>; no one else had anything like it.
₄

John liked the way the hat's wide <u>brim</u> managed to <u>shield</u>
₅   ₆

his face from the sun. When they reached Colorado, John

saw men <u>prospect</u> for gold. In some rocks they found <u>ore</u>
₇   ₈

containing silver. Mostly, though, results were so <u>meager</u>
₉

that many miners left Colorado to <u>blaze</u> a new trail to the
₁₀

California goldfields.

1. j **(1 point)**
2. f **(1)**
3. g **(1)**
4. d **(1)**
5. e **(1)**
6. a **(1)**
7. c **(1)**
8. h **(1)**
9. b **(1)**
10. i **(1)**

Name _____

Finding More Plural Nouns

Underline each plural noun in the sentences below.

1. The West offered many <u>opportunities</u> for making money. **(1 point)**
2. In Eastern <u>cities</u>, a Stetson hat wouldn't sell. **(1)**
3. In the <u>territories</u> of the West, many <u>men</u> wore one. **(1)**
4. Behind many a herd of <u>sheep</u> rode a cowboy with a Stetson. **(1)**
5. A horse might carry a settler's <u>supplies</u>, but the settler wore his Stetson. **(1)**
6. <u>Ladies</u> were impressed by a stylish broad-brimmed hat. **(1)**
7. If you picked <u>berries</u>, you could always put them in your Stetson. **(1)**
8. Did anyone ever see <u>sheep</u> or <u>deer</u> wearing headgear like that? **(1)**

On the line at the right of each singular noun given, write the correct plural form. Use a dictionary to help you.

9. duty   duties **(1)**
10. woman   women **(1)**
11. bison   bison **(1)**
12. sky   skies **(1)**
13. moose   moose **(1)**
14. child   children **(1)**
15. ditty   ditties **(1)**

Assessment Tip: Total **15** Points

Name _____

Rewriting Plural Nouns

Rewrite each sentence on the lines provided, using the plural of the noun in parentheses.

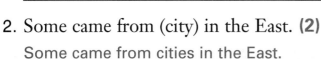

1. Many (family) went west to seek wealth. **(2 points)**

   Many families went west to seek wealth.

2. Some came from (city) in the East. **(2)**

   Some came from cities in the East.

3. Hats like (derby) were not useful in bad weather. **(2)**

   Hats like derbies were not useful in bad weather.

4. In this new land, people needed special kinds of (supply). **(2)**

   In this new land, people needed special kinds of supplies.

5. (Man) who worked in the open needed a hat to protect them. **(2)**

   Men who worked in the open needed a hat to protect them.

6. Against (sky) full of rain or snow, a Stetson offered protection. **(2)**

   Against skies full of rain or snow, a Stetson offered protection.

7. Herders of (sheep) wanted to keep the sun out of their eyes. **(2)**

   Herders of sheep wanted to keep the sun out of their eyes.

8. John Stetson's new hat pleased cowboys and (woman) alike. **(2)**

   John Stetson's new hat pleased cowboys and women alike.

9. In all the (territory) you could see Stetsons everywhere. **(2)**

   In all the territories you could see Stetsons everywhere.

10. Everyone, including (child), sported a Stetson. **(2)**

    Everyone, including children, sported a Stetson.

Name _____

Proofreading for Noun Endings

Proofread the paragraph below. Find plurals of nouns that are incorrectly spelled. Circle each misspelled plural. Then write each properly spelled plural on the lines provided. Use a dictionary to help you. (1 point for each)

Proofreading Marks  spell correctly

Would you like a hat to protect you from rainy (skyes?) How about one to keep the sun out of your (eyies?) You can use these hats to hold (grainies) for your (horsers) or to carry freshly picked (strawberris.) You can make two earholes in these hats and put them on your (sheeps) or (oxes.) What kind of hats can entire (familys) wear—men, (woman,) and (childs?) Are they (derbys?) No, these hats are (Stetsones.)

Regular	Changes *y* to *i* and adds *es*	Special plural	Same as singular
eyes	skies	oxen	sheep
grains	strawberries	women	
horses	families	children	
Stetsons	derbies		

Name _____

Writing a Business Letter

Use this page to help you plan a business letter.

My Purpose for Writing _____

Writer's Address **(1)** _____

_____

_____

_____ Inside Address **(1)**

_____

_____

_____ Greeting **(1)**

Introductory Paragraph
(2) _____

_____

Middle Paragraph
(2) _____

_____

Concluding Paragraph
(2) _____

_____

Closing
(1) _____

Signature

_____

Name _____

Improving Your Writing

Read the business letter. Find details that do not keep to the point. Mark them to be deleted. Then recopy the letter, with these details omitted on another sheet of paper. (2 points for each deleted sentence.)

1407 Green Street
Urbana, Illinois 61801
January 19, 2001

Ms. Angela O'Byrne
Public Relations Director
Kitchenwares Incorporated
920 Main Street
Mineola, New York, 11502

Dear Ms. O'Byrne:

 I am writing to request information about the new Whiz food processor. I am in the cooking class at school. ~~We are learning to bake now.~~ Our class needs a new processor. ~~We saw an advertisement in the newspaper.~~ The processor in your ad seems to be a good one.

 Our teacher asked me to write to you for information about what the processor costs and what it will do. ~~I like to write. I always get good grades on my compositions.~~ I will take the information you send and present it to our class. The class will decide if the Whiz is the one for us.

 Thank you for your help. ~~I hope the Whiz will be the food processor that we get for our class.~~ I am sure the information you send will help us make our decision.
Sincerely,
Maria Lopez

Name _____

Becoming a Citizen

Miguel's grandparents want to become citizens, but they don't know what to do. Miguel tells them what to expect. Complete Miguel's story by filling in each blank with the correct word from the list.

> ### Vocabulary
>
> allegiance
> chamber
> citizen
> citizenship
> enrich
> examiner
> oath
> petitioners

When someone wants to become a <u>citizen **(1 point)**</u> of the United States, that person must go through a special ceremony. The ceremony takes place in a United States government courthouse. The people all gather in a room called a <u>chamber **(1)**</u>. When everyone is seated, a person called an <u>examiner **(1)**</u> calls out each person's name. Then each of the <u>petitioners **(1)**</u> walks up to the desk, is given a certificate, and signs his or her name. After this is done, a judge comes into the room to administer the <u>oath **(1)**</u> of <u>citizenship **(1)**</u>. All the people stand up and pledge their <u>allegiance **(1)**</u> to the United States. After the ceremony, friends and relatives offer their congratulations to the new citizens. Hopefully, the new citizens will <u>enrich **(1)**</u> their lives and the lives of others as citizens of their new country.

Assessment Tip: Total **8** Points

Name _____

Who/What Chart

**Families and the Places They Come From
(6 points)**

Akuffo, Ghana

Baez, Dominican Republic

Batungbakal, Philippines

Castro, El Salvador

Hao, Vietnam

Huerta, Mexico

Idris, Egypt

Jimenez, Dominican Republic

Leonov, Russia

MacTaggart, Scotland

Patel, India

Soutsos, Greece

Zeng, China

Countries Where You Can Conclude That It Does Not Snow (3)

Philippines

India

Ghana

Countries Where You Can Conclude That It Snows (4)

Mexico

Russia

Greece

Scotland

Families with Grandchildren (3 points)

Batungbakal

Leonov

Patel

Families with No Children (2)

Akuffo

MacTaggart

Families Whose First Language Is English (1 point)

MacTaggart

Families with Two Children (3)

Hao

Huerta

Leonov

Families Who Need to Allow Extra Time to Get Downtown (3)

Batungbakal

Huerta

Patel

Assessment Tip: Total **25** Points

Name _____

Jacket Information

Complete the summary for the book jacket for *A Very Important Day*.

Snow is falling on New York City as different families awaken early one winter day. The members of each family worry because

they must be downtown at the courthouse

later that morning. **(2 points)**

Each family member is an immigrant who has come to America from a foreign country. Today is special because

they will become citizens of the United States. **(2)**

At the courthouse, the examiner calls out names

and gives each person a certificate. **(2)**

When the certificates are handed out, the judge leads everyone

in saying the oath of citizenship. **(2)**

When the oath is finished, the judge welcomes all the new citizens and wishes them good luck. Then everyone in the courtroom stands

to say the Pledge of Allegiance. **(2)**

All the new citizens congratulate each other and then head for home to celebrate a very special day.

Name _____

Classified Information

Read the article below and complete the chart on the following page.

Arriving at Ellis Island

Ellis Island, in New York harbor, was the first stop in the United States for millions of immigrants in the early twentieth century. When they arrived on ships, immigrants were taken there to be checked by doctors and most were then allowed to enter the United States. Among them were my grandparents, who arrived in 1913.

In Europe, my grandparents had traveled through Austria, Hungary, Germany, and France to reach the ship that brought them to New York. With them were their friends Mr. and Mrs. Radowsky, Mr. and Mrs. Graff, and Mr. Stead.

When they reached Ellis Island, they were taken to a huge hall. Around them were immigrants from Russia, China, Jamaica, Brazil, and South Africa. People were dressed in different types of clothes and spoke many different languages.

My grandparents and their friends were examined by doctors. Mr. Stead was found to be ill, and he was not allowed into the United States. Yet my grandparents and their other friends were allowed to enter. My grandparents and the Radowskys settled in Brooklyn. The Graffs settled in Chicago.

Name _____

Classified Information continued

Answer the following questions based on the article.

1. Which countries are in Europe?

   Austria, Hungary, Germany, France **(2 points)**

   _____

2. Who can be classified as friends of the grandparents?

   the Radowskys, the Graffs, Mr. Stead **(2)**

   _____

3. Who can be classified as new residents of the United States?

   the grandparents, the Radowskys, the Graffs **(2)**

   _____

4. What would you name the category that has the grandparents and the Radowskys as its only members?

   Those Who Settled in Brooklyn **(2)**

   _____

Name _____

Picturing Possessives

Write a sentence to tell about each picture. Make the noun beside each picture possessive, and use it in your sentence. Sample answers shown.

A possessive noun is a noun that shows ownership.

➤ Add an apostrophe (') and *s* to a singular noun.

➤ Add just an apostrophe (') to plural nouns ending in *s*.

➤ Add an apostrophe (') and *s* to plural nouns that do not end in *s*.

Ryan

1. Ryan's trophy made him feel proud. **(2 points)**

birds

2. The birds' nest was made of twigs. **(2)**

children

3. The children's bikes were fun to ride. **(2)**

Dora

4. Dora's sunglasses looked great! **(2)**

puppies

5. The puppies' bowls were full of food. **(2)**

Name _____

The /ôr/, /ûr/, and /yo͝or/ Sounds

When you hear the /ôr/, /ûr/, or /yo͝or/ sounds, think of these patterns and examples:

Patterns	Examples
/ôr/ *or, ore*	h**or**se, ch**ore**
/ûr/ *ur, ir, ear, or*	f**ir**m, c**ur**ve, l**ear**n, w**or**m
/yo͝or/ *ure*	p**ure**

► The /ôr/ sound is usually spelled *or* or *ore*.
► They /ûr/ sound is usually spelled *ir, ur, ear,* or *or*.
► The /yo͝or/ sound is usually spelled *ure*.
► The spelling patterns for the /ôr/ sounds in the starred words *board* and *course* are different.

Write each Spelling Word under its vowel + *r* sounds.

Order of answers for each category may vary.

/ôr/ Sounds

horse **(1 point)**   course **(1)**

chore **(1)**   score **(1)**

board **(1)**   worn **(1)**

/ûr/ Sounds

firm **(1)**   return **(1)**

learn **(1)**   worm **(1)**

dirty **(1)**   thirteen **(1)**

curve **(1)**   curl **(1)**

world **(1)**   shirt **(1)**

heard **(1)**   search **(1)**

/yo͝or/ Sounds

pure **(1)**   cure **(1)**

Theme 2: **American Stories**   135
Assessment Tip: Total **20** Points

Name _____

Spelling Spree

Word Addition Write a Spelling Word by adding the beginning of the first word to the end of the second word.

    Example: hum + part *hurt*

<table>
<tbody><tr><td>1. curb + dive</td><td>curve **(1 point)**</td></tr>
<tr><td>2. chop + store</td><td>chore **(1)**</td></tr>
<tr><td>3. wool + corn</td><td>worn **(1)**</td></tr>
<tr><td>4. seat + march</td><td>search **(1)**</td></tr>
<tr><td>5. cut + girl</td><td>curl **(1)**</td></tr>
<tr><td>6. fix + term</td><td>firm **(1)**</td></tr>
<tr><td>7. boat + hard</td><td>board **(1)**</td></tr>
<tr><td>8. cut + tore</td><td>cure **(1)**</td></tr>
<tr><td>9. ship + dart</td><td>shirt **(1)**</td></tr>
<tr><td>10. put + care</td><td>pure **(1)**</td></tr>
</tbody></table>

Spelling Words

1. horse
2. chore
3. firm
4. learn
5. dirty
6. curve
7. world
8. pure
9. board*
10. course*
11. heard
12. return
13. cure
14. score
15. worm
16. thirteen
17. worn
18. curl
19. shirt
20. search

Questions Write a Spelling Word to answer each question.

11. What number is one more than twelve?
12. What is the name for a large animal that has a long mane?
13. What word describes a room that has not been cleaned?
14. What small, soft-bodied animal crawls through the soil?
15. What do you do when you hit a home run in baseball?

11. thirteen **(1 point)**
12. horse **(1)**
13. dirty **(1)**
14. worm **(1)**
15. score **(1)**

Name _____

Proofreading and Writing

Proofreading Circle the five misspelled Spelling Words in this friendly letter. Then write each word correctly.

Dear Genya,

I have the best news in the (wurld.) I am going to become an American! Thirteen of us are taking a special (corse.) We all have to (lern) facts about our new country. Then we take a test. If I get a high score, I will become a citizen. Isn't this the greatest news you have ever (heared?)

Next year, we hope to (retern) to Russia for a visit. I can teach you a lot about America then!

Love,
Olga

Spelling Words

1. horse
2. chore
3. firm
4. learn
5. dirty
6. curve
7. world
8. pure
9. board*
10. course*
11. heard
12. return
13. cure
14. score
15. worm
16. thirteen
17. worn
18. curl
19. shirt
20. search

1. world **(2 points)**
2. course **(2)**
3. learn **(2)**
4. heard **(2)**
5. return **(2)**

✎──▸ **Write a Description** What could you tell a friend in another country about your city or town? Does it snow where you live? Are there palm trees on your street?

On a separate sheet of paper, write a paragraph telling about the place where you live. Use Spelling Words from the list.

Responses will vary. **(5)**

Name _____

One Word, Many Meanings

In each of the following sentences, the underlined word has at least two possible meanings. Choose the meaning that fits the sentence. Mark your choice with an X.

1. "We came early so we wouldn't <u>miss</u> you," said the Pitambers.

   A. __X **(1)**__ fail to meet   B. _____ avoid or escape

2. "Trinh," said her mother, "come and let's <u>board</u> the bus."

   A. _____ plank of wood   B. __X **(1)**__ get onto

3. Jorge was grateful for his father's <u>company</u> on the ferry.

   A. __X **(1)**__ companionship   B. _____ business

4. The subway ride was <u>over</u>, and it was time for breakfast.

   A. __X **(1)**__ finished   B. _____ above

5. The table had just been <u>set</u> by Veena when the doorbell rang.

   A. _____ decided on   B. __X **(1)**__ made ready

6. Nelia's son was <u>fast</u> asleep until she woke him up.

   A. __X **(1)**__ completely   B. _____ quickly

7. "She'll get <u>used</u> to snow, living here," said Kostas.

   A. _____ not new; secondhand   B. __X **(1)**__ accustomed

8. The race between Kwame and Efua ended in a <u>tie</u>.

   A. __X **(1)**__ an equal score   B. _____ make a knot

138   Theme 2: **American Stories**
    Assessment Tip: Total **8** Points

Name _____

In Search of Possessive Nouns

In each sentence, underline each possessive noun form.

1. <u>Nelia's</u> family in the Philippines had never seen snow. **(1 point)**

2. <u>Miguel's</u> family was going to the courthouse. **(1)**

3. The <u>Patels'</u> neighbors and children were invited to breakfast. **(1)**

4. <u>Eugenia's</u> whole family took the subway downtown. **(1)**

5. <u>Grandfather's</u> hands were full of wet snow. **(1)**

6. Mrs. Soutsos laughed at little <u>Kiki's</u> reaction to snowflakes. **(1)**

7. The <u>family's</u> restaurant was closed for the day. **(1)**

8. <u>Passengers'</u> bundles fell to the floor when the driver
   had to stop. **(1)**

9. The <u>judge's</u> voice was loud and clear in the courtroom. **(1)**

10. The <u>citizens'</u> voices could be heard saying the Pledge
    of Allegiance. **(1)**

**On the line at the right of each noun, write the correct
possessive form.**

11. relative   relative's **(1)**   16. sister   sister's **(1)**

12. woman   woman's **(1)**   17. mouse   mouse's **(1)**

13. children   children's **(1)**   18. babies   babies' **(1)**

14. Eugenia   Eugenia's **(1)**   19. crowd   crowd's **(1)**

15. friends   friends' **(1)**   20. city   city's **(1)**

Name _____

Replacing with Possessive Nouns

Rewrite each sentence, replacing the underlined words with a singular or plural possessive noun.

1. Nelia heard <u>the voice of the announcer</u> telling about the snow.

   Nelia heard the announcer's voice telling about the snow. **(2 points)**

2. <u>The sister of Miguel</u> woke him up. **(2)**

   Miguel's sister woke him up.

3. Niko, <u>the brother of Kiko</u>, helped her sweep snow off
   the sidewalk. **(2)**

   Niko, Kiko's brother, helped her sweep snow off the sidewalk.

4. Everyone in <u>the family of the Leonovs</u> had waited for the big day. **(2)**

   Everyone in the Leonovs' family had waited for the big day.

5. Down from the window came a gift from <u>a friend of Yujin</u>. **(2)**

   Down from the window came a gift from Yujin's friend.

6. Becoming a citizen was <u>the goal of an immigrant</u>. **(2)**

   Becoming a citizen was an immigrant's goal.

7. Everyone heard the examiner call out each of <u>the names of</u>
   <u>the Castros</u>. **(2)**

   Everyone heard the examiner call out each of the Castros' names.

8. All the people in the room could hear <u>the words of the judge</u>. **(2)**

   All the people in the room could hear the judge's words.

Assessment Tip: Total **16** Points

Name _____

Proofreading for Apostrophes

**Proofread each sentence.
Find any possessive nouns that lack apostrophes
or have apostrophes in the wrong place. Circle
each incorrect possessive noun. Then write the
corrected sentence on the line below it.**

1. The ⟨days⟩ main event for many families was becoming
   United States citizens.

   The day's main event for many families was becoming
   United States citizens. **(2 points)**
   _____

2. To one ⟨womans⟩ surprise, the DJ predicted six inches of snow.

   To one woman's surprise, the DJ predicted six inches of snow. **(2)**
   _____

3. The Huerta ⟨familys⟩ goal was to be at the courthouse early.

   The Huerta family's goal was to be at the courthouse early. **(2)**
   _____

4. ⟨Kwames⟩ wife, Efua, had her picture taken.

   Kwame's wife, Efua, had her picture taken. **(2)**
   _____

   _____

5. All the ⟨Castros⟩ signatures were on the court papers.

   All the Castros' signatures were on the court papers. **(2)**
   _____

Name _____

Writing Journal Entries

Answer these questions. Then use your answers to help write your own journal entry.

1. What new word, fact, or idea did you learn today? Now, write it down, along with a few words telling why you found it interesting. **(2 points)**

   _____

   _____

2. If you could ask anybody in the world a question, who would that person be and what question would you ask? **(2)**

   _____

   _____

3. As you look around, what object catches your eye? Name the object, and write a few words to describe it. **(2)**

   _____

   _____

4. What is a recent movie or television show that you've seen? Now, give your opinion of it. **(2)**

   _____

   _____

5. What is one thing that makes you smile? Write what it is and why it makes you smile. **(2)**

   _____

   _____

Assessment Tip: Total **10** Points

Name _____

Improving Your Writing

Read the journal entry below. Then write a journal entry as if you were one of the other characters in *A Very Important Day*. Describe the events and write your personal observations and feelings in words that give your writing your own personal voice.

From Kostas's Journal

January 18

    Today will be very special. Mother and Father are becoming United States citizens. I don't have to do that, because I'm already a citizen. I was born in this country. I feel very proud that they will become citizens, too. Tonight, we'll have a wonderful party to celebrate.

    It is snowing. I like snow. The city becomes quieter when it snows. The street sounds are muffled, and the city seems peaceful. I hope there will be enough snow to make a snowman. Maybe there will be enough snow to make two!

(10 points) _____

_____

_____

_____

_____

_____

_____

_____

Name _____

Filling in the Blank

Use the test-taking strategies and tips you have learned to help you answer fill-in-the-blank items. This practice will help you when you take this kind of test.

Read each item. At the bottom of the page, fill in the circle for the answer that best completes the sentence.

1. Tomás and his family picked fruit and vegetables for Texas farmers in the —

   A summer   **C** spring

   B winter   **D** fall

2. Right after Tomás and Enrique carried water to their parents, they —

   F visited the library

   G went to the town dump

   H picked corn in the fields

   J played with a ball

3. When Tomás got to the library, he saw —

   A that the building was closed

   B Papá Grande telling a story

   C children leaving with books

   D his brother Enrique reading a book

4. Just after Tomás went inside the library and got a drink of water, —

   F the librarian brought him some books

   G he read a book about dinosaurs

   H he listened to Papá Grande tell a story

   J the librarian told him that the library was closing

ANSWER ROWS   1 Ⓐ ● Ⓒ Ⓓ **(5 points)**   3 Ⓐ Ⓑ ● Ⓓ **(5)**

                      2 Ⓕ Ⓖ Ⓗ ● **(5)**   4 ● Ⓖ Ⓗ Ⓙ **(5)**

Name _____

Filling in the Blank continued

5. Tomás imagined he was riding one, when he read a book about —

   A horses

   B camels

   C dinosaurs

   D tigers

6. Before Tomás could leave with any of the library books, the librarian had to —

   F get him a library card

   G talk to his parents

   H check them out in her name

   J write down his address

7. When Tomás went to the town dump with his family, he looked for —

   A toys

   B iron

   C pencils

   D books

8. Before Tomás left to go back to Texas, the librarian gave him a —

   F ride on a horse

   G new book

   H package of sweet bread

   J library card

ANSWER ROWS 5 Ⓐ Ⓑ ● Ⓓ **(5 points)** 7 Ⓐ Ⓑ Ⓒ ● **(5)**

6 Ⓕ Ⓖ ● Ⓙ **(5)** 8 Ⓕ ● Ⓗ Ⓙ **(5)**

Assessment Tip: Total **40** Points

Name _____

Spelling Review

Write Spelling Words from the list on this page to answer the questions.

Order of answers in each category may vary.

1–14. Which fourteen words have the /ou/, /ô/, /ŏŏ/, or /ōō/ sounds?

1. howl **(1 point)**
2. bounce **(1)**
3. jaw **(1)**
4. couch **(1)**
5. dawn **(1)**
6. false **(1)**
7. sauce

8. wood **(1)**
9. put **(1)**
10. push **(1)**
11. tool **(1)**
12. full **(1)**
13. roof **(1)**
14. pull **(1)**

15–22. Which eight words have the /îr/, /är/, or /âr/ sounds?

15. gear **(1)**
16. year **(1)**
17. spare **(1)**
18. hardly **(1)**

19. dairy **(1)**
20. alarm **(1)**
21. cheer **(1)**
22. charge **(1)**

23–30. Which eight words have the /ôr/ or /ûr/ sounds?

23. search **(1)**
24. world **(1)**
25. chore **(1)**
26. curl **(1)**

27. dirty **(1)**
28. horse **(1)**
29. heard **(1)**
30. return **(1)**

Spelling Words

1. gear
2. howl
3. wood
4. bounce
5. jaw
6. put
7. year
8. false
9. couch
10. dawn
11. push
12. sauce
13. spare
14. tool
15. full
16. search
17. roof
18. pull
19. hardly
20. world
21. dairy
22. chore
23. curl
24. dirty
25. alarm
26. cheer
27. charge
28. horse
29. heard
30. return

Assessment Tip: Total **30** Points

Name _____

Spelling Spree

Context Clues Write the Spelling Word that completes each sentence.

1. You rode a black horse **(1 point)** _____ at the farm.

2. When I come back, I return **(1)** _____.

3. I put **(1)** _____ my coat in the closet.

4. We heard **(1)** _____ noises in the kitchen.

5. Mom likes to curl **(1)** _____ her hair.

Rhyme Time Write the Spelling Word that makes sense and rhymes with the word in dark print.

6. **Thirty** dirty **(1)** _____ rabbits hopped.

7. We always **yawn** at dawn **(1)** _____.

8. **Ouch**! I fell off of the couch **(1)** _____.

9. Choose **good** wood **(1)** _____ for the fire.

10. Wolves sometimes **growl** or howl **(1)** _____.

American Places Use the Spelling Words to complete these sentences about American cities.

11. New York is one of the biggest cities in the world **(1)** _____.

12. There are many dairy **(1)** _____ farms in Wisconsin.

13. Many people visit Austin, Texas, each year **(1)** _____.

14. Sometimes you can hardly **(1)** _____ see in the fog of San Francisco.

15. Boston chefs make delicious spaghetti sauce **(1)** _____.

Spelling Words

1. howl
2. couch
3. dawn
4. sauce
5. wood
6. put
7. hardly
8. year
9. dairy
10. horse
11. dirty
12. curl
13. heard
14. world
15. return

Assessment Tip: Total **15** Points

Name _____

Proofreading and Writing

Proofreading Circle the six misspelled Spelling Words in this advertisement. Then write each word correctly.

Come visit a real log cabin. You will (bownce) along an old lane for about one mile. Then you will see smoke from the chimney on the (ruf). The (charg) is three dollars.

In the 1700s, people had little (spair) time. Each child had at least one (chor) to do. Every day was (ful) of work.

1. bounce **(1 point)**   4. spare **(1)**

2. roof **(1)**   5. chore **(1)**

3. charge **(1)**   6. full **(1)**

What's the Message? **After his visit, Harry e-mailed his cousin. Use Spelling Words to complete the message. (1 point each)**

Is it true or 7. false **(1)** that you are sick? I hope this note will 8. cheer **(1)** you up. My 9. jaw **(1)** dropped when we visited a log cabin. No 10. tool **(1)** in the cabin was electric! You would need muscles to 11. push **(1)** and 12. pull **(1)** logs into place! Except for a fire 13. alarm **(1)** in the roof, it is the same as it was long ago. We can 14. search **(1)** for a place like this where we can bring our camping 15. gear **(1)** .

✏️➤ **Write a Diary Entry** **On a separate sheet of paper, write a diary entry about life in a log cabin. Use the Spelling Review Words.** Responses will vary. **(5)**

Name _____

Adapting a Book to a Play

Choose a book (or one of the selections from the previous themes) to adapt into a play. Explain why you have chosen it. Make a list of all the elements of a play that must be included.

Answers will vary. **(5 points)**

_____

_____

_____

_____

_____

Next write the cast of characters, the setting, and the time of the play.

Answers will vary. **(5 points)**

_____

_____

_____

_____

_____

_____

_____

_____

_____

_____

Name _____

Write a Character Analysis

Write a character analysis, or description, for the following characters from *Tales of a Fourth Grade Nothing*. Describe what kind of person the character is. Be sure to use descriptive adjectives that tell about the character's personality. Refer to the play for examples to support your descriptions.

1. Peter: _Answers will vary. (5 points)_____

_____

_____

_____

_____

_____

_____

_____

_____

2. Mrs. Yarby: _Answers will vary. (5 points)_____

_____

_____

_____

_____

_____

_____

_____

_____

Assessment Tip: Total **10** Points

Name _____

Make It Amazing!

Change the underlined words in the paragraph below to make it amazing. The first one is done for you. Accept reasonable answers, sample answers provided.

When I walked into my house yesterday, I saw my mother on the sofa. She was reading the newspaper. When she looked up, I told her about my day at school.

When I ___*flew*___ into my _castle, pond_ **(2 points)** yesterday, I saw _a frog, an elephant_ **(2)** on the _refrigerator, moon_ **(2)**. She was _singing a song, dancing a jig_ **(2)**. When she _did a cartwheel, bounced up and down_ **(2)**, I told her about my day _on a spaceship, on Mars_ **(2)**.

Continue the story to tell about your amazing day!

Answers will vary. **(8)**

_____
_____
_____
_____
_____
_____

★ **Bonus To make your story even more amazing, rewrite the paragraph, adding adjectives to describe the important nouns. Here are two examples: "my upside down house" and "the floating sofa."** Answers will vary. **(5)**

Name _____

That's Amazing!

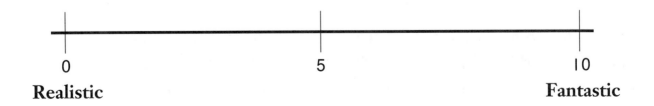

	What in the story was realistic?	What amazing things happened in the story?
The Stranger	Most things from the story are realistic: the family, their house, their activities, and some of the stranger's behavior. **(4 points)**	The stranger has many odd traits: his low temperature breaks the thermometer; the rabbits are not afraid of him; leaves have stopped changing color.**(4)**
Cendrillon	People lead everyday lives; they have realistic attitudes; the island of Martinique is described realistically. **(4)**	Nannin's wand changes everyday items into special things. Things miraculously change back. **(4)**
Heat Wave!	The family lives on a farm, and the surroundings and possessions are all realistic at first: geese, cows, flowers, corn, crows. **(4)**	Everything that happens to these normal items is fantastic: geese are cooked by the heat wave, flowers walk, cow's milk turns to butter, lettuce cools air. **(4)**

Which of these stories was most amazing to you? Put a mark on the line for each story, labeled with the story's title, to show how realistic you think each one was! Answers will vary. **(2)**

```
0                          5                         10
```
Realistic   **Fantastic**

Name _____

Chilly Crossword

Complete the puzzle using words from the vocabulary list. Write the word that fits each clue.

Across

2. season of year between summer and winter (**1 point**)
4. very thin covering of ice (**1**)
6. an instrument that measures temperature (**1**)
8. a flow of air (**1**)

Down

1. strange, odd (**1**)
3. silvery metal used in thermometers (**1**)
5. made a design by cutting lines (**1**)
7. shy; easily frightened (**1**)

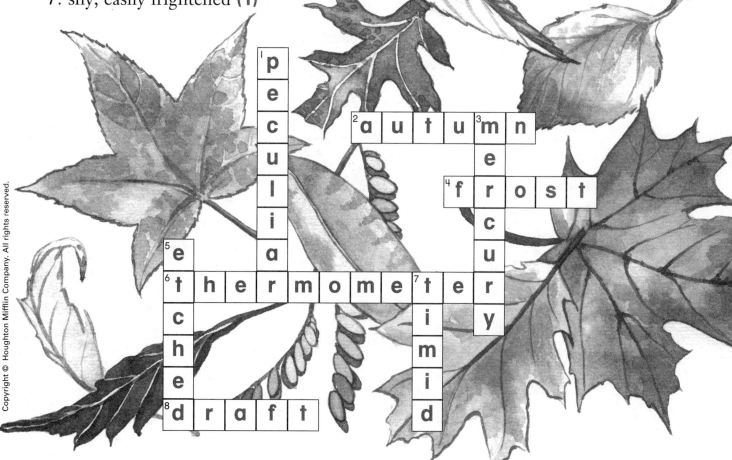

Vocabulary

autumn
draft
etched
frost
mercury
peculiar
thermometer
timid

Name _____

Detail Map

(page 306)

doesn't talk **(1)**

_____

(page 306)

wears odd rough leather

clothing **(1 point)**

(page 308)

is confused by buttons **(1)**

_____

**Stranger
Details**

(page 308)

is friends with the rabbits **(1)**

_____

(page 314)

blows on a leaf **(1)**

(page 310)

works hard and never tires **(1)**

_____

(page 302)

summer turning to fall, cool

breeze blowing **(1 point)**

(page 308)

shivering cold in the house **(1)**

_____

**Weather
Details**

(page 314)

air turns cold **(1)**

(page 312)

feels like summer **(1)**

Name _____

A Nose for Details

Think about the selection. Then answer these questions.

1. What time of year does the story take place?
   fall, autumn **(2 points)**

2. What happens when Mr. Bailey is driving his truck?
   He hits a man. **(2)**

3. What was the stranger wearing?
   odd rough leather clothing **(2)**

4. What does the stranger **not** do?
   talk **(2)**

5. The stranger pulls a leaf off a tree and does what?
   He blows on it. **(2)**

6. What happens to the weather and the leaves after the stranger leaves?
   The air becomes cold and the leaves change color. **(2)**

7. What words are etched in frost on the farmhouse windows every year?
   "See you next fall." **(2)**

Name _____

Think About It

Read the story. Then complete the detail map on the next page.

What's Your Name?

Mr. Downing's first attempt at a garden since his retirement was a huge disappointment. He had tried everything—plant food, pruning, bug control, and water. It still looked like even the smallest field mouse couldn't get a meal from it.

One day an elderly lady wearing a large hat covered with flowers passed by the fence in front of Mr. Downing's house. She called over to him, "Looks like you could use a little help there." The lady walked over to the garden, tucked her long, curly, gray hair up into her hat, bent down, and immediately began tending the plants.

As Mr. Downing watched her in stunned silence he noticed that the flowers in her hat were real. "How odd," he thought. Then he heard the lady softly talking. He was about to ask her to speak up when he realized she wasn't talking to him but the plants instead.

Mr. Downing focused his eyes on the lady for quite some time. Finally she stood up and spoke to him. "Remember, a little conversation never hurts." She began to walk away.

A little confused, Mr. Downing looked from her to his garden. He was amazed at the sight before his eyes. The flowers were blooming and there were vegetables on the vines. He turned back, thanked the lady and asked her name.

"Everybody just calls me Mother," she said, with a smile full of sunshine.

Name _____

Think About It

Complete this Detail Map for the story "What's Your Name?"

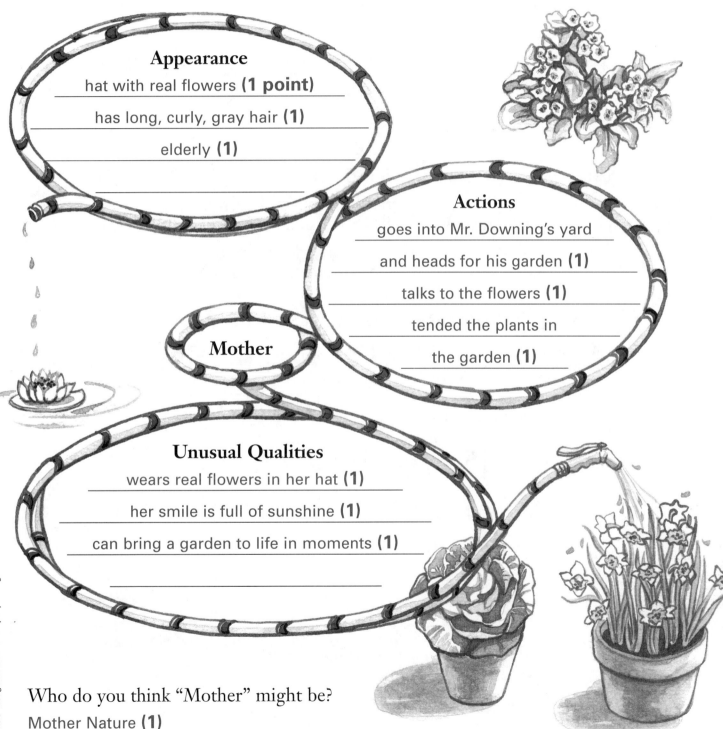

Appearance

hat with real flowers **(1 point)**

has long, curly, gray hair **(1)**

elderly **(1)**

_____

Actions

goes into Mr. Downing's yard

and heads for his garden **(1)**

talks to the flowers **(1)**

tended the plants in

the garden **(1)**

Mother

Unusual Qualities

wears real flowers in her hat **(1)**

her smile is full of sunshine **(1)**

can bring a garden to life in moments **(1)**

_____

Who do you think "Mother" might be?

Mother Nature **(1)**

Name _____

Compound Challenge

**Write the compound word that matches each clue. Then write
the circled letters in order at the bottom of the page to spell a
word that describes the Stranger.**

1. carousel m e r r y - g o - r o u n d **(1 point)**

2. a yard at the back of a house b a c k y a r d **(1)**

3. the first meal of the day b r e a k f a s t **(1)**

4. light coming from stars s t a r l i g h t **(1)**

5. Saturday and Sunday w e e k e n d **(1)**

6. a truck used by firefighters f i r e e n g i n e **(1)**

7. a bank shaped like a pig p i g g y b a n k **(1)**

8. a coat worn to protect against rain r a i n c o a t **(1)**

9. a house for a dog d o g h o u s e **(1)**

10. a walk on the side of a road s i d e w a l k **(1)**

A word to describe the Stranger:

m y s t e r i o u s **(2)**

     Assessment Tip: Total **12** Points

Name _____

Compound Words

A **compound word** is made up of two or more smaller words. To spell a compound word correctly, you must know if it is written as one word, as two words joined by a hyphen, or as two separate words.

rail + **road** = railroad   **ninety** + **nine** = ninety-nine
seat + **belt** = seat belt

► In the starred word *already*, an *l* was dropped in *all* to make one word.

Write each Spelling Word under the heading that tells how the word is written. Order of answers for each category may vary.

One Word

railroad **(1 point)**   fireplace **(1)**

airport **(1)**   ourselves **(1)**

everywhere **(1)**   forever **(1)**

homesick **(1)**   breakfast **(1)**

understand **(1)**   whenever **(1)**

background **(1)**   everything **(1)**

anything **(1)**   meanwhile **(1)**

already **(1)**   afternoon **(1)**

With a Hyphen   **Two Words**

ninety-nine **(1)**   seat belt **(1)**

make-believe **(1)**   all right **(1)**

Spelling Words

1. railroad
2. airport
3. seat belt
4. everywhere
5. homesick
6. understand
7. background
8. anything
9. ninety-nine
10. already*
11. fireplace
12. ourselves
13. all right
14. forever
15. breakfast
16. whenever
17. everything
18. meanwhile
19. afternoon
20. make-believe

Theme 3: **That's Amazing!**   161
Assessment Tip: Total **20** Points

Name _____

Spelling Spree

What Am I? Write the Spelling Word that answers each riddle.

1. I'm cereal and juice, and I happen before lunch.
   What am I? breakfast **(1)**

2. I'm really quite old, but less than one hundred.
   What am I? ninety-nine **(1)**

3. I'm the part of the day between morning and night.
   What am I? afternoon **(1)**

4. Fasten me and I'll save you from crashes.
   What am I? seat belt **(1)**

5. If going by plane, you must pass through me.
   What am I? airport **(1)**

1. railroad
2. airport
3. seat belt
4. everywhere
5. homesick
6. understand
7. background
8. anything
9. ninety-nine
10. already*
11. fireplace
12. ourselves
13. all right
14. forever
15. breakfast
16. whenever
17. everything
18. meanwhile
19. afternoon
20. make-believe

Finish the word Each of the words below forms part of a Spelling Word. Write the Spelling Words on the lines.

6. any anything **(1)**

7. home homesick **(1)**

8. under understand **(1)**

9. back background **(1)**

10. where everywhere **(1)**

11. our ourselves **(1)**

12. all all right **(1)**

13. when whenever **(1)**

14. while meanwhile **(1)**

15. believe make-believe **(1)**

    Assessment Tip: Total **15** Points

Name _____

Proofreading and Writing

Proofreading Circle the five misspelled Spelling Words in the newspaper article. Then write each word correctly.

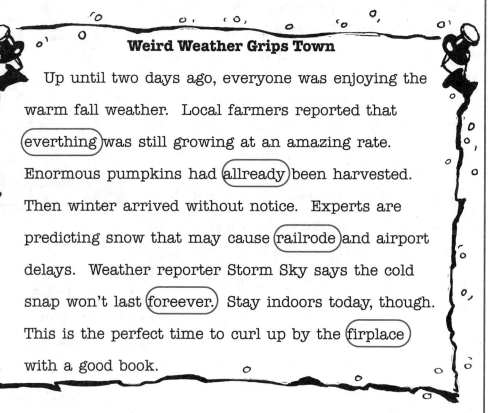

Weird Weather Grips Town

Up until two days ago, everyone was enjoying the warm fall weather. Local farmers reported that (everthing) was still growing at an amazing rate. Enormous pumpkins had (allready) been harvested. Then winter arrived without notice. Experts are predicting snow that may cause (railrode) and airport delays. Weather reporter Storm Sky says the cold snap won't last (foreever.) Stay indoors today, though. This is the perfect time to curl up by the (firplace) with a good book.

1. everything **(1 point)**
2. already **(1)**
3. railroad **(1)**
4. forever **(1)**
5. fireplace **(1)**

1. railroad
2. airport
3. seat belt
4. everywhere
5. homesick
6. understand
7. background
8. anything
9. ninety-nine
10. already*
11. fireplace
12. ourselves
13. all right
14. forever
15. breakfast
16. whenever
17. everything
18. meanwhile
19. afternoon
20. make-believe

Write Helpful Hints The stranger in the story was unfamiliar with many things in the Bailey house. Have you ever helped a person in an unfamiliar situation? What information would be helpful to that person?

On a separate sheet of paper, write a list of helpful tips for newcomers to your town or neighborhood. You might include information such as where to get the best pizza. Use Spelling Words from the list. Responses will vary. **(10 points)**

Name _____

Strange Synonyms

Mrs. Fields, a neighbor of the Baileys, wrote this letter to a cousin. She uses the word *strange* in almost every sentence. From the word list below, choose synonyms to add variety to Mrs. Fields's letter. Some of the words are exact synonyms for *strange*, while others are words that give a better sense of the sentence. Some words will fit in more than one sentence, but use each word only once. Use the sentence context to help decide which words fit best.

Dear Cousin Joe,

   Our town had a very 1. strange autumn. Every leaf stayed green for weeks, which is 2. strange for these parts. A 3. strange wind blew in the trees, making it feel just like summer. Everyone noticed the 4. strange weather, even the new person in town. He was a little 5. strange — he didn't talk much, but he sure could play the fiddle! He had a 6. strange gift with animals. But the weather must have been too 7. strange for him, because he left suddenly. The town felt 8. strange without him. We missed him a lot. Shortly after he left, the 9. strange summer weather turned to fall. It's too bad that the 10. strange stranger left so soon. I think he would have liked autumn.

Answers will vary.

Your cousin,
Freda Fields

Vocabulary

unusual
shy
unique
warm
unknown
rare
unfamiliar
new
odd
special
cool
weird
sad
uncommon
timid
quiet
different
lonely

1. **(1 point)** _____
2. **(1)** _____
3. **(1)** _____
4. **(1)** _____
5. **(1)** _____

6. **(1)** _____
7. **(1)** _____
8. **(1)** _____
9. **(1)** _____
10. **(1)** _____

Assessment Tip: Total **10** Points

Name _____

Letter with Action Verbs

Read Katy Bailey's letter to her cousin. Circle each action verb and write it on the lines below.

Dear Eva,

We (have) a new guest at our house. I (think) he (lives) in the forest near us. He (wears) a leather shirt and pants. His breath (makes) things cold. I (call) him "Jack Frost." He (likes) my mother's cooking, though. He especially (enjoys) her homemade vegetable soup. I (hope) you (meet) him soon.

Love,

Katy

have **(1 point)** _____

think **(1)** _____

lives **(1)** _____

wears **(1)** _____

makes **(1)** _____

call **(1)** _____

likes **(1)** _____

enjoys **(1)** _____

hope **(1)** _____

meet **(1)** _____

Name _____

Take Action!

Katy tells the class about the stranger who came to stay with her family. Complete Katy's story by filling each blank with an action verb. Choose verbs from the box or use action verbs of your own.
(1 point for each answer.)

change
disappears
drives
grows
hears
jams
helps
jumps
listens
works

    One fall day as my father _drives **(1 point)**_ his truck along the road, he _hears **(1)**_ a loud thump. He _jams **(1)**_ on the brakes and _jumps **(1)**_ out of the truck. Father _helps **(1)**_ the stranger into his truck.

    The doctor _listens **(1)**_ to the stranger's heart. The stranger _grows **(1)**_ stronger and _works **(1)**_ with Father on the farm. When the stranger _disappears **(1)**_, the leaves _change **(1)**_ color and the weather turns cold.

Name _____

Using Action Verbs

Using Exact Verbs Good writers use verbs that name specific actions to produce a vivid image in the reader's mind. Read each sentence below. Then rewrite the sentence. Substitute an exact verb for the general word or phrase in parentheses.

1. The doctor (looks at) the man's body.

   The doctor examines the man's body. **(2 points)**

2. The doctor (finds) a lump on the man's head.

   The doctor discovers a lump on the man's head. **(2)**

3. The stranger (does the same thing as) Katy as she cools her soup.

   The stranger imitates Katy as she cools her soup. **(2)**

4. The cold breath (makes) a chill up Mrs. Bailey's spine.

   The cold breath sends a chill up Mrs. Bailey's spine. **(2)**

5. The rabbits do not (act frightened by) the stranger.

   The rabbits do not fear the stranger. **(2)**

6. The stranger (goes) along when Mr. Bailey works in the fields.

   The stranger tags along when Mr. Bailey works in the fields. **(2)**

7. Two weeks (go by) and the stranger can't remember his name.

   Two weeks pass and the stranger can't remember his name. **(2)**

8. The stranger (wondered about) the colors of the leaves on the trees.

   The stranger puzzled over the colors of the leaves on the trees. **(2)**

Name _____

Writing an Explanation

Use this page to plan your explanation. You can explain why something happens or how something happens. Then number your reasons or facts in the order you will use them.

| **Topic: (1 point)** |
| **Title: (1)** |

| **Topic Sentence: (2)** |
| |

Reason / Fact: (2)	**Reason / Fact: (2)**

Reason / Fact: (2)	**Reason / Fact: (2)**

Assessment Tip: Total **12** Points

Audience

Writers are always aware of their audience. A good writer will adapt the style of writing to fit the reader.

▶ Formal writing is used for reports, presentations, many school assignments, and business letters.

Formal: Deer can be found in almost all regions of the United States. Although they are wild animals, they can become quite used to the presence of human beings.

▶ Informal writing is for friendly letters, postcards, or e-mails between friends.

Informal: We saw the most incredible deer today. I was careful to walk up to it really slowly. I stretched out my hand, and it sniffed my palm. It felt really funny!

Write two short paragraphs about the change of seasons. Make the first one formal, as if you were giving a report. Make the second one informal, as if you were writing a postcard to a good friend.

The Change of Seasons

Formal:

Responses will vary. **(6 points)**

_____

_____

_____

Informal:

Responses will vary. **(6)**

_____

_____

_____

Name _____

Evaluating Your Story

**Reread your story. What do you need to make it better? Use this
page to help you decide. Put a checkmark in the box for each
sentence that describes your story.**

Rings the Bell!

☐ The setting and characters are well defined.

☐ My story has an interesting beginning, middle, and end.

☐ I made good use of dialogue in my story.

☐ The main character solves the story's problem in an
interesting way.

☐ There are almost no mistakes.

Getting Stronger

☐ The setting and characters are described in a general way.

☐ The plot could be more interesting.

☐ I could add more details and dialogue to the story.

☐ The main character's solution to the problem could be
more interesting.

☐ There are a few mistakes.

Try Harder

☐ The plot is not interesting.

☐ There is no clear problem.

☐ I haven't included details or dialogue.

☐ There are a lot of mistakes.

Name _____

Using Possessives

A **possessive** shows ownership.

► Add 's to make nouns possessive.

► For plurals that end in *s*, add an apostrophe.

Rewrite each phrase, using a possessive noun. Then use the new phrase in a sentence of your own.

1. the pouch of the kangaroo the kangaroo's pouch **(1 point)**

   Sentences will vary. **(1)** _____

   _____

2. the roar of the lion the lion's roar **(1)**

   Sentences will vary. **(1)** _____

   _____

3. the buzz of the flies the flies' buzz **(1)**

   Sentences will vary. **(1)** _____

   _____

4. the cleverness of the foxes the foxes' cleverness **(1)**

   Sentences will vary. **(1)** _____

   _____

5. the prey belonging to the tiger the tiger's prey **(1)**

   Sentences will vary. **(1)** _____

   _____

6. the symphony of the frogs the frogs' symphony **(1)**

   Sentences will vary. **(1)** _____

   _____

Assessment Tip: Total **12** Points

Name _____

Spelling Words

Words Often Misspelled Look for familiar spelling patterns to help you remember how to spell the Spelling Words on this page. Think carefully about the parts that you find hard to spell in each word.

Write the missing letters in the Spelling Words below.

1. ton __i__ __g__ __h__ t (**1 point**)
2. __w__ __h__ ole (**1**)
3. __w__ __h__ ile (**1**)
4. c __o__ __u__ __l__ d (**1**)
5. w __o__ __r__ ld (**1**)
6. __w__ __r__ iting (**1**)
7. b __u__ __i__ ld (**1**)
8. s __c__ __h__ ool (**1**)
9. fini __s__ __h__ ed (**1**)
10. mo __r__ __n__ ing (**1**)
11. c __o__ __m__ ing (**1**)
12. sto __p__ __p__ ed (**1**)
13. ge __t__ __t__ ing (**1**)
14. g __o__ __e__ s (**1**)
15. g __o__ ing (**1**)

Study List **On a separate piece of paper, write each Spelling Word. Check your spelling against the words on the list.** Order of words may vary. (**5 points**)

Name _____

Spelling Spree

Write a Spelling Word to fit each clue.

1. a word meaning "at the same time as" while **(1 point)**
2. a two-syllable synonym for *done* finished **(1)**
3. the opposite of *going* coming **(1)**
4. a pencil helps you with this writing **(1)**
5. what the car did at the red light stopped **(1)**
6. the whole wide world **(1)**
7. a synonym for *leaving* going **(1)**
8. what carpenters do build **(1)**
9. a place for learning school **(1)**
10. not broken into smaller pieces whole **(1)**

Spelling Words
1. tonight
2. whole
3. while
4. could
5. world
6. writing
7. build
8. school
9. finished
10. morning
11. coming
12. stopped
13. getting
14. goes
15. going

Word Addition **Combine the first part of the first word with the second part of the second word to write a Spelling Word.**

11. goat + sees   goes **(1)**
12. couch + mold   could **(1)**
13. tons + light   tonight **(1)**
14. more + inning   morning **(1)**
15. germ + sitting   getting **(1)**

Theme 3: **That's Amazing!**   173
Assessment Tip: Total **15** Points

Name _____

Proofreading and Writing

Proofreading Circle the five misspelled Spelling Words in this newspaper item. Then write each word correctly.

The latest episode of *Amazing and Incredible* will be on (tonigt) at eight o'clock. It (coud) be an interesting program. Most of the show is about a woman who tried to build a house out of old soft drink bottles. Apparently, she (finnished) most of two stories. However, she (stoped) when she realized that the bottles wouldn't be able to support a roof. There will also be an interview with a person who's trying to row a boat around the (werld.) This show can be seen on Channel 9.

Spelling Words

1. tonight
2. whole
3. while
4. could
5. world
6. writing
7. build
8. school
9. finished
10. morning
11. coming
12. stopped
13. getting
14. goes
15. going

1. tonight **(1 point)** _____
2. could **(1)** _____
3. finished **(1)** _____
4. stopped **(1)** _____
5. world **(1)** _____

✏ **Rhyming Sentences** Pick five Spelling Words from the list. Then write a sentence for each word. In each sentence, include a word that rhymes with the Spelling Word. Underline the rhyming words. Responses will vary. **(5 points)**

174   Theme 3: **That's Amazing!**
Assessment Tip: Total **10** Points

Name _____

A Perfect Match

Write the letter to match each word with its definition.

d **(1)**   **crossly**   a. a woman who acts as a child's parent

f **(1)**   **elegant**   b. relating to a poor farm worker

a **(1)**   **god-mother**   c. thinking highly of oneself

e **(1)**   **orphan**   d. in a grumpy or grouchy way

b **(1)**   **peasant**   e. a child whose parents are dead

c **(1)**   **proud**   f. marked by good taste

Write your own sentence for each vocabulary word. Answers will vary.

1. orphan: **(1 point)** _____

_____

2. god-mother: **(1)** _____

_____

3. elegant: **(1)** _____

_____

4. proud: **(1)** _____

_____

5. crossly: **(1)** _____

_____

6. peasant: **(1)** _____

_____

Name ______________________________

Venn Diagram

Vitaline and Cendrillon

(accept reasonably varied answers)

Vitaline

is younger than Cendrillon
is spoiled
is invited to ball
is jealous of Cendrillon and Paul
foot doesn't fit the shoe
(5 points)

How They Are Alike

have same father
are sisters
live in same house
go to the ball
want to marry Paul
(5)

has a godmother
hands are blistered
works all day
is called lazy
dances with Paul
marries Paul
(5)

Cendrillon

Assessment Tip: Total **15** Points

Name _____

Memory Check

Think about the selection. Then complete the sentences.

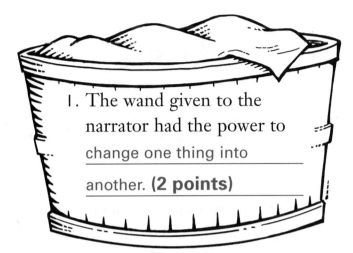

1. The wand given to the narrator had the power to

   change one thing into

   another. **(2 points)**

2. One day, Cendrillon came sad-faced to the river because

   she wanted to go to Paul's

   birthday ball. **(2)**

3. Cendrillon's godmother turned breadfruit and six agoutis into

   a carriage and six horses. **(2)**

4. While running from the ball, Cendrillon stumbled and left behind

   one embroidered slipper. **(2)**

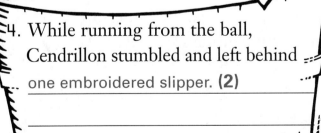

5. Cendrillon told her godmother "No more spells" because

   she wanted Paul to love her for

   who she really was. **(2)**

Name _____

A Resourceful Parent

Read the story. Then complete the Venn diagram on the following page.

A Costume for the Carnival

It was carnival time and everyone was hurrying to make or find the most original costume to win the grand prize. Pantaloon, a rich boy, and Harlequin, a poor boy, both wanted to win.

Pantaloon's rich father ordered a costume from a famous tailor. When completed, the costume was spectacular. It was made of gold cloth, trimmed with yellow diamonds, complete with purple gloves and a hat with feathers.

Since Harlequin was poor, he didn't know what to do. His mother suggested, "Why don't you ask if you can borrow an extra costume from one of your friends?"

Harlequin ran to the house of every one of his friends, but at every house it was the same. "I'm sorry, Harlequin, I don't have an extra costume. But I have these scraps of cloth left over. You may have them—if they will help."

Sadly, Harlequin brought the scraps to his mother. His mother had an idea and sent him off to bed. Harlequin did as he was told. The next morning there, at the foot of his bed, lay the most beautiful costume he had ever seen! His mother had used the scraps and cut them into diamond shapes. Then she had sewn all the shapes together to create a costume with every color of the rainbow! She had sewn on sequins so the costume caught the light and shined and sparkled. He even had a matching hat with feathers!

Harlequin pulled on his costume and hurried to the Square. Did his costume win the prize for the most original? Well, what do you think?

Name _____

A Resourceful Parent continued

Complete the Venn Diagram for the story "A Costume for the Carnival."

Harlequin's Costume

1. made of diamond shapes sewn together **(1)**

2. made from scraps **(1)**

3. all the colors of the rainbow **(1)**

How the Costumes are Alike

1. shined and sparkled **(1)**

2. hats with feathers **(1)**

Pantaloon's Costume

1. all of gold cloth **(1)**

2. trimmed in yellow diamonds **(1)**

3. purple gloves **(1)**

If you were one of the costume judges, would you award the prize to Harlequin or Pantaloon? Why? Use complete sentences.

Answers will vary. **(2)**

_____

_____

_____

Name _____

A Suffix Story

**Fill in each blank with a word from the box and the suffix
-able. Then finish the fairy tale by writing what happens
next. Try to use at least one word with the suffix -able in
your story ending.**

Once upon a time, Angelina was given a magic wand
by her fairy godmother. This magic wand was the most
marvelous thing <u>imaginable **(1 point)**</u>. It could
make a hard wooden chair <u>comfortable **(1)**</u>.
It could make the most difficult book
<u>readable **(1)**</u>. One wave of the wand, and
an old game became <u>playable **(1)**</u> or a
shirt that was too small became <u>wearable **(1)**</u>
again. Even a lost jewel or a tiny charm became
<u>findable **(1)**</u>.

But one day, the <u>valuable **(1)**</u> wand
disappeared! Angelina looked everywhere. Finally she cried,
"This is not <u>acceptable **(1)**</u>! Where is my
wand?" Was the problem <u>solvable **(1)**</u>?

<u>Endings will vary. **(1)**</u>

_____

_____

_____

_____

Name _____

Final /ər/ and Final /l/ or /əl/

A syllable is a word or word part that has one vowel sound. The final syllable of some words ends with a weak vowel sound + *r* or *l*. This weak vowel sound is called **schwa** and is shown as /ə/. When you hear the final /ər/ sounds in a two-syllable word, think of the patterns *er, or,* and *ar.* When you hear the final /l/ or /əl/ sounds in a two-syllable word, think of the patterns *el, al,* and *le.*

final /ər/	*er, or, ar* (weath**er**, harb**or**, sug**ar**)
final /l/ or /əl/	*el, al, le* (mod**el**, fin**al**, midd**le**)

Write each Spelling Word under its spelling of the final /ər/, /l/, or /əl/ sounds. Order of answers for each category may vary.

Spelling Words

1. harbor
2. final
3. middle
4. weather
5. labor
6. model
7. chapter
8. special
9. sugar
10. bottle
11. medal
12. collar
13. proper
14. towel
15. beggar
16. battle
17. trouble
18. shower
19. uncle
20. doctor

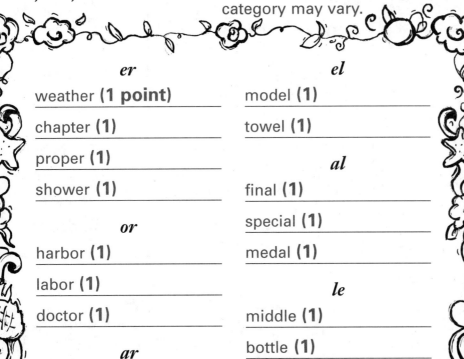

er

weather **(1 point)**

chapter **(1)**

proper **(1)**

shower **(1)**

or

harbor **(1)**

labor **(1)**

doctor **(1)**

ar

sugar **(1)**

collar **(1)**

beggar **(1)**

el

model **(1)**

towel **(1)**

al

final **(1)**

special **(1)**

medal **(1)**

le

middle **(1)**

bottle **(1)**

battle **(1)**

trouble **(1)**

uncle **(1)**

Assessment Tip: Total **20** Points

Name _____

Spelling Spree

Crossword Use the Spelling Words from the box to complete the crossword puzzle.

Across

2. a brother of your mother or father
4. cloth used to dry things
7. unusual or exceptional
8. polite
9. home for a boat
11. a small copy
13. a brief rain
14. work

Down

1. container for liquids
3. part of a shirt
5. a section of a book
6. rain, sun, or snow
10. someone who begs
12. someone who pratices medicine
13. a substance used to sweeten food

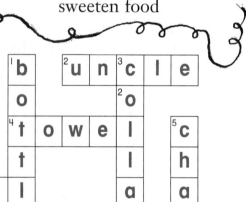

Crossword grid solution:

- 2 Across: **uncle**
- 4 Across: **towel**
- 7 Across: **special**
- 8 Across: **proper**
- 9 Across: **harbor**
- 11 Across: **model**
- 13 Across: **shower**
- 14 Across: **labor**
- 1 Down: **bottle**
- 3 Down: **collar**
- 5 Down: **chapter**
- 6 Down: **weather**
- 10 Down: **beggar**
- 12 Down: **doctor**
- 13 Down: **sugar**

Assessment Tip: Total **15** Points

Name _____

Proofreading and Writing

Proofreading Circle the five misspelled Spelling Words in this diary entry. Then write each word correctly.

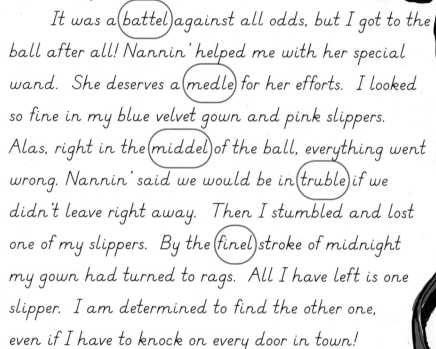

Dear Diary,

It was a ⟨battel⟩ against all odds, but I got to the ball after all! Nannin' helped me with her special wand. She deserves a ⟨medle⟩ for her efforts. I looked so fine in my blue velvet gown and pink slippers. Alas, right in the ⟨middel⟩ of the ball, everything went wrong. Nannin' said we would be in ⟨truble⟩ if we didn't leave right away. Then I stumbled and lost one of my slippers. By the ⟨finel⟩ stroke of midnight my gown had turned to rags. All I have left is one slipper. I am determined to find the other one, even if I have to knock on every door in town!

Spelling Words

1. harbor
2. final
3. middle
4. weather
5. labor
6. model
7. chapter
8. special
9. sugar
10. bottle
11. medal
12. collar
13. proper
14. towel
15. beggar
16. battle
17. trouble
18. shower
19. uncle
20. doctor

1. battle **(1 point)**
2. medal **(1)**
3. middle **(1)**
4. trouble **(1)**
5. final **(1)**

✏️ **Write an Explanation** Think about *Cendrillon* and other fairy tales you have read. What do you like about these stories? Are there things about fairy tales that you don't like?

On a separate sheet of paper, write a paragraph giving reasons why you like or dislike fairy tales. Use some of the Spelling Words from the list. Responses will vary. **(10 points)**

Name _____

Make a Spelling Table Pronunciation Key

Write the words in the correct blanks to complete the spelling table/pronunciation key below. Then underline the letters in those words that match the sound.

wand	fruit	chime
coach	round	guests
lost	spoil	gasp
blaze	scarf	stood

Spelling Table / Pronunciation Key

Sound	Sample Words
/ă/	hand, g<u>a</u>sp **(1 point)**
/ā/	face, bl<u>aze</u> **(1)**
/ä/	march, sc<u>ar</u>f **(1)**
/ĕ/	bread, g<u>ue</u>sts **(1)**
/ī/	my, ch<u>i</u>me **(1)**
/ŏ/	hot, w<u>a</u>nd **(1)**
/ō/	most, c<u>oa</u>ch **(1)**
/ô/	fall, l<u>o</u>st **(1)**
oi	boy, sp<u>oi</u>l **(1)**
/o͝o/	cook, st<u>oo</u>d **(1)**
/o͞o/	move, fr<u>ui</u>t **(1)**
ou	crowd, r<u>ou</u>nd **(1)**

Name _____

Identifying Verbs

Underline the whole verb in each sentence. Then write the main verb and the helping verb on the lines below.

1. Cendrillon's stepmother has made the girl a servant.

   Main verb: made **(1 point)**

   Helping verb: has **(1)**

2. Cendrillon and her godmother have washed clothes at the river.

   Main verb: washed **(1)**

   Helping verb: have **(1)**

3. Cendrillon has suffered without complaint.

   Main verb: suffered **(1)**

   Helping verb: has **(1)**

4. Who has arrived at the ball?

   Main verb: arrived **(1)**

   Helping verb: has **(1)**

5. Her godmother has accompanied her to the ball.

   Main verb: accompanied **(1)**

   Helping verb: has **(1)**

Name _____

Writing Helping Verbs

**Change each verb in the sentences below by adding *has* or
have. Write the new sentence on the lines.**

1. Cendrillon's stepmother scolded her.

   Cendrillon's stepmother has scolded her. **(2 points)**

   _____

2. Cendrillon and her godmother washed clothes for the family

   Cendrillon and her godmother have washed clothes for the family. **(2)**

   _____

3. The godmother changed the agoutis into horses.

   The godmother has changed the agoutis into horses. **(2)**

   _____

4. The carriage traveled over the bridge.

   The carriage has traveled over the bridge. **(2)**

   _____

5. Cendrillon and the handsome young man danced all evening.

   Cendrillon and the handsome young man have danced all evening. **(2)**

   _____

Name _____

Using Helping Verbs

Good writers often combine two sentences that have the same subject and helping verb but different main verbs. Read each pair of sentences below. Then rewrite the two sentences as one sentence by combining the main verbs and helping verbs. Write your new sentence on the lines provided.

1. Cendrillon's godmother has tapped the breadfruit with her wand. She has turned it into a gilded coach.

   Cendrillon's godmother has tapped the breadfruit and turned

   it into a gilded coach. **(2 points)**

2. The godmother has turned the agoutis into carriage horses. She has changed the lizards into tall footmen.

   The godmother has turned the agoutis into carriage horses and

   changed the lizards into tall footmen. **(2)**

3. The carriage has crossed the bridge. The carriage has arrrived at the mansion.

   The carriage has crossed the bridge and arrived at the mansion. **(2)**

4. All the guests have looked at Cendrillon. They have talked about her.

   All the guests have looked at Cendrillon and talked about her. **(2)**

5. Cendrillon has heard the bells. She has run from the ball.

   Cendrillon has heard the bells and run from the ball. **(2)**

Name _____

Writing an Announcement

Use the chart to organize your ideas for an announcement. Then
write an announcement about a birth, wedding, concert, fair,
parade, or other special event.

Who? **(1 point)**	**What?** **(1)**	**Where?** **(1)**
When? **(1)**	**Why?** **(1)**	**How?** **(1)**

Answers will vary. **(6 points)**

_____

_____

_____

_____

_____

_____

    Assessment Tip: Total **12** Points

Name _____

Ordering Important Information

► When writing an announcement, first decide what information is most important. Put that information first.
► Put other information in order of importance from most important to least important.
► Be sure your announcement includes all the necessary information that answers some or all of these questions: who, what, where, when, why, how.

Use the following outline to write a wedding announcement for Cendrillon and Paul. Fill in the information in the outline. Then put the information in the order that makes the most sense.

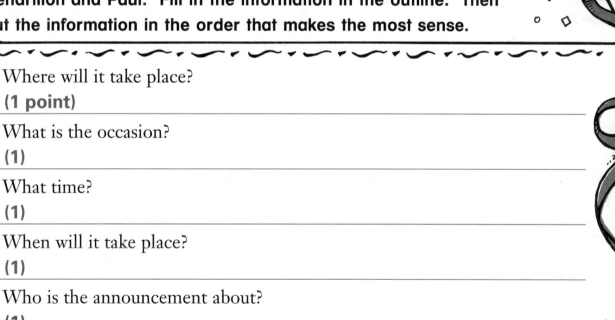

Where will it take place?
(1 point)
_____

What is the occasion?
(1)
_____

What time?
(1)
_____

When will it take place?
(1)
_____

Who is the announcement about?
(1)
_____

Answers will vary. Suggested order of events: who, what, when,
_____
where, what time. **(5 points)**
_____
_____
_____

Name —————————————————————————

What Do You Mean?

Write the word from the box that fits each definition.

1. to burn slightly
   singe **(1 point)** ————————————————

2. moveable pointer that shows wind direction
   weather vane **(1)** ———————————————

3. figured incorrectly
   miscalculated **(1)** ——————————————

4. measure of heat or coldness
   temperature **(1)** ————————————————

5. the line along which the sky and the earth seem to meet
   horizon **(1)** ——————————————————

6. caused a change in
   affected **(1)** —————————————————

**Write the word from the vocabulary list that belongs
in each group.**

7. Words about fire
   burn   char   scorch   singe **(1)** ——————————

8. Words that tell about making mistakes
   misspelled   misjudged   mistaken   miscalculated **(1)** —————

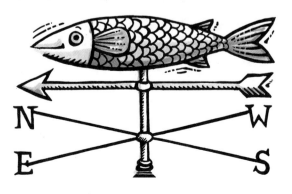

Name _____

Fantasy/Realism Chart

Page	Story Detail (accept varied answers)	Fantasy (F)/ Realism (R)
361	Geese are plucked, stuffed, and roasted. Geese are cooked in the sky. **(2 points)**	R F **(1 point)**
367	Milk is churned into butter. Cows jumping causes the milk to become butter. **(2)**	R F **(1)**
368	Getting oats wet makes oatmeal. Oatmeal makes fine glue. **(2)**	R F **(1)**
371	Adding water to flour and yeast makes dough. The rising dough picks up the tractor and the mule. **(2)**	R F **(1)**
375	They plant lettuce seeds and lettuce grows. Lettuce grows as soon as the seeds hit the dirt. **(2)**	R F **(1)**

Name _____

Interview Time

You're the narrator being interviewed by reporters after you defeat the Heat Wave. Answer the reporters' questions.

What is your name?

What happened here?

I don't have one in the story.

(2 points)

A Heat Wave got snagged on our weather vane. (Students can tell as many of the other main events as they wish.) **(2)**

Why is your ma knitting?

Who beat the Heat Wave?

She's knitting sweaters for the cows whose coats got singed.

(2)

We all worked together to deal with the mess. Sally, our mule, gave me the idea that worked. **(2)**

How did you beat the Heat Wave?

We planted iceberg lettuce, and it cooled off the air. **(2)**

Assessment Tip: Total **10** Points

Name _____

That's Fantastic!

Read the story and complete the chart on the next page.

The Big Little Machine

My name is Julius G. Malone. My middle initial stands for *genius*. Why? I have invented a machine that makes big things little. You simply place an object inside the machine, turn the dial, and *presto!* Big to little, large to small.

I made sure it worked by turning my dad's golf clubs into toothpicks. I also made my sister's new school clothes just the right size for her doll. I even made two ceiling lights into glow-in-the-dark earrings for my mother.

I was really excited about my new invention. Just as I was bragging about it to my sister, my mother called, "Everybody to the kitchen! We need to have a family meeting to solve a big problem!"

My dad began the meeting by saying, "Julius, perhaps you should limit your experiments to your own belongings." My sister, Lily, stuck her tongue out at me. When I promised to no longer shrink any of their things, Dad said, "Good. Thank you. This family meeting is officially over."

Just then our dog, Gruffly, ran into the room, chasing our cat. Before anyone could stop him, Gruffly ran right into the Big Little Machine as my hand slipped on the dial. In a second, he went from the size of a giant sheepdog down to the size of a pencil eraser.

Lily began crying. My mother frowned. And my dad said, "Attention, please. This family meeting is NOT officially over!"

Theme 3: **That's Amazing!**   193

That's Fantastic! continued

Complete this chart for the story "The Big Little Machine." Label the details with an F if it's *fantasy* or R if it is *realism*. Write in other details when the letter F or R is provided for you.

Story Detail (Answers may vary.)	Fantasy (F) or Realism (R)?
golf clubs becoming toothpicks	F **(1 point)**
sister's clothes fitting her doll	F **(1)**
Julius bragging to his sister **(1)** _____	R
having a family meeting to solve a problem	R **(1)**
Lily sticking her tongue out at Julius **(1)** _____	R
Gruffly, the dog, chasing the cat	R **(1)**
Gruffly becoming the size of an eraser **(1)** _____	F
lights made into glow-in-the-dark earrings **(1)** _____	F

Assessment Tip: Total **8** Points

Name _____

Add the Ending

▶ When a base word ends with *e*, the *e* is dropped before adding *-ed* or *-ing*.   *move/moved/moving*

▶ When a base word ends with one vowel followed by a single consonant, the consonant is doubled before adding *-ed* or *-ing*.   *pop/popped/popping*

Read each sentence. Choose a word from the box similar in meaning to the word or words in dark type. Complete the puzzle by adding *-ed* or *-ing* to your word.

turn
rise
bake
stir
race
drive
switch
grab
hop
scrub

Across

1. My brother **changed** his tune when the Heat Wave hit. **(1)**
4. Pa started **washing** the cows as hard as he could. **(1)**
6. The cows were **jumping** around like rabbits. **(1)**
7. The dough was **going up** so fast we ran for our lives. **(1)**
8. We **hurried** into the barn, but it was too late. **(1)**
9. I **snatched** a shovel and ran to the cornfield. **(1)**

Down

2. Ma was **steering** the truck out to the cornfield. **(1)**
3. We watched the Heat Wave **twisting** in the sky. **(1)**
4. I **mixed** the water and the flour in a trough. **(1)**
5. The dough **cooked** in the heat. **(1)**

Name _____

Words with *-ed* or *-ing*

Each of these words has a base word and an ending. A **base word** is a word to which a beginning or an ending can be added. If a word ends with *e*, drop the *e* before adding *-ed* or *-ing*. If a one-syllable word cnds with one vowel followed by a single consonant, double the consonant before adding *-ed* or *-ing*.

race + **ed** = rac**ed**   land + **ed** = land**ed**

sna**p** + **ing** = sna**pping**

Write each Spelling Word under the heading that tells what happens to its spelling when *-ed* or *-ing* is added.

Order of answers for each category may vary.

No Spelling Change

landed **(1 point)**

checking **(1)**

smelling **(1)**

fainted **(1)**

Final Consonant Doubled

skipped **(1)**

flipped **(1)**

snapping **(1)**

dimmed **(1)**

rubbing **(1)**

stripped **(1)**

tanning **(1)**

Final *e* Dropped

dancing **(1)**

hiking **(1)**

raced **(1)**

pleasing **(1)**

dared **(1)**

striped **(1)**

wasting **(1)**

traced **(1)**

phoning **(1)**

Assessment Tip: Total **20** Points

Name _____

Spelling Spree

Spelling Words

1. dancing
2. skipped
3. hiking
4. flipped
5. snapping
6. raced
7. landed
8. pleasing
9. checking
10. dared
11. dimmed
12. rubbing
13. striped
14. wasting
15. traced
16. stripped
17. tanning
18. smelling
19. phoning
20. fainted

Word Factory Write Spelling Words by adding *-ed* or *-ing* to each word below.

1. flip   flipped **(1 point)**
2. please   pleasing **(1)**
3. land   landed **(1)**
4. stripe   striped **(1)**
5. check   checking **(1)**
6. trace   traced **(1)**
7. rub   rubbing **(1)**
8. tan   tanning **(1)**
9. strip   stripped **(1)**

Meaning Match Write a Spelling Word that has each meaning and ending below.

Example: repair + ing *fixing*

10. pass out + ed   fainted **(1)**
11. detect an odor + ing   smelling **(1)**
12. run at top speed + ed   raced **(1)**
13. go on a long walk + ing   hiking **(1)**
14. challenge someone + ed   dared **(1)**
15. make a cracking sound + ing   snapping **(1)**

Name _____

Proofreading and Writing

Proofreading Circle the five misspelled Spelling Words in the following memo. Then write each word correctly.

To: All city workers
From: Mayor Cole Breeze

Summer's first heat wave is here, and
I ask all city workers to follow these guidelines:

- Carry on with all normal work. The heat is no excuse for (skiped) tasks.
- Shut fire hydrants to avoid (wasteing) water.
- Save energy by keeping office lights (dimed.)
- Keep checking on anyone doing heavy outdoor work.
- Avoid (foning) my office for the latest bulletins.

Finally, don't miss the official heat wave party on
Saturday. Bring your (danceing) shoes!

1. dancing
2. skipped
3. hiking
4. flipped
5. snapping
6. raced
7. landed
8. pleasing
9. checking
10. dared
11. dimmed
12. rubbing
13. striped
14. wasting
15. traced
16. stripped
17. tanning
18. smelling
19. phoning
20. fainted

1. skipped **(1 point)**
2. wasting **(1)**
3. dimmed **(1)**
4. phoning **(1)**
5. dancing **(1)**

Write a Funny Weather Report Have you ever experienced a long period of hot or cold weather, snow, or heavy rain? Try to remember what it was like. Then imagine what might happen if the weather's effects were greatly exaggerated.

On a separate sheet of paper, write a funny weather report predicting severe weather. Use Spelling Words from the list.
Responses will vary. **(10 points)**

Name _____

Divide and Conquer

Here are sixteen words from *Heat Wave!* Divide each word into syllables. Then write each word in the correct column on the chart below.

disappeared	everyone	brother	girls
feeding	lettuce	miserable	horizon
Hank	altogether	commotion	tease
farmers	everybody	thermometer	fight

Words with One Syllable

Hank **(1 point)**

tease **(1)**

fight **(1)**

girls **(1)**

Words with Three Syllables

ho•ri•zon **(1)**

com•mo•tion **(1)**

eve•ry•one **(1)**

dis•ap•peared **(1)**

Words with Two Syllables

broth•er **(1)**

farm•ers **(1)**

feed•ing **(1)**

let•tuce **(1)**

Words with Four Syllables

al•to•geth•er **(1)**

eve•ry•bod•y **(1)**

mis•er•a•ble **(1)**

ther•mom•e•ter **(1)**

Name _____

Getting the Tense

Underline the verb in each sentence. Then write each verb in the correct column, under *Present Tense,* *Past Tense,* **or** *Future Tense.*

1. Hank will tease me again.
2. I feed the chickens every day.
3. The clump of yellow air rolled across the sky.
4. The heat roasted the geese in midair.
5. The flowers will wilt soon in this heat.
6. I wrap a blanket around the hound dog.
7. The cows hopped around like rabbits.
8. The cows' milk will turn to butter.
9. We pour butter over the popcorn.
10. The oats dried in the field.

Present Tense	**Past Tense**	**Future Tense**
feed **(1 point)**	rolled **(1)**	will tease **(1)**
wrap **(1)**	roasted **(1)**	will wilt **(1)**
pour **(1)**	hopped **(1)**	will turn **(1)**
	dried **(1)**	

Reporting in the Past Tense

**Help the reporter complete the news story by writing the correct
past-tense forms of the verbs in parentheses.**

Last week an unusual thing happened **(1 point)**_____.
(happen) We suffered **(1)**_____ a very sudden heat
wave. (suffer) No one quite believed **(1)**_____ the
temperature. (believe) The mercury just
blasted **(1)**_____ out of the thermometer at one
farm here. (blast) The ground was so hot, cows
jumped **(1)**_____ up and down. (jump) Their
movements turned **(1)**_____ their milk to butter.
(turn) The farmer's daughter hosed **(1)**_____ the
hot cows down and cooled **(1)**_____ them. (hose)
(cool) She tried **(1)**_____ wetting down the oats
but she only created **(1)**_____ a huge, lumpy field
of oatmeal. (try) (create) If you have any other stories about
the heat wave, call the newspaper immediately.

**Write three sentences of your own about the heat wave,
using past tense verbs.**

Responses will vary. **(2 points each)** _____

_____

_____

_____

Name _____

Using the Correct Tense

Good writers make sure to choose the verb tense that correctly shows the time of the action described. Read the diary entry below. Then, on the lines, rewrite the entry so that all of the verbs show that the events have already happened.

> *Dear Diary,*
> *Yesterday a friend of mine visits our farm. It turns out to be a strange day. It will start with a hot wind blowing in. The wind sounds like the roar of a lion. The wind quickly heats up everything.*
> *This wind created lots of trouble. It nearly burns all the crops. We save the popcorn, though. At one point, I almost will drown in oatmeal. Finally, some crows flap their wings and cool us off.*

Yesterday a friend of mine **visited (1 point)** our farm. It **turned (1)** out to be a strange day. It **started (1)** with a hot wind blowing in. The wind **sounded (1)** like the roar of a lion. The wind quickly **heated (1)** up everything.

This wind created lots of trouble. It nearly **burned (1)** all the crops. We **saved (1)** the popcorn, though. At one point, I almost **drowned (1)** in oatmeal. Finally, some crows **flapped (1)** their wings and **cooled (1)** us off.

Assessment Tip: Total **10** Points

Name _____

Writing a Summary

Use this page to plan a summary of the first few pages of *Heat Wave!* Write the main idea for the story in the top box. Then write an important detail for each page of the story.

Main Idea

(2 points) _____

_____

_____

Page 361 Detail

(2) _____

_____

_____

Page 363 Detail

(2) _____

_____

_____

Page 365 Detail

(2) _____

_____

_____

Name _____

Paraphrasing

► Writers use paraphrasing when they write a summary or notes for a report.

► Paraphrasing is restating an idea in your own words, without changing the author's meaning.

"Then we heard a commotion in the pasture."

Which paraphrasing does not change the author's meaning?

☑ Then we heard noise coming from the pasture.

☐ Then we saw something in the pasture.

Paraphrase each sentence. Answers will vary. Sample answers given.

1. The ground had gotten too hot, so we herded the cows inside the barn.

   The ground was too hot for the cows to stay outside, so we brought

   them into the barn. **(2 points)**

2. As it turned out, the cows had jumped so much, they'd churned their milk to butter.

   The cows jumped around so much that their milk turned into

   butter. **(2)**

3. We scrubbed a couple of shovels and the beds of the pickup trucks.

   We cleaned some shovels and the back of the pickup trucks. **(2)**

4. I sent Pa and Hank to the field to fill the pickups with popcorn.

   I told Pa and Hank to fill the pickups with the popcorn in the

   cornfield. **(2)**

5. In no time at all, they sold every last bit of that popcorn, then hurried home.

   They sold all the popcorn quickly and then returned home. **(2)**

Name _____

Writing a Personal Response

Use the test-taking strategies and tips you have learned to help you answer this kind of question. Then read your answer and see how you may make it better. This practice will help you when you take this kind of test.

Write one or two paragraphs about one of the following topics.

a. You have just read *Heat Wave!* What do you think would happen if it could really get hot enough for corn to start popping while it is growing in the field? What other crops might be affected by this kind of heat? What would happen to those crops?

b. In the story, the narrator came up with unbelievable solutions for cooling the Heat Wave. Use your imagination to think of another way to cool the Heat Wave. What would you do? How would it work? Answers will vary. **(15 points)**

_____

_____

_____

_____

_____

_____

_____

_____

_____

_____

Name _____

Writing a Personal Response continued

Read your answer. Check to be sure that it

- focuses on the topic
- is well organized
- has details that support your answer
- includes vivid and exact words
- has few mistakes in capitalization, punctuation, grammar, or spelling

Now pick one way to improve your response. Make your changes below. Answers will vary. **(5)**

_____

_____

_____

_____

_____

_____

_____

_____

_____

_____

_____

_____

_____

_____

     Assessment Tip: Total **20** Points

Name _____

Spelling Review

Write Spelling Words from the list on this page to answer the questions.

Order of answers in each category may vary.

1–10. Which ten words are compound words? They can be written as one word, as hyphenated words, or as two words.

1. airport **(1 point)**
2. understand **(1)**
3. anything **(1)**
4. ninety-nine **(1)**
5. seat belt **(1)**
6. all right **(1)**
7. make-believe **(1)**
8. whenever **(1)** ✓ **(2)**
9. homesick **(1)**
10. railroad **(1)**

11–20. Which ten words end with the /ər/, /l/, or /əl/ sounds? Bonus: Put a check mark beside the compound word above that ends with the /ər/ sound.

11. weather **(1)**
12. doctor **(1)**
13. uncle **(1)**
14. beggar **(1)**
15. final **(1)**
16. proper **(1)**
17. battle **(1)**
18. towel **(1)**
19. trouble **(1)**
20. medal **(1)**

21–30. Which ten words end with *-ed* or *-ing*?

21. raced **(1)**
22. smelling **(1)**
23. pleasing **(1)**
24. fainted **(1)**
25. snapping **(1)**
26. skipped **(1)**
27. hiking **(1)**
28. striped **(1)**
29. dimmed **(1)**
30. checking **(1)**

Spelling Words

1. weather
2. doctor
3. airport
4. understand
5. raced
6. smelling
7. anything
8. uncle
9. pleasing
10. ninety-nine
11. fainted
12. beggar
13. seat belt
14. final
15. all right
16. proper
17. battle
18. make-believe
19. towel
20. snapping
21. whenever
22. skipped
23. hiking
24. trouble
25. medal
26. striped
27. homesick
28. railroad
29. dimmed
30. checking

Assessment Tip: Total **32** Points

Name _____

Spelling Spree

Book Titles Write the Spelling Word that best completes each book title. Remember to use capital letters.

1. *Aunt Angela and* <u>Uncle</u> **(1 point)** _____ *Ed*
   by Watt A. Life

2. *Fasten Your* <u>Seat Belt</u> **(1)** _____ *! Blast Off!*
   by Rock Ottship

3. *Our* <u>Final</u> **(1)** _____ *Day in the Jungle*
   by I. M. Lost

4. *Now I* <u>Understand</u> **(1)** _____ *: Science Made*
   Simple by Sy N. Smaster

5. *The Mystery of the* <u>Airport</u> **(1)** _____
   Without Planes by A. D. Tektiv

6. *The* <u>Railroad</u> **(1)** _____ *Station at the End*
   of the Tracks by Steem N. Jin

7. *Eat Vegetables* <u>Whenever</u> **(1)** _____ *You Like:*
   A Guide to Healthy Eating by Dr. Eetmore Greenes

Spelling Words

1. battle
2. airport
3. all right
4. homesick
5. railroad
6. understand
7. anything
8. make-believe
9. whenever
10. trouble
11. ninety-nine
12. seat belt
13. final
14. proper
15. uncle

The Next Word Write the Spelling Word that belongs with each group of words.

8. seventy-seven, eighty-eight, <u>ninety-nine</u> **(1)** _____

9. correct, right, fitting, <u>proper</u> **(1)** _____

10. nothing, something, <u>anything</u> **(1)** _____

11. fight, struggle, war, <u>battle</u> **(1)** _____

12. good, okay, <u>all right</u> **(1)** _____

13. lonesome, sad, <u>homesick</u> **(1)** _____

14. fantasy, pretend, <u>make-believe</u> **(1)** _____

15. problem, worry, <u>trouble</u> **(1)** _____

        Assessment Tip: Total **15** Points

Name _____

Proofreading and Writing

Proofreading Circle the six misspelled Spelling Words in Professor Mick Stupp's diary of backward adventures. Then write each word correctly.

August 32nd At ten this morning it was just getting dark. The (wether) was fine, but it was raining hard. Now I've seen anything! I met a (begger) sitting on a (towle.) I gave him a million-dollar bill, and he (faynted.) I went (hikeing) down the street to find him a (docter.) What a day!

1.	weather **(1 point)**	4.	fainted **(1)**
2.	beggar **(1)**	5.	hiking **(1)**
3.	towel **(1)**	6.	doctor **(1)**

Spelling Words

1. fainted
2. checking
3. beggar
4. towel
5. hiking
6. dimmed
7. weather
8. snapping
9. pleasing
10. doctor
11. medal
12. raced
13. smelling
14. striped
15. skipped

Mixed-up News Use Spelling Words to complete the following paragraph of a TV news report.

Our reporter has been 7. checking **(1)** on Professor Stupp's latest adventure. She has not 8. skipped **(1)** any details. The professor was 9. smelling **(1)** like fish, after he fell into a fish barrel. The mayor awarded him a 10. medal **(1)** on a blue-and-white 11. striped **(1)** ribbon. The ribbon was 12. pleasing **(1)** to most, but Professor Stupp's smile 13. dimmed **(1)** when he saw it wasn't red! Still, he 14. raced **(1)** quickly offstage, 15. snapping **(1)** his fingers and saying, "Time for adventure!"

✏️ **Create an Adventure** On a separate sheet of paper, write about another adventure of Professor Mick Stupp. Use the Spelling Review Words. Responses will vary. **(5)**

Name _____

Be a Problem Solver!

Many problems have more than one solution. For each of the following problems, write down at least two different ways to solve it!

Problem #1: One of the wheels on your bicycle breaks.

Possible answers: Fix the wheel, bring it to a bike shop, buy a new

bicycle. **(5 points)**

Problem #2: You're having a hard time understanding your math homework.

Possible answers: Ask your teacher for help, reread the lesson in the

book, ask an older sibling/parent to explain it to you. **(5)**

Problem #3: Your parents won't give you money to buy the game you want.

Possible answers: Offer to do some chores to earn money, ask for

the game as a present, play a different game. **(5)**

Name _____

Problem Solvers

	Who is the main character? What problem does he or she have?	What are some benefits that result from solving the problem?
My Name Is María Isabel	María Isabel; she does not have a part in the winter pageant; in class, she is not called by her correct name. **(3 points)**	María gets to participate in the pageant; can sing her song; makes her parents proud. **(3)**
Marven of the Great North Woods	Marven; he is in a strange place without his family; has to figure out the bookkeeping; food not kosher. **(3)**	Marven figures out a system for bookkeeping; makes friends with loggers; has a great time; does not get influenza.**(3)**
The Last Dragon	Peter; he doesn't want to spend the summer in Chinatown; has many difficulties in fixing his dragon; has to figure out a way to fix each part of the dragon. **(3)**	Peter learns to like Chinatown; discovers his heritage; has a sense of achievement because he worked hard to make a beautiful dragon. **(3)**
Sing to the Stars	Ephram; he is afraid to play the violin in front of an audience. **(3)**	Ephram overcomes his fear; Mr. Washington plays the piano once again. **(3)**

Name _____

Vocabulary Scramble

Unscramble the vocabulary words and write them on the lines.

ddppiisantoe d i s a (p) p o (i) n t e d
(2 points)

Hint: means "having unsatisfied hopes or wishes"

youvernsl n e (r) v o u s l y **(2)**

Hint: means "with worry or concern"

aeeiytttnvl (a) t t e n t i v e l y **(2)**

Hint: means "alertly or with great attention"

lbreetoosum (t) r o u b l e s o (m) e **(2)**

Hint: means "causing trouble or difficulty"

uddsstmiinnnerag

m i s (u) n d e r (s) t a n d i n g **(2)**

Hint: means "a failure to understand"

Unscramble the circled letters to answer the question.

What does the chorus do before a winter concert?

i t **w** a r m s u p **(2)**

Theme 4: **Problem Solvers**   213
Assessment Tip: Total **12** Points

Name _____

Prediction Chart

Details about María
Accept reasonable answers.

María at School	**What María Likes**
doesn't have part in Winter	her full name (p. 394)
Pageant (p. 396)	the Hanukkah song (p. 396)
shy toward classmates (p. 396)	singing (p. 396)
reads during class (p.403)	the library book (p. 396) **(4)**
(4 points)	
María's Life at Home	**What María Wishes**
makes dinner, sets table (p. 396)	to make a snowman (p. 396)
parents excited about the	to be a famous singer (p. 396)
pageant (p. 398)	to have a part in the Winter
unable to tell parents truth about	Pageant (p. 403)
pageant (p. 398)	to be called by her full name
helps with dishes (p. 401)	(p. 403) **(4)**
father gives her a gift (p. 404) **(4)**	

What will happen in next year's school pageant?

I predict that María Isabel will be the lead actress in the

pageant. If I were her, I'd be feeling really proud and confident about

saying what I feel. That's why I think nothing will stop her. **(4)**

Name _____

A Diary Entry

Help María Isabel finish this page in her diary by completing the sentences.

Because there are two other girls named María in my class, my teacher doesn't call me by my real name. **(1 point)** _____

Tony, Johnathan, and I **(1)** _____ are the only three kids who don't have parts in the play.

The others don't mind, but I feel sad. **(1)** _____

My only comfort is reading my book *Charlotte's Web.* **(1)** _____

My problems don't seem so bad compared with Wilbur's. **(1)** _____

When I rode the bus home today, I sang the Hanukkah _____ song **(1)** _____ and I felt a little better.

I cannot tell Mama and Papa **(1)** _____ that I am not in the pageant, because they will be so disappointed.

I'm so glad I wrote an essay on my greatest wish **(1)** _____ because it led me to get a part in the pageant.

Name _____

What Might Happen?

**Read this story and then answer the questions
on the following page.**

My Mean Brother

It was the first day of the new school year, and my first
day of fifth grade. This meant going to a new school, the same
one as my older brother, Kevin. He was in seventh grade.

Kevin had been trying to scare me all summer about Mrs. D.,
my new teacher. He'd say things such as, "Look out, Bryan,
Mean Mrs. D. doesn't like kids. She once sent me to the
principal's office for sneezing! She doesn't let you erase your
mistakes. And she even does surprise fingernail checks to make
sure they are neat and clean!" I laughed at Kevin, wondering if
he was telling the truth.

Being really nervous about the first day of school, I couldn't
believe my luck when I missed the bus. Kevin made me go
back in the house to get his lunch, but when I did, the bus
drove by and Dad told me Kevin already took his lunch!

My dad took me to school that day, telling me not to let
Kevin bother me. But I was bothered by the fact that we were
late! All I could think about was what Mean Mrs. D. was
going to do to me!

When we arrived, I ran up and down the hallway, searching
for Mrs. D.'s classroom. I guess I was making a lot of noise because
Mrs. D. opened her door as I skidded to a stop in front of her.

"Oh, you must be Bryan," she said. "I was worried about you.
Glad you made it. Why don't you get a drink of water, and then
come to class."

216   Theme 4: **Problem Solvers**

Name _____

What Might Happen? continued

Answer each of the following questions with a prediction about what will happen and the details from the story that support that prediction.

1. What do you think Bryan will do when he and Kevin return home from school?

   Prediction: _Bryan will laugh at Kevin and tell him he_ _was wrong about Mrs. D._ **(2 points)**

   _____

   Supporting Details: _Bryan laughs at Kevin's description of_ _Mrs. D. over the summer._ **(1)**

   Mrs. D. treats Bryan nicely even though he is late for class. **(1)**

2. What kind of student do you think Bryan will be in Mrs. D.'s class?

   Prediction: _I think he will be a very good student._ **(2)**

   _____

   Supporting Details: _Bryan thinks school is exciting._ **(1)**

   Mrs. D. treats him nicely. **(1)**

3. What do you think Bryan would be like as an older brother?

   Prediction: _I think Bryan would be nice to his younger brother._ **(2)**

   _____

   Supporting Details: _Kevin lies to Bryan._ **(1)**

   Bryan doesn't like the way Kevin treats him. **(1)**

Name _____

Is It Poss*ible?*

**Write T if the statement is true. Write F if the statement is false.
If you are unsure of a word's meaning, use a dictionary.**

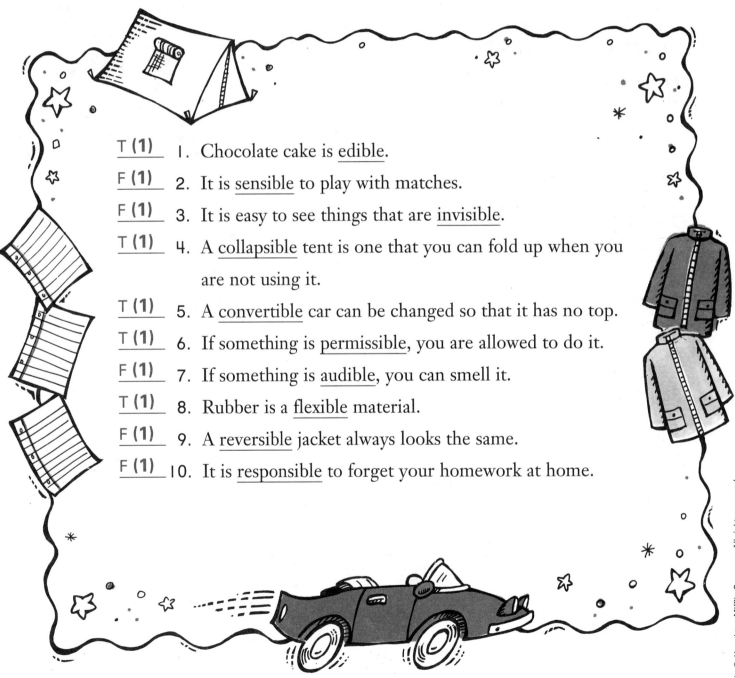

T **(1)**   1. Chocolate cake is <u>edible</u>.

F **(1)**   2. It is <u>sensible</u> to play with matches.

F **(1)**   3. It is easy to see things that are <u>invisible</u>.

T **(1)**   4. A <u>collapsible</u> tent is one that you can fold up when you
are not using it.

T **(1)**   5. A <u>convertible</u> car can be changed so that it has no top.

T **(1)**   6. If something is <u>permissible</u>, you are allowed to do it.

F **(1)**   7. If something is <u>audible</u>, you can smell it.

T **(1)**   8. Rubber is a <u>flexible</u> material.

F **(1)**   9. A <u>reversible</u> jacket always looks the same.

F **(1)**   10. It is <u>responsible</u> to forget your homework at home.

Name _____

The /k/, /ng/, and /kw/ Sounds

Remember these spelling patterns for the /k/, /ng/, and /kw/ sounds:

/k/	k, ck, c	(shar**k**, atta**ck**, publi**c**)
/ng/	(before k) n	(si**n**k)
/kw/	qu	(**qu**estion)

▶ In the starred words *ache* and *stomach*, /k/ is spelled *ch*.

Write each Spelling Word under the correct heading.
Circle the words with the /ng/ sound. Order of answers
for each category may vary. **(1 point for each circle)**

/k/ Spelled *ck*

attack **(1 point)**   track **(1)**

jacket **(1)**   struck **(1)**

/k/ Spelled *k* or *c*

shark **(1)**   crooked **(1)**

risk **(1)**   (drink) **(1)**

public **(1)**   topic **(1)**

(sink) **(1)**   (blanket) **(1)**

electric **(1)**   mistake **(1)**

(blank) **(1)**   (junk) **(1)**

Other Spellings for /k/

ache **(1)**   stomach **(1)**

/kw/

question **(1)**   squirrel **(1)**

Spelling Words

1. shark
2. attack
3. risk
4. public
5. sink
6. question
7. electric
8. jacket
9. blank
10. ache*
11. crooked
12. drink
13. topic
14. track
15. blanket
16. struck
17. mistake
18. junk
19. squirrel
20. stomach*

Name _____

Spelling Spree

Daily News Write the Spelling Word that best completes each sentence.

Swimmer Bumped by Unidentified Object

Vacationers were upset by a report that a
(1) <u>shark **(1 point)**</u> had been spotted in the water.
Fred Finn was (2) <u>struck **(1)**</u> in the leg by "a huge
white fish." A family that had just spread out their
(3) <u>blanket **(1)**</u> on the sand nearby claimed the fish
was indeed a "great white." Police Chief Ann Summer
wasn't convinced this was an actual (4) <u>attack **(1)**</u>.
"Unless there's a real (5) <u>risk **(1)**</u> of someone
getting bitten, the beach will remain open," she declared.
Mr. Finn escaped with an (6) <u>ache **(1)**</u> in his leg.
He said, "I'm just glad I didn't end up as a meal in that
monster's (7) <u>stomach **(1)**</u>!"

**Write a Spelling Word by adding the beginning of the
first word to the end of the second word.**

8. topcoat + music	12. job + trunk
9. size + think	13. election + metric
10. jackpot + bonnet	14. squirm + barrel
11. crooning + wicked	15. blue + tank

8. <u>topic **(1)**</u>	12. <u>junk **(1)**</u>
9. <u>sink **(1)**</u>	13. <u>electric **(1)**</u>
10. <u>jacket **(1)**</u>	14. <u>squirrel **(1)**</u>
11. <u>crooked **(1)**</u>	15. <u>blank **(1)**</u>

Spelling Words

1. shark
2. attack
3. risk
4. public
5. sink
6. question
7. electric
8. jacket
9. blank
10. ache*
11. crooked
12. drink
13. topic
14. track
15. blanket
16. struck
17. mistake
18. junk
19. squirrel
20. stomach*

Assessment Tip: Total **15 Points**

Name _____

Proofreading and Writing

Proofreading Circle the five misspelled Spelling Words in this billboard advertisement. Then write each word correctly. (**5 points** for correct placement of circles.)

There's no (kwestion) about it!

Potato latkes are great! They're crispy and tasty and easy to make. It doesn't matter whether you're celebrating Hanukkah or just want to enjoy a fantastic treat. Serve them with a tall (drinck) and a mound of applesauce. Make no (misstake!) An admiring (publick) will sing your praises. Be careful cooking, though. There's always a risk of getting splattered with hot oil, and remember to keep (trak) of hot cookware at all times.

1. question **(1 point)**
2. drink **(1)**
3. mistake **(1)**
4. public **(1)**
5. track **(1)**

1. shark
2. attack
3. risk
4. public
5. sink
6. question
7. electric
8. jacket
9. blank
10. ache*
11. crooked
12. drink
13. topic
14. track
15. blanket
16. struck
17. mistake
18. junk
19. squirrel
20. stomach*

Write a Letter How does your family celebrate a special day? Do you exchange presents? Do you cook special food or sing special songs? Do friends and relatives come to visit?

On a separate sheet of paper, write a letter to tell a friend what happens at your house on the special day. Use Spelling Words from the list. Responses will vary. **(10)**

My Name Is María Isabel

Vocabulary Skill Dictionary:
Base Words and Inflected
Forms -s, -es, -ing, -er, -est

Will You Find the Word in the Entry?

Read each sentence. In the space write *yes* if you think the underlined word would be part of a dictionary entry for the base word. Write *no* if you think it would not be part of the base word entry. Then circle the base words for *yes* answers in the word find box.

1. Everything at school <u>revolved</u> around plans for the
   Winter Pageant. <u>yes **(1 point)**</u>

2. The class <u>talked</u> about Hanukkah and other holidays. <u>no **(1)**</u>

3. María Isabel's problems were <u>smaller</u> than Wilbur's. <u>yes **(1)**</u>

4. Wilbur was in danger of <u>becoming</u> the holiday dinner. <u>yes **(1)**</u>

5. She felt herself getting <u>sadder</u> each day. <u>yes **(1)**</u>

6. What was <u>waiting</u> for her in the next few days? <u>no **(1)**</u>

7. The teacher asked, "What is your <u>greatest</u> wish? <u>yes **(1)**</u>

8. The boy <u>dropped</u> his crutch only once during rehearsal. <u>yes **(1)**</u>

```
R  O  M  I  H  O  M  A  W
E  S  A  D  E  Y  R  P  A
V  M  A  H  L  R  O  O  N
O  A  L  K  G  R  E  A  T
L  L  D  P  D  A  I  G  R
V  L  I  B  E  C  O  M  E
E  R  D  T  H  B  N  E  F
```

Name _____

Completing with *be*

Complete each sentence by filling in the blank with the form of
***be* that goes with the subject. Use the correct form for the**
tense named in parentheses.

1. This photo <u>is **(1 point)**</u> a picture of my mother and father.
   (present)

2. We <u>were **(1)**</u> in Santo Domingo for the holidays. (past)

3. My family <u>was **(1)**</u> there two years ago. (past)

4. Those two melodies <u>are **(1)**</u> very familiar to me. (present)

5. Many of the songs <u>are **(1)**</u> from other countries. (present)

6. Three students <u>were **(1)**</u> not in the play. (past)

7. What <u>is **(1)**</u> your favorite story about animals? (present)

8. Wilbur <u>is **(1)**</u> the main character in María's favorite
   story. (present)

9. What <u>was **(1)**</u> your wish for the new year? (past)

10. What <u>is **(1)**</u> María's full name? (present)

Name _____

To be in the Past or the Present

**Complete the sentences by writing a form of the verb
be. In the first four sentences, use the past. In the last
four sentences, use the present.**

1. María __was **(1 point)**__ troubled about Wilbur.

2. María __was **(1)**__ unhappy about not being in the pageant.

3. Her parents __were **(1)**__ there two years ago.

4. __Was **(1)**__ María nervous in front of the class?

5. María __is **(1)**__ happy about leading the song.

6. The butterfly barrettes __are **(1)**__ a present from María's father.

7. The Hanukkah song __is **(1)**__ María's favorite.

8. María wrote, "Most of all, I __am **(1)**__ proud of my name."

**Now make up two sentences of your own, telling
something about María and her experiences at school.
Use a different tense of *be* in each sentence.**

Responses will vary. **(1 point for each sentence)**

_____

_____

_____

_____

_____

224   Theme 4: **Problem Solvers**
       Assessment Tip: Total **10** Points

Name _____

Writing with the Verb *be*

Using Forms of the Verb *be* Good writers are careful to use tense forms of *be* that match the subjects. Read the paragraph below. Rewrite the paragraph, correcting tense forms of *be* so that they match the subject of the sentence

I think that holiday songs is my favorite kind of music. These songs be very tuneful. Our school program will have a lot of them. The first song on the program are for guitar and voice. It were once a lullaby. You and I know the music by heart. We is in the chorus.

I think that holiday songs are **(2 points)** my favorite kind of music. These songs are **(2)** very tuneful. Our school program will have a lot of them. The first song on the program is **(2)** for guitar and voice. It was **(2)** once a lullaby. You and I know the music by heart. We are **(2)** in the chorus.

Name _____

Writing an Opinion

Use this page to plan how you will write a paragraph expressing your *opinion* in a convincing way. Use facts or reasons to support your opinion. Number your facts or reasons in the order you will present them. Finally, restate your opinion.

Topic Sentence: Opinion

(2 points) _____

_____

Fact/Reason:

(2) _____

_____

_____

_____

_____

Fact/Reason:

(2) _____

_____

_____

_____

_____

Fact/Reason:

(2) _____

_____

_____

_____

_____

Opinion Restated:

(2) _____

_____

Assessment Tip: Total **10** Points

Name _____

Using Commas with Introductory Phrases

A phrase is a small group of words that acts as a part of speech. A phrase at the beginning of a sentence is called an **introductory phrase**. Good writers use introductory phrases to vary sentence length and make sentences interesting. Introductory phrases should be set off with a comma.

At first, María Isabel Lopez Salazar did not know she was being addressed.

Read the following sentences. If the sentence has an introductory phrase, write the sentence on the lines below and add a comma to set off the introductory phrase.

1. After helping with the dishes she finished her homework.
   After helping with the dishes, she finished her homework. **(2 points)**

   _____

2. In time María Isabel told her parents about her problem.
   In time, María Isabel told her parents about her problem. **(2)**

   _____

3. The teacher agreed to the request made by María Isabel's parents.
   no introductory phrase; no comma needed. **(2)**

   _____

4. Pleased to be called by her full name María Isabel agreed to sing her favorite song.
   Pleased to be called by her full name, María Isabel agreed to sing her

   favorite song. **(2)**

5. María Isabel's mother and father were there to hear her sing.
   no introductory phrase; no comma needed **(2)**

   _____

Name _____

Evaluating Your Persuasive Essay

Reread your persuasive essay. What do you need to do to make it better? Use this page to help you decide. Put a checkmark in the box for each sentence that describes your persuasive essay.

Rings the Bell!

☐ My essay has a beginning that will get my readers' attention.

☐ I stated my goal clearly and gave reasons to support the goal.

☐ I used facts and examples to support my opinion.

☐ The essay is interesting to read and convincing.

☐ There are almost no mistakes.

Getting Stronger

☐ I could make the beginning more attention grabbing.

☐ I stated my goal, but I could add some reasons to support it.

☐ I need to add more facts and examples to make this convincing.

☐ There are a few mistakes.

Try Harder

☐ I need a better beginning.

☐ I didn't state my goals or reasons for my opinion.

☐ I need to add facts and examples.

☐ This isn't very convincing.

☐ There are a lot of mistakes.

Name _____

Subject-Verb Agreement

► Add *-s* or *-es* to most verbs to show the present tense if the subject is singular.

That frog jump**s** high.   He watch**es** frogs all day.

► Do not add *-s* or *-es* to most verbs to show the present tense if the subject is plural or the word *I*.

Frogs swim in our pond.   I watch**es** frogs all day.

Complete each sentence.   Circle the correct form of each verb.

1. Frogs (is/are) amphibians. **(1 point)**

2. An amphibian (has/have) wet skin. **(1)**

3. Amphibians (live/lives) both on land and in the water. **(1)**

4. Toads (is/are) actually a type of frog. **(1)**

5. Toads (has/have) dry skin and a stumpy body. **(1)**

6. Both frogs and toads (breathe/breathes) through their skin. **(1)**

7. Scientists (worry/worries) about frogs. **(1)**

8. One scientist (blame/blames) ozone loss for the problem. **(1)**

9. Gaps in the ozone layer (let/lets) dangerous UV rays through. **(1)**

10. The UV rays (damage/damages) frogs. **(1)**

Name _____

Spelling Words

Words Often Misspelled Look for familiar spelling patterns to help you remember how to spell the Spelling Words on this page. Think carefully about the parts that you find hard to spell in each word.

Write the missing letters in the Spelling Words below.

1. <u>s</u><u> </u> ure **(1 point)**

2. h <u>e</u><u> </u> r <u> </u> e <u> </u> **(1)**

3. <u>k</u><u> </u> <u>n</u><u> </u> ew **(1)**

4. m <u>i</u><u> </u> <u>g</u><u> </u> <u>h</u><u> </u> t **(1)**

5. pre <u>t</u><u> </u> <u>t</u><u> </u> y **(1)**

6. rea <u>l</u><u> </u> <u>l</u><u> </u> y **(1)**

7. v <u>e</u><u> </u> <u>r</u><u> </u> y **(1)**

8. <u>w</u><u> </u> <u>h</u><u> </u> ere **(1)**

9. lit <u>t</u><u> </u> <u>l</u><u> </u> <u>e</u><u> </u> **(1)**

10. unt <u>i</u><u> </u> <u>l</u><u> </u> **(1)**

11. int <u>o</u><u> </u> **(1)**

12. o <u>f</u><u> </u> <u>f</u><u> </u> **(1)**

13. s <u>a</u><u> </u> <u>i</u><u> </u> d **(1)**

14. <u>o</u><u> </u> <u>u</u><u> </u> r **(1)**

15. let <u>t</u><u> </u> <u>e</u><u> </u> r **(1)**

Spelling Words

1. sure
2. here
3. knew
4. might
5. pretty
6. really
7. very
8. where
9. little
10. until
11. into
12. off
13. said
14. our
15. letter

Study List **On a separate piece of paper, write each Spelling Word. Check your spelling against the words on the list. (5 points)** Order of words may vary.

Name _____

Spelling Spree

Contrast Clues The second part of each clue contrasts with the first part. Write a Spelling Word for each clue.

1. not there, but <u>here **(1 point)**</u>

2. not ugly, but <u>pretty **(1)**</u>

3. not on, but <u>off **(1)**</u>

4. not a phone call, but a <u>letter **(1)**</u>

5. not big, but <u>little **(1)**</u>

6. not your, but <u>our **(1)**</u>

7. not out of, but <u>into **(1)**</u>

Word Magic Replace or add one letter in each word below to make a Spelling Word. Write it on the line.

8. untie <u>until **(1)**</u>

9. rally (add one letter) <u>really **(1)**</u>

10. knee <u>knew **(1)**</u>

11. right <u>might **(1)**</u>

12. sand <u>said **(1)**</u>

13. vary <u>very **(1)**</u>

14. pure <u>sure **(1)**</u>

15. here <u>where **(1)**</u>

Spelling Words

1. sure
2. here
3. knew
4. might
5. pretty
6. really
7. very
8. where
9. little
10. until
11. into
12. off
13. said
14. our
15. letter

Name _____

Proofreading and Writing

Proofreading Circle the five misspelled Spelling Words in this dialogue. Then write each word correctly.

Pam: Well, they said that was the last bus (untill) 6:15.

Zack: So I guess we're stuck (hear) for another three hours.

Pam: I guess you (mite) say that.

Zack: I'm sorry—I was (shur) I'd have time to run and get a

   snack. Who (new) that the bus would leave on time?

Pam: There's *got* to be some other way of getting home.

Spelling Words

1. sure
2. here
3. knew
4. might
5. pretty
6. really
7. very
8. where
9. little
10. until
11. into
12. off
13. said
14. our
15. letter

1. until **(1 point)** _____

2. here **(1)** _____

3. might **(1)** _____

4. sure **(1)** _____

5. knew **(1)** _____

✏️ **Stating the Problem** What are some problems you would like to see someone try to solve? On a separate piece of paper, write four sentences that describe problems you think need solving. Use Spelling Words from the list.

Responses will vary. **(5 points)**

Name _____

Words in the Woods

Vocabulary

bunkhouse	cords (of wood)	immense	landscape
lumberjacks	snowshoes	timber	woodsman

The woods are full of words from the vocabulary list. Write each word above the tree trunk that shows its meaning.

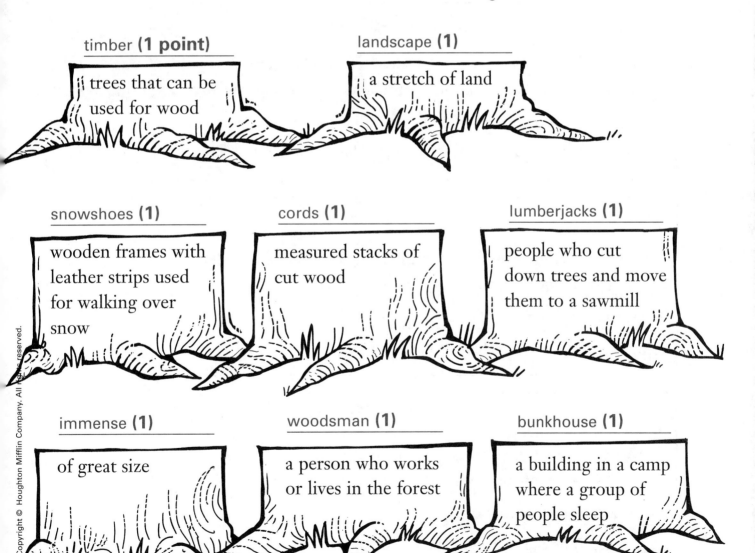

timber **(1 point)**

trees that can be used for wood

landscape **(1)**

a stretch of land

snowshoes **(1)**

wooden frames with leather strips used for walking over snow

cords **(1)**

measured stacks of cut wood

lumberjacks **(1)**

people who cut down trees and move them to a sawmill

immense **(1)**

of great size

woodsman **(1)**

a person who works or lives in the forest

bunkhouse **(1)**

a building in a camp where a group of people sleep

Theme 4: **Problem Solvers**   233
Assessment Tip: Total **8** Points

Name _____

Problem-Solution Frame

Page 419

Problem: How can Marven learn French?

Steps: **(3 points)** listen to the language being spoken, learn what certain words mean, practice the words he knows

Solution: Marven learns enough French to get by. **(2)**

Page 430

Problem: How can Marven eat food that isn't kosher?

Steps: **(3)** eat only flapjacks and oatmeal with milk one day, eat steak and oatmeal without milk the next day, never eat the bacon

Solution: Marven is able to obey Jewish law and still eat. **(2)**

Page 433

Problem: How can Marven organize the bookkeeping system?

Steps: **(3)** list loggers' names and dates of pay period, code each chit with dates, make a chart

Solution: Marven does his job very well. **(2)**

Page 436–437

Problem: How can Marven avoid worrying about his family?

Steps: **(3)** learn the lumberjacks' songs, play games with the lumberjacks, dance with the lumberjacks

Solution: Time flies by and it's time for Marven to go home. **(2)**

Assessment Tip: Total **20** Points

Name _____

Write a Letter

Mail from the Forest

Help Marven complete this letter he wrote to his aunt and uncle.

Dear Aunt Ghisa and Uncle Moishe,

    I know it was a good idea for me to leave the city to make sure I didn't get <u>influenza **(2 points)**</u>, but I miss all of you.

    Here at the logging camp, Mr. Murray asked me to <u>keep the books **(2)**</u> since I have a good head for numbers.

    One of the scariest things I had to do my first morning at camp was to <u>wake up the lumberjacks **(2)**</u>.

    Now I have lots of fun with <u>Jean Louis **(2)**</u>, a huge lumberjack, because we are friends.

    No matter how much fun I have in the great north woods, I will be happy in spring when I can <u>come home to Duluth and be with you, Mama, Papa, and my sisters. **(2)**</u>

Your nephew,
Marven

Name _____

A Cold Adventure

Read the story. Then complete the chart on the following page.

Race to the Pole

In the far north, a group of men struggled against icy wind. It was 60 degrees below zero. It was so cold that frostbite could occur in minutes. The explorers wore thick fur parkas, gloves, and boots to protect themselves against the cold. Robert Peary and Matthew Henson would not give up. They wanted to be the first explorers to reach the North Pole.

In 1909, no one had ever been to the North Pole. People believed it was somewhere in the Arctic Ocean at the very top of the world. That far north it is light for six months and dark for six months. The explorers could not cross the ice in the dark. But if they waited too long to leave, the summer sun would melt the ice before they could cross it coming back.

The Arctic Ocean this far north also contains great chunks of ice. The men had to cut through the ice to move on. They carried their supplies on sledges, long sleds pulled by teams of dogs. The dogs had to be fed, too, which meant the men had to carry a lot of food.

The pull of the moon's gravity and the movement of Earth often crack the ice in the Arctic. This creates lanes of water called leads, which can split open at any time, plunging the explorers into the freezing water. So the team must always be prepared to get out of the water and change clothes quickly. If they did not get into dry clothes, they could freeze to death in minutes.

Peary and Henson had tried to reach the North Pole twice before. Both times they had been beaten by the freezing winds, huge blocks of ice, and starvation. Could they make it this time? They would not have another chance.

Name _____

A Cold Adventure continued

Problem	Solution
The extreme cold could cause frostbite.	The men wear parkas, gloves, and boots. **(2 points)**
In the Arctic, it is light for six months and dark for six months.	The men must time their trip carefully. **(2)**
The men need help carrying their supplies.	The men use sleds pulled by teams of dogs. **(2)**
The moon's gravity and Earth's movement cause lanes of water in the ice to open up.	The men must be prepared to pull themselves out of the water and change their clothes. **(2)**

If you were exploring a cold and icy place like the North Pole, what do you think would be the greatest problem you would face? Why? How would you solve it? Answers will vary. **(2)**

_____

_____

_____

_____

Prefix Precision

Answer the questions. Answers will vary.

1. Why might a **misprinted** book need to be **reprinted**?
   (2 points)
   _____

   _____

2. Why is it an **excellent** idea to recycle?
   (2)
   _____

   _____

3. Why should you try to **respell** a word that you have
   misspelled?
   (2)
   _____

   _____

4. Why is it important to **reread** the directions during an **exam**?
   (2)
   _____

   _____

5. Why should you **retrace** your steps when you **misplace**
   something?
   (2)
   _____

   _____

Write the word in dark type above next to its meaning.

put in the wrong place	misplace **(1)**
outstanding	excellent **(1)**
printed again	reprinted **(1)**
read again	reread **(1)**

Name _____

Final /ē/

When you hear the final /ē/ sound in a two-syllable word, think of the spelling patterns *y* and *ey*.

beau**ty**   hon**ey**

► In the starred word *movie*, the final /ē/ sound is spelled *ie*.

Write each Spelling Word under its spelling of final /ē/.

Order of answers for each category may vary.

y

beauty **(1 point)**

ugly **(1)**

lazy **(1)**

marry **(1)**

ready **(1)**

sorry **(1)**

empty **(1)**

duty **(1)**

hungry **(1)**

lonely **(1)**

body **(1)**

twenty **(1)**

fifty **(1)**

ey

honey **(1)**

valley **(1)**

alley **(1)**

turkey **(1)**

hockey **(1)**

monkey **(1)**

Another Spelling

movie **(1)**

Copyright © Houghton Mifflin Company. All rights reserved.

Spelling Words

1. beauty
2. ugly
3. lazy
4. marry
5. ready
6. sorry
7. empty
8. honey
9. valley
10. movie*
11. duty
12. hungry
13. lonely
14. alley
15. body
16. twenty
17. turkey
18. hockey
19. fifty
20. monkey

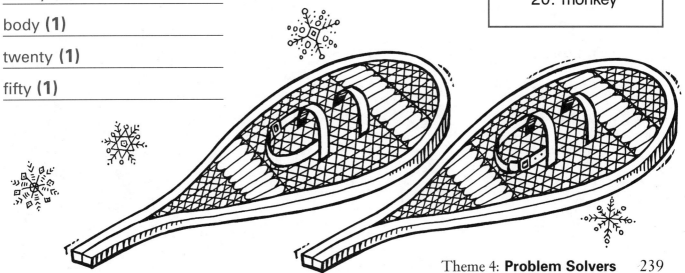

Theme 4: **Problem Solvers**   239

Assessment Tip: Total **20** Points

Name _____

Spelling Spree

Word Search Circle the 15 Spelling Words in the puzzle. Then write them on the lines below.

Spelling Words

1. beauty
2. ugly
3. lazy
4. marry
5. ready
6. sorry
7. empty
8. honey
9. valley
10. movie*
11. duty
12. hungry
13. lonely
14. alley
15. body
16. twenty
17. turkey
18. hockey
19. fifty
20. monkey

```
L R E E A S H O C K E Y T H E
A C L A S P W S T T R I P T M
Z F I S H H U T H U L E E H P
Y O V E U K T U E S S M A R T
E A E Y N A F R Y L H O N E Y
T H S U G H H K I M O V E E S
S H Y R R O S E E A P I X E L
F I F T Y L E Y A Y B E T A N
U P V S H Y U L H M S W E E T
M A T I E U G L Y O U E N Y W
A L I M Y S L O A N B N O S E
R R A L A K E T W K I T T E N
R B O D Y Y L O N E L Y I V T
Y N Q U E E S T A Y A L L E Y
```

1. ugly **(1 point)**
2. lazy **(1)**
3. marry **(1)**
4. empty **(1)**
5. honey **(1)**
6. movie **(1)**
7. hungry **(1)**
8. lonely **(1)**
9. alley **(1)**
10. body **(1)**
11. twenty **(1)**
12. turkey **(1)**
13. hockey **(1)**
14. fifty **(1)**
15. monkey **(1)**

Assessment Tip: Total **15** Points

Name _____

Proofreading and Writing

Proofreading Circle the five misspelled Spelling Words in this poem. Then write each word correctly.

Marven's Adventure

His father said, "My son, go forth."

So ten-year-old Marven headed north.

Met in a (vally) by a stranger

Far from the city, out of danger.

He took a break from his daily (dutie,)

Skied in search of woodland (beuty.)

Though the lumberjack life was steady,

He missed his family and he was (readey)

To ski home over the springtime snow.

And his friends were (sory) to see him go.

5 points for correct placement of circles.

1. valley **(1 point)**   4. ready **(1)**
2. duty **(1)**   5. sorry **(1)**
3. beauty **(1)**

Spelling Words

1. beauty
2. ugly
3. lazy
4. marry
5. ready
6. sorry
7. empty
8. honey
9. valley
10. movie*
11. duty
12. hungry
13. lonely
14. alley
15. body
16. twenty
17. turkey
18. hockey
19. fifty
20. monkey

✏️ **Write a Journal Entry** Pick your favorite incident or picture from *Marven of the Great North Woods*.

On a separate sheet of paper, write a journal entry that describes what happened in the scene from Marven's point of view. Use Spelling Words from the list.

Responses will vary. **(10)**

Name _____

All in the Word Family

In each box, read the clues and add endings to the underlined word to make words that fit the word family. Remember, an ending sometimes changes the spelling of the base word. The first word family is written for you.

t o w e r
two or more: t o w e r s
very tall: t o w e r i n g
in the past: t o w e r e d

f i d d l e
two or more: f i d d l e s **(1 point)**
person who plays a fiddle: f i d d l e r **(1)**
playing a fiddle: f i d d l i n g **(1)**
played in the past: f i d d l e d **(1)**

t h i c k
more thick: t h i c k e r **(1)**
most thick: t h i c k e s t **(1)**
in a thick way: t h i c k l y **(1)**

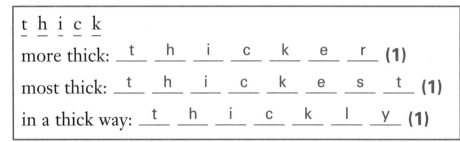

f r e e z e
turning to ice: f r e e z i n g **(1)**
a very cold place for food: f r e e z e r **(1)**
becomes ice: f r e e z e s **(1)**

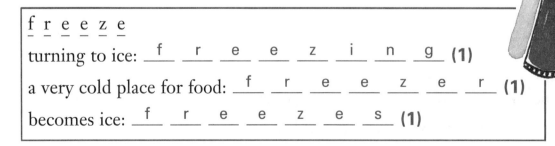

Challenge Use the base word "camp" or "wild" and write clues for other words in the same family. Swap puzzles with a classmate. **(5)**

Assessment Tip: Total **15** Points

Name _____

Irregular Completion

Complete each sentence by writing the correct form of the verb named in parentheses.

1. All the jacks have <u>worn **(1 point)**</u> snowshoes every day this winter. (wear)

2. The jack <u>threw **(1)**</u> the axe directly at the tree. (throw)

3. Marven's family <u>took **(1)**</u> him to the train station. (take)

4. The train <u>came **(1)**</u> to a full stop at Bemidji. (come)

5. Marven had <u>begun **(1)**</u> a new part of his life now. (begin)

6. Marven's father had <u>given **(1)**</u> him skis for his sixth birthday. (give)

7. Marven's skis never <u>broke **(1)**</u> on his way from the station. (break)

8. Marven <u>brought **(1)**</u> latkes and knishes with him. (bring)

9. The days have <u>grown **(1)**</u> much shorter now. (grow)

10. Marven never <u>knew **(1)**</u> snow could stay white so long. (know)

Name _____

Verbs in a Letter

Write a letter to the author, Kathryn Lasky, to tell her why you enjoyed *Marven in the Great North Woods*. Use as least five of the verbs on the verb tree in your letter. Vary the verb tenses. A sample has been done for you.
(**1 point** for each verb)

Dear Ms. Lasky,

When I began to read your story about Marven at the lumber camp, I couldn't stop. I knew Marven would come to enjoy life in the north woods. I even brought the story home to show my parents. Thanks for writing such a good story. You have given me lots of interesting information about what it was like to grow up in the early 1900s.

give
wear
know
take
begin
come
break
throw
bring
grow

_____

_____

_____

_____

_____

_____

Assessment Tip: Total **10** Points

Name _____

Using Irregular Verbs

Using the Correct Verb Form **Read the first draft of the report on one day in Marven's life at the logging camp. On the lines below, rewrite the report, replacing any incorrect forms of irregular verbs with correct forms. (1 point** for each correct verb)

Marven had bring his skis along. One Friday, Marven put the skis on and taked off on the sled paths into the woods. He wear his heavy coat. Everything growed still and white. When he come to a frozen lake, he stopped. He know the scenery would be beautiful. He heard a growl. He begun to tremble. Was it a bear? Had a branch broke off? It give him quite a scare. Luckily, the noise had came from his friend Jean Louis.

Marven had **brought** his skis along. One Friday, Marven put the skis

on and **took** off on the sled paths into the woods. He **wore** his heavy coat.

Everything **grew** still and white. When he **came** to a frozen lake, he

stopped. He **knew** the scenery would be beautiful. He heard a growl.

He **began** to tremble. Was it a bear? Had a branch **broken** off? It **gave**

him quite a scare. Luckily, the noise had **come** from his friend Jean

Louis.

Name _____

How to Take Notes

Use this page to *take notes* on a winter activity. Research a
sport or hobby that interests you, or take notes on the article
about snowshoeing on pages 446–449 of your anthology.

Research Question:
(2 points) _____

_____

Main idea 1: (1) _____

supporting detail: (1) _____

supporting detail: (1) _____

supporting detail: (1) _____

Main idea 2: (1) _____

supporting detail: (1) _____

supporting detail: (1) _____

supporting detail: (1) _____

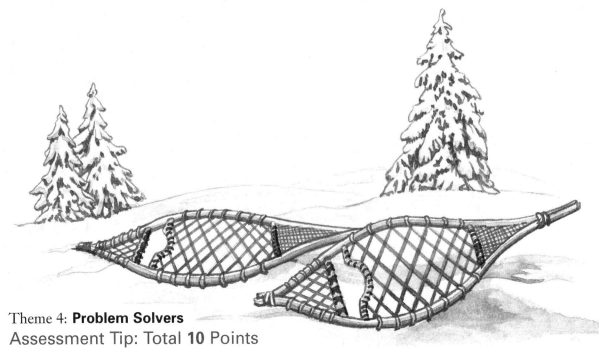

Assessment Tip: Total **10** Points

Name _____

Choosing What's Important

When writers take notes, they list main ideas and the important details that support the main ideas. To check whether a detail supports the main idea, reread the main idea. Ask: *Is this detail about the main idea?*

> **Main idea:** use safety when snowshoeing
> **supporting detail:** go with a partner
> **supporting detail:** tell an adult where you are going
> **supporting detail:** ~~snowshoes are 6,000 years old~~   *This detail is not about snowshoe safety.*

Read the following sets of notes. Use this proofreading mark ✗ **to delete the details that do not support the main idea.**

1. **Main idea:** some mammals are well-adapted to life in the arctic regions

   detail: musk oxen and reindeer have large feet that allow them to walk on snow

   detail: lemmings, arctic fox, and gray wolves grow white winter coats

   detail: ~~some kinds of whales are endangered worldwide~~ **(3 points)**

2. **Main idea:** some animals hibernate during the winter
   detail: bears and bats hibernate in caves
   detail: ~~certain fish are found only in tropical waters~~
   detail: animals fatten up to hibernate

Theme 4: **Problem Solvers**   247
Assessment Tip: Total **6** Points

Name _____

Scrambled Dragons

Unscramble the letters to make a word from the vocabulary list. Then solve the riddle.

gheoma <u>h</u> <u>o</u> <u>m</u> <u>a</u> <u>g</u> <u>e</u> **(1 point)**
            1
Hint: means "honor or respect"

lessac <u>s</u> <u>c</u> <u>a</u> <u>l</u> <u>e</u> <u>s</u> **(1)**
                2
Hint: means "small, thin, flat parts that cover a reptile"

densak <u>s</u> <u>n</u> <u>a</u> <u>k</u> <u>e</u> <u>d</u> **(1)**
                        3
Hint: means "moved like a snake"

ecefir <u>f</u> <u>i</u> <u>e</u> <u>r</u> <u>c</u> <u>e</u> **(1)**
            4
Hint: means "wild and mean"

crachearts <u>c</u> <u>h</u> <u>a</u> <u>r</u> <u>a</u> <u>c</u> <u>t</u> <u>e</u> <u>r</u> <u>s</u> **(1)**
                5   6
Hint: means "marks or signs used in writing"

gniemet <u>t</u> <u>e</u> <u>e</u> <u>m</u> <u>i</u> <u>n</u> <u>g</u> **(1)**
             7   8
Hint: means "to be full or crowded"

sterc <u>c</u> <u>r</u> <u>e</u> <u>s</u> <u>t</u> **(1)**
            9
Hint: means "something that grows out of an animal's head"

Write each numbered letter in the space with the same number to solve the riddle.

What does a dragon's breath feel like?
<u>h</u> <u>o</u> <u>t</u> <u>a</u> <u>s</u> <u>f</u> <u>i</u> <u>r</u> <u>e</u> **(3)**
 5   1   7   2   6   4   8   9   3

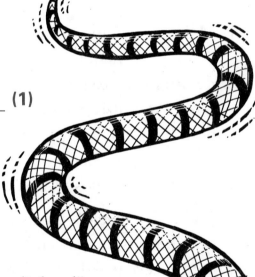

Name _____

Conclusions Chart

	Details Answers may vary.	**Conclusions** Accept reasonably varied answers.
page 455 **The dragon**	covered in dust, cobwebs, and bug skeletons mouth is wired shut only its tail, empty crates, and a jar of salted duck eggs are near it **(3 points)**	No one wants the dragon. **(2)**
page 459 **Peter's** **reaction**	asks if dragon is for sale strokes its whiskers says he'll clean it himself **(3)**	Peter is very excited about fixing the dragon. **(2)**
pages **467–468** **The** **dragon's** **eyes**	Dr. Fong does not have any dragon eyes. Dragon eyes need to be blessed by a priest. The eyes cannot be painted by an artist. **(3)**	The dragon's eyes are the most difficult part to fix. **(2)**

Name _____

Peter's Adventure

Complete the story map to tell about *The Last Dragon*.

Setting

Where does the story take place?
Chinatown **(1 point)**

Events

What does Peter find?
a ragged old dragon costume **(1)**

What is the problem with what he finds?
It is falling apart. **(1)**

Who helps Peter? List at least four people.
Great Aunt; her friends; the tailor, Mr. Pang; the kite maker, Miss Rose

Chiao; the herb shop owner, Dr. Fong; the sign painter, Mr. Sung **(4)**

Ending

What happens on the last night of Peter's visit with Great Aunt?
Great Aunt has a party, and the Last Dragon appears. A priest paints his

eyes, and the dragon parades through the streets. **(3)**

Name _____

A Snapshot of America

Read the article. Then read the statements. Decide if the statement is *true, false*, or if *not enough information* is given to draw a conclusion.

United States Population to Double

Washington, DC — By the year 2100, there will be twice as many Americans as there are today. Imagine twice as many cars on the highways. Imagine twice as many people in line at the supermarket. Can our nation handle the change?

Today about 275 million people live in the United States. According to the Census Bureau, by 2100 that number will be about 571 million. That would make our population density (people per area) a bit over 160 people per square mile. In comparison, the density of Germany today is over 400 people per square mile. It's a good thing that our country is large and vast.

Today there are around 65,000 people age 100 or older. In 2100, there may be 5 million. The elderly will make up one-fifth of our population. The median age (the age at which half the population is older and half younger) will rise by 2100 to over 40, compared to around 36 today.

The Hispanic population of the United States is expected to triple in the next 50 years. The Asian and Pacific Islander population will more than triple. Today, non-Hispanic white people make up about three-quarters of the population. Although that group will grow, too, by 2050, they will make up only about one-half of the total.

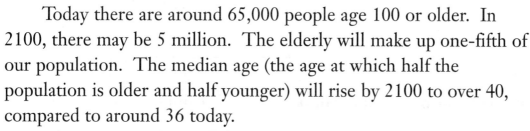

Name _____

A Snapshot of America continued

1. The Hispanic population in the United States is expected to double in the next 50 years. **(1 point)**

   true   (false)   not enough information

2. The population density of Germany is greater than the population density of the United States. **(1)**

   (true)   false   not enough information

3. Germany has a larger population than the United States has. **(1)**

   true   false   (not enough information)

4. There are more Asian Americans than Hispanic Americans in the United States today. **(1)**

   true   false   (not enough information)

5. In the year 2100, there will be more people in the United States over 100 years old than today. **(1)**

   (true)   false   not enough information

6. Doubling the amount of cars will cause terrible gridlock. **(1)**

   true   false   (not enough information)

7. By the year 2050, our population will be around 571 million. **(1)**

   true   (false)   not enough information

8. The United States is vaster than Germany. **(1)**

   (true)   false   not enough information

Assessment Tip: Total **8** Points

Name _____

Complete Prefix Control

Write two words from the box that together match each description. Use each word only once. Use a dictionary if you need help.

Example:

No one "exactly expected" how the dragon would look when finished. In other words, no one **precisely predicted** how it would look.

commercial	concert	congratulations	preowned
committee	concise	constant	prerecorded
companion	concrete	construction	preserved
completely	condition	consumer	preteen
computer	confused	prehistoric	preventable

1. steady friend: <u>constant companion **(2 points)**</u>

2. mixed-up group: <u>confused committee **(2)**</u>

3. advertisement taped earlier: <u>prerecorded commercial **(2)**</u>

4. buyer between the ages of 9 and 12:
    <u>preteen consumer **(2)**</u>

5. totally saved from an earlier time:
    <u>completely preserved **(2)**</u>

6. used machine that runs programs:
    <u>preowned computer **(2)**</u>

7. very old musical performance:
    <u>prehistoric concert **(2)**</u>

8. brief words to express joy for someone's good luck:
    <u>concise congratulations **(2)**</u>

Name _____

Final /j/ and /s/

Remember these spelling patterns for the final /j/, /ĭj/, and /s/ sounds:

/j/ in a one-syllable word	*dge, ge*	(bri**dge**, stran**ge**)
/ĭj/ in a word of more than one syllable	*age*	(vill**age**)
/s/	*ce*	(en**ce**)

Remember that in words with a short vowel sound, final /j/ is spelled *dge*. In words with a long vowel sound, final /j/ is spelled *ge*.

Write each Spelling Word under the correct heading.

Order of answers for each category may vary.

/j/ in One-Syllable Words

bridge **(1 point)**

strange **(1)**

cage **(1)**

change **(1)**

ridge **(1)**

edge **(1)**

lodge **(1)**

dodge **(1)**

/ĭj/ in Two-Syllable Words

village **(1)**

cottage **(1)**

carriage **(1)**

manage **(1)**

damage **(1)**

marriage **(1)**

cabbage **(1)**

Final /s/ Spelled *ce*

fence **(1)**

chance **(1)**

twice **(1)**

glance **(1)**

since **(1)**

Spelling Words

1. village
2. cottage
3. bridge
4. fence
5. strange
6. chance
7. twice
8. cage
9. change
10. carriage
11. glance
12. ridge
13. manage
14. damage
15. since
16. marriage
17. edge
18. lodge
19. cabbage
20. dodge

Assessment Tip: Total **20** Points

Name _____

Spelling Spree

Rhyming Pairs Complete each sentence by writing a pair of rhyming Spelling Words.

1-2. I had to duck and _____ snowboarders on my way to the ski _____.

3-4. The bride and groom rode off in a horse-drawn _____ to begin their _____.

5-6. I know this outfit looks a little _____, so I think I'll go back home and _____.

7-8. We must cross the _____ to get to the _____ on the other side of the river.

	Spelling Words
1.	village
2.	cottage
3.	bridge
4.	fence
5.	strange
6.	chance
7.	twice
8.	cage
9.	change
10.	carriage
11.	glance
12.	ridge
13.	manage
14.	damage
15.	since
16.	marriage
17.	edge
18.	lodge
19.	cabbage
20.	dodge

1. dodge **(1 point)**

2. lodge **(1)**

3. carriage **(1)**

4. marriage **(1)**

5. strange **(1)**

6. change **(1)**

7. bridge **(1)**

8. ridge **(1)**

Quick Pick Write the Spelling Word that best matches the meaning of each word or group of words below.

Example: courtroom official   *judge*

9. animal carrier cage **(1)**

10. vegetable cabbage **(1)**

11. barrier around a garden fence **(1)**

12. small town village **(1)**

13. small house cottage **(1)**

14. quick look glance **(1)**

15. rim or border edge **(1)**

Assessment Tip: Total **15** Points

Name _____

Proofreading and Writing

Proofreading Circle the five misspelled Spelling Words in this ad. Then write each word correctly.

5 points for correct placement of circles

HELP WANTED

Experts Needed to Repair Dragon

At first (glanse) he might not look like much. All this Chinese dragon needs, though, is tender loving care to repair a little (damidge.) If you can (manige) to spare some time to help, please ask for Peter at the noodle factory. In return for sewing, painting, frame repair, and blessings, I promise to run errands and do small jobs ((sins) I don't have any money for payment). Don't think twice. All the dragon needs is a (chanse!)

1. glance **(1 point)** _____

2. damage **(1)** _____

3. manage **(1)** _____

4. since **(1)** _____

5. chance **(1)** _____

Spelling Words
1. village
2. cottage
3. bridge
4. fence
5. strange
6. chance
7. twice
8. cage
9. change
10. carriage
11. glance
12. ridge
13. manage
14. damage
15. since
16. marriage
17. edge
18. lodge
19. cabbage
20. dodge

✏️➤ **Write a Thank-You Note** Peter had help from a tailor, his great-aunt and her friends, a kite maker, a painter, and others. Choose one of the people who worked on the dragon and write that person a thank-you note that Peter might have written.

On a separate sheet of paper, write your note. Be sure to include the task the person performed and why the person's help was important. Use Spelling Words from the list. Responses will vary. **(10)**

Name _____

Add the Correct Suffix

Rewrite each sentence below, replacing the words in italics with one word. Make the new word by adding the suffix *-ful*, *-less*, or *-ly* to the underlined word. Use a dictionary if you need help remembering the meanings of the suffixes.

1. Great Aunt thought the old dragon was *without <u>hope</u>*.

   Great Aunt thought the old dragon was <u>hopeless **(1 point)**</u>.

2. *Full of <u>cheer</u>*, Great Aunt's friends repaired the dragon's crest.

   <u>Cheerfully **(1)**</u>, Great Aunt's friends repaired the dragon's crest.

3. Peter waited *in a <u>patient</u> way* for Mr. Pang to repair the dragon's body.

   Peter waited <u>patiently **(1)**</u> for Mr. Pang to repair the dragon's body.

4. *With respect to <u>fortune</u>*, Dr. Fong located eyes for the dragon.

   <u>Fortunately **(1)**</u>, Dr. Fong located eyes for the dragon.

Add *two* suffixes to the underlined word in each sentence below.

5. The dragon moved *in a manner without <u>effort</u>* on silken legs.

   The dragon moved <u>effortlessly **(2)**</u> on silken legs.

6. Peter and his friends restored the dragon *in a way full of <u>beauty</u>*.

   Peter and his friends restored the dragon <u>beautifully **(2)**</u>.

Assessment Tip: Total **8** Points

Name _____

Being Specific with Adjectives

Complete each sentence with the adjective from the box that fits best. Use each adjective only once. Underline the noun each adjective modifies. Write whether the adjective tells *what kind* or *how many*.

| two | tasty | loud | big | new |

1. Its mouth opened with a <u>loud **(1 point)**</u> sound.
   <u>what kind **(1)**</u>

2. Fixing the dragon will be a <u>big **(1)**</u> job.
   <u>what kind **(1)**</u>

3. Miss Tam made <u>tasty **(1)**</u> dumplings.
   <u>what kind **(1)**</u>

4. Peter did <u>two **(1)**</u> things for Miss Rose.
   <u>how many **(1)**</u>

5. The kite shop was not far from the <u>new **(1)**</u>
   restaurant. <u>what kind **(1)**</u>

Complete each sentence by choosing the correct article in parentheses. Then write your choice in the blank.

6. Peter noticed <u>the **(1)**</u> severed tail. (an, the)

7. Miss Rose had <u>an **(1)**</u> idea. (a, an)

      Assessment Tip: Total **12** Points

Name _____

Dragon Menu

The pictures below show what foods were served at Peter's farewell dinner at the Golden Palace Restaurant. Write a caption for each picture, describing the food shown and how it tastes. Use adjectives to tell what kind and how many. Color the pictures to show what the foods look like and to help you describe them.

Answers will vary.

Won-ton Soup

(2 points) _____

_____

_____

_____

Noodles

(2) _____

_____

_____

_____

Peppery Shrimp

(2) _____

_____

_____

_____

Vegetables

(2) _____

_____

_____

_____

On a separate sheet of paper, write a description of something else you would like to see on the menu. (2)

Name _____

Expanding with Adjectives

Good writers add interest and detail to their sentences by including adjectives that tell what kind and how many. Read the sentences below. Rewrite each sentence using specific adjectives that tell what kind or how many. (Answers may vary. Sample answers shown. 1 point for each word.)

1. The crest on the dragon's head was _____ and _____.

   The crest on the dragon's head was scraggly and worn.

2. Peter didn't like Great Aunt's _____, _____ apartment.

   Peter didn't like Great Aunt's tiny, cramped apartment.

3. Peter was carrying a sack of _____, _____ crabs.

   Peter was carrying a large sack of squirming, black crabs.

4. The _____ jaw could move easily now.

   The mended jaw could move easily now.

5. Miss Rose sewed _____, _____ scales on the tail.

   Miss Rose sewed bright, shining scales on the tail.

6. The _____ streets of Chinatown were filled with people.

   The teeming streets of Chinatown were filled with people.

Assessment Tip: Total **10** Points

Name _____

Writing a Comparison/ Contrast Composition

Use this page to plan your *comparison/contrast composition*. Fill In the graphic organizer with details about how two places, activities, or books are alike and different. Then, on a separate sheet of paper, write a comparison/contrast composition. When you have finished your composition, exchange papers with a partner.

Comparison/Contrast of

1. **(1 point)** _____ and 2. **(1)** _____

I.

(2) _____

How It Is Different

_____

_____

_____

_____

_____

_____

_____

How They're Alike

(2)

_____

_____

_____

_____

_____

2.

(2) _____

How It Is Different

_____

_____

_____

_____

_____

_____

_____

Name _____

Correcting Sentence Fragments

Writers know that **sentence fragments** can be used for any note-taking graphic organizer. Good writers also know to use complete sentences when writing paragraphs, essays, or reports. Complete sentences have subjects and predicates.

      subject   predicate

The English teacher / suggested showing the dragon to a kite maker.

Sentence fragments that only have a subject need a predicate.
> **subject:** Great Aunt's apartment
> **needs predicate:** is in Chinatown.

Sentence fragments that only have a predicate need a subject.
> **predicate:** made a new crest for the dragon.
> **needs subject:** Great Aunt's downstairs neighbor, Mrs. Li

Read each group of words. If it is a complete sentence, write Complete Sentence on the lines below. If it is a sentence fragment, change it into a complete sentence by adding a missing subject or predicate. Responses will vary.

1. Did chores and ran errands.

   Every day Peter did chores and ran errands. **(2 points)**

2. Something special about that dragon.

   Everyone felt there was something special about that dragon. **(2)**

3. Dr. Fong's herb shop.

   Dr. Fong's herb shop has hundreds of different herbs. **(2)**

4. Blessed by a priest or the dragon will stay blind.

   Dragon eyes must be blessed by a priest or the dragon will stay blind. **(2)**

5. The dragon paraded through the restaurant.

   Complete Sentence **(2)**

taking out the trash doing chores running errands

Name _____

Musical Meanings

Fill in the blanks with words from the vocabulary list to complete the news article.

Vocabulary

amplifiers
blaring
classical
debut
murmur
rhythm
strides
jazz

The News

Student Band Gives First Concert

The student band is warming up for its

debut **(1 point)** _____. The leader checks the

amplifiers **(1)** _____ to make sure the music can be

heard at the back of the hall. Then the concert begins. The

drummer sets the rhythm **(1)** _____ with his flying

drumsticks. The trumpets are blaring **(1)** _____

out a jazz **(1)** _____ tune. The final song they

played is an updated version of an old

classical **(1)** _____ melody. There was not a

murmur **(1)** _____ from the audience as the band

played. Everyone agreed the band has made great

strides **(1)** _____ since they first began playing

together.

On the lines below write a sentence that uses two of the vocabulary words.

Answers will vary. **(2)** _____

_____

_____

Name _____

Story Structure Map

Characters

Ephram
girls jumping rope
Mr. Washington
rappers
Grandma
neighbors
(3 points)

Main Characters

Ephram
Mr. Washington
(2)

Settings

sidewalk
street corner
Ephram's home
rooftop
park
(3)

Main Setting

the neighborhood
(2)

Problems

Main Character #1	**Main Character #2**
Ephram **(1)**	Mr. Washington **(1)**
how to overcome stage fright **(2)**	how to regain joy in his life **(2)**

Solution

play together at concert **(2)**

264   Theme 4: **Problem Solvers**
Assessment Tip: Total **18** Points

Name _____

Hear the Music

Complete each sentence to tell about *Sing to the Stars*.

1. Mr. Washington always knew that Ephram was coming because
   he recognized the rhythm of Ephram's walk and the swinging of
   his violin case. **(2 points)**

2. When a rapper on the corner yelled to Ephram to get himself
   an electric guitar, Ephram
   pretended to play his violin case as if it were a guitar. **(2)**

3. Mr. Washington stopped playing the piano when
   his daughter was killed in a car accident, he was blinded, and the
   joy went out of his life. **(2)**

4. Ephram said that he did not think he would play at the benefit
   concert because
   he didn't know if he could play on a stage in front of many people.
   (2)

5. The title of this story, *Sing to the Stars*, refers to
   the fact that Ephram plays outdoors on the roof and at the benefit
   concert, as well as the beauty of the music as it spreads through
   the crowd and up to the stars. **(2)**

Name _____

What Did You Say?

Read the story. Then complete the following page.

The Talking Yam

Once upon a time, a long time ago, not far from the city of Accra, a farmer went to dig some yams from his garden. While he was digging, one of the yams said to him, "Go away and leave me alone!" The farmer turned and looked at the cow in amazement. "Did you say something?"

The cow didn't answer, but the dog said, "The yam spoke to you. The yam says leave him alone."

The man became angry, so he kicked a stone. The stone yelled, "Hey, cut that out!" Frightened, the man ran to the village. On the way, he met a fisherman carrying a large fish. "What's your hurry?" the fisherman asked.

"My yam is talking to me! My dog is talking to me! The rock is talking to me!" screamed the farmer.

"So what's the fuss?" the fish answered. "Besides," the fishing pole added, "you shouldn't kick rocks." The farmer jumped, yelled, and went running to the king.

"My yam is talking to me! My dog is talking to me! The rock is talking to me!" screamed the farmer. "Then a fish talked to me and a fishing pole, too!"

The king listened to the farmer. Finally, he said, "This is a wild story. Go back to your work before I punish you for disturbing the peace." The farmer went away and the king shook his head. "What a silly story. Stories like this upset all the people."

"You're right," answered his throne. "Imagine, a talking yam!"

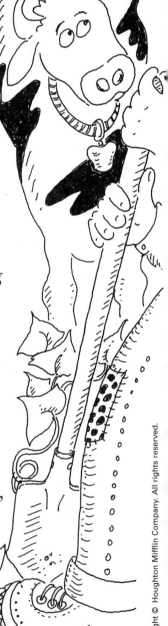

Name _____

What Did You Say? continued

Complete the chart for the story "The Talking Yam."

Main Character
the farmer **(1)**

Setting
once upon a time, a long time ago,
not far from the city of Accra **(1)**

Farmer's Problem
The talking yam upsets him. **(1)**

Beginning

The farmer gets upset when a yam, dog, and stone talk to him. **(1)**

Middle

The farmer gets more upset when a fish and a fishing pole also start

talking to him. **(1)**

End

The farmer goes to the king for help. **(1)**

Solution

The king tells the farmer to stop telling such wild tales and return

home. The farmer obeys. The throne starts talking to the king. **(2)**

Name _____

Syllable Sort

Pair up the syllables in the box to make words, then write the word that matches each clue and draw a line between the syllables.

1. a tooth doctor ___den/tist **(1 point)**___

2. a tool for hitting nails ___ham/mer **(1)**___

3. a windy snowstorm ___bliz/zard **(1)**___

4. a marriage ceremony ___wed/ding **(1)**___

5. the opposite of before ___af/ter **(1)**___

6. a hat used to protect the head ___hel/met **(1)**___

7. A cricket is a kind of ___in/sect **(1)**___

8. a person who has great skill ___ex/pert **(1)**___

9. Six and nine are both ___num/bers **(1)**___

10. having no mistakes ___per/fect **(1)**___

wed	fect	hel	mer	ding	den	in	per	zard	tist
sect	bers	ham	ter	af	num	pert	bliz	met	ex

Theme 4: **Problem Solvers**
Assessment Tip: Total **10** Points

Name _____

VCCV Pattern

Knowing how to divide a word into syllables can help you spell it. Remember these rules for dividing two-syllable words with the VCCV pattern:

► Divide most VCCV words between the consonants, whether the consonants are different or the same.

► Divide a VCCV word before the consonants if those consonants form a cluster.

► Divide a VCCV word after the consonants if those consonants spell one sound.

VC | CV	**pic | ture, at | tend**
V | CCV	**a | fraid**
VCC | V	**oth | er**

Spelling Words

1. bottom
2. picture
3. other
4. attend
5. capture
6. common
7. danger
8. afraid
9. borrow
10. office
11. arrow
12. suppose
13. escape
14. whether
15. pillow
16. dinner
17. thirty
18. degree
19. allow
20. corner

Write each Spelling Word under the heading that shows where its syllables divide. Draw a line between its syllables. Order of answers for each category may vary.

VC | CV

bot | tom **(1 point)**

pic | ture **(1)**

at | tend **(1)**

cap | ture **(1)**

com | mon **(1)**

dan | ger **(1)**

bor | row **(1)**

of | fice **(1)**

ar | row **(1)**

sup | pose **(1)**

es | cape **(1)**

pil | low **(1)**

din | ner **(1)**

thir | ty **(1)**

al | low **(1)**

cor | ner **(1)**

V | CCV

a | fraid **(1)**

de | gree **(1)**

VCC | V

oth | er **(1)**

wheth | er **(1)**

Assessment Tip: Total **20** Points

Name _____

Spelling Spree

Write the Spelling Word in each word below.

1. officer <u>office</u> **(1 point)**
2. uncommon <u>common</u> **(1)**
3. supposed <u>suppose</u> **(1)**
4. bottomless <u>bottom</u> **(1)**
5. swallow <u>allow</u> **(1)**
6. borrower <u>borrow</u> **(1)**
7. pillowcase <u>pillow</u> **(1)**

Write the Spelling Word that answers each riddle.

8. You might find me inside a frame. Who am I?

9. I'm speeding cars and thin ice. Who am I?

10. Along with breakfast and lunch, I'm a winner. Who am I?

11. I have a point, and I'm very narrow. Who am I?

12. I'm smaller than forty and bigger than twenty. Who am I?

13. If I'm not one thing, I'm the _____.

14. I'm hot or cold, high or low. Who am I?

8. <u>picture</u> **(1)**   12. <u>thirty</u> **(1)**

9. <u>danger</u> **(1)**   13. <u>other</u> **(1)**

10. <u>dinner</u> **(1)**   14. <u>degree</u> **(1)**

11. <u>arrow</u> **(1)**

Spelling Words

1. bottom
2. picture
3. other
4. attend
5. capture
6. common
7. danger
8. afraid
9. borrow
10. office
11. arrow
12. suppose
13. escape
14. whether
15. pillow
16. dinner
17. thirty
18. degree
19. allow
20. corner

Assessment Tip: Total **14** Points

Name _____

Proofreading and Writing

Proofreading Circle the six misspelled Spelling Words in this neighborhood flyer. Then write each word correctly. **6 points** for correct placement of circles.

Concert After Dark Series

You're invited to (atend) a concert in the park
every Saturday in August!
Ninety-degree temperatures got you down? Enjoy a
concert and (ekscape) the summer heat. Come one, come all,
(wether) young or old. Don't be (afriad) to leave work early.
Invite your boss or bring a friend. Take the opportunity to
(capshur) the sounds of summer to remember all winter long.
Concerts are held right around the (korner) in Davis Park.

1. attend **(1 point)**	4. afraid **(1)**
2. escape **(1)**	5. capture **(1)**
3. whether **(1)**	6. corner **(1)**

Spelling Words

1. bottom
2. picture
3. other
4. attend
5. capture
6. common
7. danger
8. afraid
9. borrow
10. office
11. arrow
12. suppose
13. escape
14. whether
15. pillow
16. dinner
17. thirty
18. degree
19. allow
20. corner

✏️ **Write a Character Sketch** Mr. Washington was kind and encouraging to Ephram. Were you surprised when Mr. Washington came and played at the concert? How would describe Mr. Washington to someone who hasn't read the story?

On a separate sheet of paper, describe the kind of person Mr. Washington was. Use Spelling Words from the list.

Responses will vary. **(8)**

Name _____

All the Good News That's Fit to Print

Merry Times, the editor of the *Good News Gazette*, is having a problem with a new reporter, Peter Downhill. He wrote an article that uses many words with negative connotations. Help Merry replace each underlined word with one that has a more positive connotation. Write the new word on the line that has the same number. Answers will vary

Traffic along Maple Street today was <u>horrible</u>, all because
₁

of a family of <u>silly</u> geese. One driver described how traffic
₂

<u>screeched</u> safely to a halt when a <u>stubborn</u> mother goose and her
₃ ₄

family walked across the road. School children <u>escaped</u> their school
₅

bus to watch. The bus driver explained that the <u>nosy</u> students
₆

had never seen geese crossing a road. The students stood on the

sidewalk and <u>screamed</u> hello to the goose and her chicks. A police
₇

officer stepped past the <u>mob</u> of people to <u>push</u> the geese
₈ ₉

across the street. Everyone agreed that they would have an <u>odd</u>
₁₀

story to tell their families.

1. slow, backed up **(1 point)**

2. confused, lost, mixed-up **(1)**

3. came, slowed **(1)**

4. determined **(1)**

5. left, got off **(1)**

6. curious, excited **(1)**

7. shouted, called **(1)**

8. crowd, group **(1)**

9. help, guide **(1)**

10. interesting **(1)**

      Assessment Tip: Total **10** Points

Name _____

Making Comparisons

Write the correct comparing form of the adjective in parentheses

1. Ephram thought this evening was <u>warmer **(1 point)**</u> than yesterday evening. (warm)

2. During the day, the streets were <u>noisier **(1)**</u> than they were at night. (noisy)

3. The <u>sweetest **(1)**</u> sounds of all come from a well-played violin. (sweet)

4. On stage, Ephram saw the <u>largest **(1)**</u> piano he had ever seen. (large)

5. Mr. Washington's fingers were <u>stiffer **(1)**</u> than they had been before. (stiff)

6. As he thought about playing in public, Ephram felt <u>more nervous **(1)**</u> than when he played on the roof. (nervous)

7. The <u>happiest **(1)**</u> moment of all came when Mr. Washington went up on stage with him. (happy)

8. One of the two singers on the program was <u>thinner **(1)**</u> than the other. (thin)

Complete the chart with the correct form of the adjective.

Adjective	Compare 2	Compare 3 or more
hot	→ hotter →	hottest **(1)**
beautiful	more beautiful **(1)**	most beautiful

Name _____

Comparing with Music

Help Ephram complete his diary entry by writing the correct forms of the adjectives in the box. Use -er, -est, more, or most.

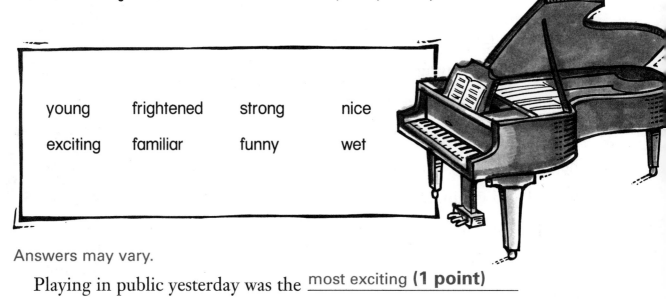

young	frightened	strong	nice
exciting	familiar	funny	wet

Answers may vary.

Playing in public yesterday was the _most exciting **(1 point)**_ thing I have done in my life. When I went up on stage, someone said I was the _youngest **(1)**_ person to play at a concert there. I was a lot _more frightened **(1)**_ than when I play by myself on the roof. Grandma said that the sound of my violin was _stronger **(1)**_ than she ever had heard it. The _nicest **(1)**_ thing of all was getting Mr. Washington to play the piano with me. I discovered that he was once one of the _most famous **(1)**_ pianists in our city. I won't forget this, either. I can't think of anything _funnier **(1)**_ than feeling Shiloh's wet nose on my elbow. That dog has the _wettest **(1)**_ nose of any dog I know!

Name _____

Using Comparisons

Good writers are careful to use the correct forms of *good*
and *bad* when comparing two, three, or more.

**Read the following paragraph. Then rewrite it, replacing any
incorrect forms of *good* and *bad*.**

Hot weather is more bad for a violin than cold weather. The
better temperature of all is around 72°F. One of the worse things
that can happen is for a violin string to break in the middle of a
performance. If the violin bow makes squeaky sounds, the better
thing of all to do is to rub resin on it. Some people think that the
cello has a more good sound than the violin. One thing for sure is
that flat notes sound worst than sharp notes. The baddest sound of
all is a squeaky violin. Personally, I think that the better music of all
is written for the violin.

Hot weather is **worse (1 point)** for a violin than cold weather.

The **best (1)** temperature of all is around 72°F. One of the **worst (1)**

things that can happen is for a violin string to break in the middle of a

performance. If the violin bow makes squeaky sounds, the **best (1)**

thing of all to do is to rub resin on it. Some people think that the cello

has a **better (1)** sound than the violin. One thing for sure is that flat

notes sound **worse (1)** than sharp notes. The **worst (1)** sound of all is

a squeaky violin. Personally, I think that the **best (1)** music of all is

written for the violin.

_____

_____

_____

_____

Name ______________________

Writing a Message

Use this page to take a telephone *message.*

Date: (1 point) ______________ Time: (1) ______

For: (1) ______________________

From: (1) ______________________

Phone Number: (1) ______________________

Message: (2) ______________________

____

____

____

____

____

____

____

____

____

Message taken by:

(1) ______________________

Assessment Tip: Total **8** Points

Name _____

Using Complete Information

When you take a message, always listen carefully and write the information exactly. Write down all the details. Do not leave anything out.

First "listen" to the following recordings left on a telephone answering machine. Then read the written messages that were taken. Make the written messages complete and exact by correcting any inaccuracies and adding any missing information.

1. Hey, Sam, it's Rick, on Sunday, at 5:00. Cheerleading practice has been changed from Monday and Wednesday to Tuesday and Thursday. Same place, the gym, same time, 3:15. I have to go to the library after practice. Call me, 555-1577.

Date: Sun. **Time:** 5:00
For: Sam   **Caller:** Rick
Caller's number: 555-5177 **555-1577**
　　　　　　　　day (not time) change
Message: Cheerleading practice time
　　　　　　Tuesday (not Monday)
change. Now it's Monday and Thursday.

Same time and place. He has to go to the
　　　　　　　　　　He has to go to the library
library. Call him. after practice. **(6 points)**
Message taken by: Tom

2. Hi, Jason. It's me, Yasko, and it's Wednesday, 7:30. Can you bring the cake for the cheerleaders' party? Let me know by Friday. Oh, yeah, the party will be at Suzanne's house after the game on May 18, probably about 5 or 6:00. My number 556-3672. Bye now.

Date: Fri. **Time:** 7:30 Wed.
For: Jason   **Caller:** Yasko
Caller's number: 556-3672

Message: Can you bring the cake and
just cake, not plates
plates for the cheerleaders' party? It's at
Suzanne's house　　　　　　　May 18 **(8)**
Yasko's house, after the game on May 8,

about 5 or 6:00. Let Yasko know by Fri.
Message taken by: Mom

Name _____

Vocabulary Items

Use the test-taking strategies and tips you have learned to help you answer vocabulary items. This practice will help you when you take this kind of test.

Read each sentence. Choose the word that means about the same as the underlined word. Fill in the circle for the correct answer at the bottom of the page.

1. The dragon's only <u>companions</u> were his severed tail, two empty shipping crates, and a jar of salted duck eggs.

   <u>Companions</u> means —

   A enemies **C** friends

   B cousins **D** pieces

2. Peter thought Chinatown seemed old and <u>alien</u> and strange.

   <u>Alien</u> means —

   F foreign **H** unique

   G familiar **J** exciting

3. Peter stroked the dragon's <u>tangled</u> whiskers and wondered how long it would take to unknot them.

   <u>Tangled</u> means —

   A straight **C** curly

   B twisted **D** short

4. Great Aunt told Peter that the dragons of her childhood received the <u>homage</u> of every living thing.

   <u>Homage</u> means —

   F interest **H** honesty

   G respect **J** anger

ANSWER ROWS 1 Ⓐ Ⓑ Ⓒ Ⓓ **(5 points)** 3 Ⓐ Ⓑ Ⓒ Ⓓ **(5)**

2 Ⓕ Ⓖ Ⓗ Ⓙ **(5)** 4 Ⓕ Ⓖ Ⓗ Ⓙ **(5)**

Theme 4: **Problem Solvers** 279

Name _____

Vocabulary Items continued

5. Mr. Pang peered <u>suspiciously</u> over his newspaper as Peter walked up with the dragon.

   <u>Suspiciously</u> means —

   A approvingly   **C** angrily

   B happily   **D** distrustfully

6. Mr. Pang told Peter not to be <u>impatient</u> since repairing the dragon was a big job that would take quite a bit of time.

   <u>Impatient</u> means —

   F anxious   **H** upset

   G sorry   **J** disappointed

7. Peter learned to fly a fighting kite, which <u>entertained</u> his Great Aunt and her friends.

   <u>Entertained</u> means —

   A bothered   **C** amused

   B injured   **D** scared

8. The dragon looked <u>fierce</u> with its bold eyebrows, red cheeks, and sharp teeth.

   <u>Fierce</u> means—

   F gentle   **H** active

   G threatening   **J** silly

ANSWER ROWS   5 Ⓐ Ⓑ Ⓒ ⬤**D** **(5 points)**   7 Ⓐ Ⓑ ⬤**C** Ⓓ **(5)**

6 ⬤**F** Ⓖ Ⓗ Ⓙ **(5)**   8 Ⓕ ⬤**G** Ⓗ Ⓙ **(5)**

Name _____

Spelling Review

Write Spelling Words from the list on this page to answer the questions.

Order of answers in each category may vary.

1–9. Which nine words have the final /ē/ sound?

1. alley **(1 point)**

2. lonely **(1)**

3. thirty **(1)**

4. monkey **(1)**

5. beauty **(1)**

6. degree **(1)**

7. honey **(1)**

8. twenty **(1)**

9. ready **(1)**

10–17. Which eight words have the /k/, /ng/, or /kw/ sound?

10. sink **(1)**

11. squirrel **(1)**

12. mistake **(1)**

13. question **(1)**

14. attack **(1)**

15. blanket **(1)**

16. crooked **(1)**

17. monkey **(1)**

18–25. Which eight words have the final /j/, /ĭj/, or /s/ sound?

18. ridge **(1)**

19. twice **(1)**

20. chance **(1)**

21. strange **(1)**

22. glance **(1)**

23. cottage **(1)**

24. since **(1)**

25. village **(1)**

26–32. What letters are missing from each word below? Write each word.

26. of—— office **(1)**

27. wheth—— whether **(1)**

28. af—— afraid **(1)**

29. oth—— other **(1)**

30. sup—— suppose **(1)**

31. cor—— corner **(1)**

32. beau—— beauty **(1)**

Spelling Words

1. village
2. corner
3. office
4. sink
5. squirrel
6. alley
7. whether
8. ridge
9. mistake
10. afraid
11. question
12. other
13. lonely
14. attack
15. thirty
16. blanket
17. monkey
18. twice
19. chance
20. suppose
21. beauty
22. degree
23. crooked
24. honey
25. strange
26. glance
27. twenty
28. cottage
29. since
30. ready

Name _____

Spelling Spree

Riddles **Write the Spelling Word that answers each
question.**

1. What is a place where people wash dishes?
   sink **(1 point)** _____

2. What word sounds like *weather* and means "if"?
   whether **(1)** _____

3. What animal eats nuts and chatters? squirrel **(1)** _____

4. What is a long, narrow edge? ridge **(1)** _____

5. What is a narrow street? alley **(1)** _____

6. What is the place where two lines, meet? corner **(1)** _____

7. What kind of sentence are you reading? question **(1)** _____

8. What kind of animal is a baboon? monkey **(1)** _____

1. whether
2. afraid
3. ridge
4. alley
5. squirrel
6. degree
7. strange
8. sink
9. ready
10. question
11. twenty
12. corner
13. monkey
14. honey
15. chance

Be a Poet **Finish the rhymes by writing a Spelling Word in
each blank line. The Spelling Word should rhyme with the
underlined word.**

9. In their home on the <u>range</u>, those cows are so strange **(1)** _____!

10. Don't be afraid **(1)** _____! That stranger is just the <u>maid</u>.

11. Hold the baseball bat <u>steady</u>. Then your swing will be ready **(1)** _____.

12. We've had four cookies, and that should be <u>plenty</u>,
    But Jenny says no — she wants to have twenty **(1)** _____!

13. The temperature says it is just twenty-<u>three</u>.
    Maybe we should turn the heat up one degree **(1)** _____!

14. Do we have enough <u>money</u> to buy that new kind of honey **(1)** _____?

15. This is your last chance **(1)** _____ to get up and <u>dance</u>.

Assessment Tip: Total **15** Points

Proofreading and Writing

Proofreading Circle the six misspelled Spelling Words in this plan. Then write each word correctly.

This school year I will try to (atak) a new problem every day. I want to be (reddy) to do my best thinking. I will read each question at least (twise). I won't just (glanss) at it. If I have to look at a problem (thurty) times before I solve it, I will. I (suppoze) this will be difficult, but I am prepared.

1. attack **(1 point)**
2. ready **(1)**
3. twice **(1)**
4. glance **(1)**
5. thirty **(1)**
6. suppose **(1)**

Speech, Speech Use context clues to help you write the Spelling Word that belongs next to each number.

In the 7. _____ of Pineville, there is a narrow, 8. _____ road near the pretty 9. _____ of the Wilson family. It is a quiet and 10. _____ area with natural 11. _____. Some people wanted to tear down the Wilson's house to widen the road. I said we should try this 12. _____ idea: turn the area into a park. At first no one liked the idea. I wanted to get into bed and pull a 13. _____ over my head! Then I met with the mayor in her 14. _____. The mayor agreed that it would be a 15. _____ to widen the road.

7. village **(1)**
8. crooked **(1)**
9. cottage **(1)**
10. lonely **(1)**
11. beauty **(1)**
12. other **(1)**
13. blanket **(1)**
14. office **(1)**
15. mistake **(1)**

Spelling Words

1. ready
2. mistake
3. crooked
4. glance
5. village
6. cottage
7. other
8. beauty
9. office
10. attack
11. twice
12. suppose
13. thirty
14. blanket
15. lonely

Write a Persuasive Paragraph Write a paragraph about a problem and how to solve it. Use the Spelling Review Words.

Responses will vary. **(3)**

Name ______________________________

Comparing Poems

Think about the elements of poetry. Choose three poems to compare and contrast. Then complete the chart below.

Answers will vary.

	_______ (title)	_______ (title)	_______ (title)
What kind of language is used in each poem?	**(2 points each)**		
Does the poem express a feeling? If so, what feeling does it express?			
What images are in each poem?			

Tell which of these poems is your favorite and why. **(4 points)**

Answers will vary.

____

____

Assessment Tip: Total **22** Points

Name _____

May the Best Poems Win!

You are hosting an awards ceremony for poetry. Choose one of the poems from this theme to receive the Best Rhythm Award, another to get the Best Rhyme Prize, and a third for Best Imagery. Explain why each poem won that prize, giving an example from that poem.

Rhythm Award

Winning Poem: **(1 point)** _____

Why: **(2)** _____

_____

Example: **(2)** _____

_____

Rhyme Prize

Winning Poem: **(1)** _____

Why: **(2)** _____

_____

Example: **(2)** _____

_____

Best Imagery

Winning Poem: **(1)** _____

Why: **(2)** _____

_____

Example: **(2)** _____

_____

Name ______________________________

Heroes

Fill in the information to show what you think about heroes.

What is a hero?

Possible answers: someone who has achieved something important, a good person, someone who helps others **(3 points)**

HEROES

Who are some of your heroes?

Accept reasonable varied answers. **(3)**

Possible answers: hard-working, brave, courageous, kind, a leader, helps others **(6)**

What are some characteristics of a hero?

Assessment Tip: Total **12** Points

Name _____

Heroes

	Name the hero or heroes in each story. What are their achievements?	What qualities helped them achieve their goals?
Happy Birthday, Dr. King!	Rosa Parks: started important civil rights protest by refusing to give up her bus seat to a white man; Dr. Martin Luther King, Jr.: was a great leader of the civil rights movement, supported fighting injustice peacefully. **(4 points)**	Rosa Parks: had courage, would not give in to injustice; Dr. King: a great leader, earned people's respect, gave powerful speeches; fearless. **(4)**
Gloria Estefan	Gloria Estefan: is a very successful singer; uses her talents to help others, especially children; overcame injury and pain. **(4)**	determined and works hard to get what she wants; caring about her family, friends, and other people; doesn't give up in school, in work, in illness **(4)**
Lou Gehrig: The Luckiest Man	Lou Gehrig: was one of baseball's greatest players; never missed a game; although famous, always remained humble; after he was diagnosed with illness, worked with former prisoners. **(4)**	supported his family; was an excellent team player; showed good sportsmanship; modest; worked hard at everything; never gave up; optimistic, even when ill **(4)**

Assessment Tip: Total **24** Points

Name _____

Civil Rights Crossword

Complete the crossword puzzle using words from the vocabulary box.

Vocabulary

boycott   civil rights   fare   protest   stupendous

Across

3. the money paid to travel **(1 point)**
4. a refusal to use, buy from, or deal with a company **(1)**
5. to strongly object to something **(1)**

Down

1. relates to the legal privileges of a citizen **(1)**
2. amazing **(1)**

Write a sentence using at least two of the vocabulary words.

Answers will vary. **(1)**

_____

_____

Name _____

Cause and Effect Chart

Cause	Effect
page 536 Jamal gets a note from the principal.	Jamal is afraid he is in trouble and tries to sneak quietly into his house. **(2 points)**
page 539 Jamal tells Grandpa Joe about the fight. **(2)**	Grandpa Joe gets angry at Jamal.
page 541 Jamal apologizes to Grandpa Joe for fighting. She wouldn't give up her seat at the front of the bus. **(2)**	Grandpa Joe tells Jamal about Rosa Parks. **(2)** Rosa Parks got arrested.
page 542 African Americans heard about Rosa Parks's arrest.	African Americans boycotted the buses. **(2)**
page 544 Dr. King headed the bus boycott and became a great civil rights leader. **(2)**	Dr. King's birthday is honored and celebrated with a national holiday.
page 547 Dad explains to Jamal that Dr. King worked in peaceful ways.	Jamal has an idea to put on a skit about solving problems peacefully. **(2)**

290   Theme 5: **Heroes**
Assessment Tip: Total **14** Points

Name _____

Knowing Dr. King

Read and answer the questions.

1. Why was Grandpa Joe so angry that Jamal got into a fight to sit in the back of the bus?

   It reminded him of how hard African Americans had fought to sit

   at the front of a bus. **(1 point)**

2. Which two famous African Americans did Jamal and Grandpa Joe talk about?

   Rosa Parks and Martin Luther King, Jr. **(1)**

3. What did Jamal's father say about the way Dr. King made things happen?

   Dr. King made things happen in peaceful ways. **(1)**

4. What was the Montgomery Bus Boycott?

   African Americans refused to ride the buses because they

   were not allowed to sit anywhere they wanted on a bus. **(1)**

5. Dr. King become a leader of what movement?

   Dr. King became a leader of the civil rights movement. **(1)**

6. What did Jamal decide to do for the Martin Luther King, Jr., assembly?

   He decided to do a skit to show that fighting is not the way to get

   something done. **(1)**

Theme 5: **Heroes**   291
Assessment Tip: Total **6** Points

The Effects of Hard Work

Read the story below and then complete the chart on the next page.

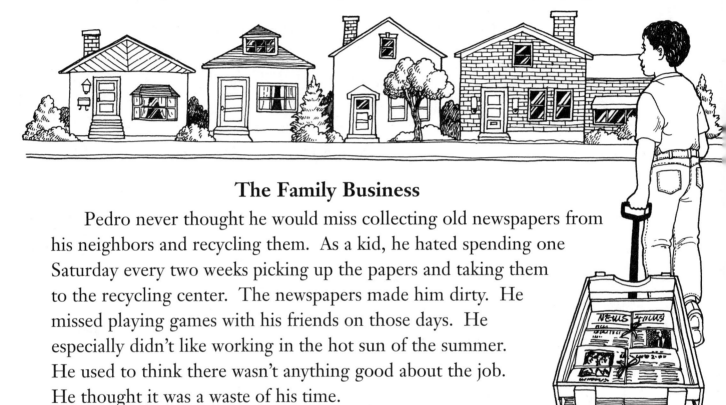

The Family Business

Pedro never thought he would miss collecting old newspapers from his neighbors and recycling them. As a kid, he hated spending one Saturday every two weeks picking up the papers and taking them to the recycling center. The newspapers made him dirty. He missed playing games with his friends on those days. He especially didn't like working in the hot sun of the summer. He used to think there wasn't anything good about the job. He thought it was a waste of his time.

But now that he was moving with his family to a new neighborhood, he thought back on all the good things that happened because of the job. His sisters, who started the business, each saved enough money to pay for their own summer vacations to Europe. Pedro was able to buy a stereo for his room and send himself to summer camp.

"Hey, Pedro! Come in here please," his mother called from the kitchen. "Grampa's on the phone and he wants to say good-bye."

"Hello, Grampa! I was just thinking about the paper recycling business you convinced Anna and Katrina to begin. It sure brought us many good things."

"I'm glad to hear that, Pedro," his grandfather said. "It just goes to show you that all it takes is a good idea."

Name _____

The Effects of Hard Work

continued

Complete the chart below based on "The Family Business."

Cause	Effect

Cause

Pedro hated working on Saturdays. **(2 points)**

The newspapers made him dirty. **(2)**

He missed playing games with his friends. **(2)**

He didn't like working in the hot summer sun. **(2)**

He thought the job was a waste of time. **(2)**

Effect

Pedro didn't like his recycling job.

His sisters saved enough money to go to Europe.

He bought a stereo.

He paid for summer camp.

He misses the recycling job. **(2)**

Name _____

Searching for Prefixes and Suffixes

In the puzzle below, find and circle the hidden words in the box. Then recall what you know about prefixes and suffixes and write each word by its meaning.

wasteful	disinfect
unprepared	amazement
priceless	tasteless
measurement	emptiness
research	dishonest

T	V	P	R	I	C	E	L	E	S	S	B
F	J	G	M	G	B	S	R	E	S	E	S
M	E	A	S	U	R	E	M	E	N	T	T
Y	U	D	R	B	I	V	W	I	Y	A	O
U	D	I	S	H	O	N	E	S	T	S	N
N	R	I	E	W	E	K	K	N	Y	T	L
P	E	Q	S	M	A	O	L	N	U	E	I
R	S	U	M	I	P	S	Y	L	X	L	Z
E	E	Y	H	Y	N	T	T	M	A	E	J
P	A	M	O	F	K	F	I	E	K	S	R
A	R	D	P	I	B	R	E	N	F	S	T
R	C	M	S	P	F	N	E	C	E	U	M
E	H	P	L	H	H	K	A	H	T	S	L
D	A	M	A	Z	E	M	E	N	T	B	S

1. to get rid of germs
   disinfect **(1 point)**

2. not ready
   unprepared **(1)**

3. great surprise
   amazement **(1)**

4. careful study
   research **(1)**

5. nothingness
   emptiness **(1)**

6. untruthful
   dishonest **(1)**

7. without flavor
   tasteless **(1)**

8. using more than is needed
   wasteful **(1)**

9. size or amount
   measurement **(1)**

10. very valuable
    priceless **(1)**

Words with a Prefix or a Suffix

A **prefix** is a word part added to the beginning of a base word. A **suffix** is a word part added to the end of a base word. Both prefixes and suffixes add meaning.

Prefixes: **re**build, **dis**like, **un**lucky

Suffixes: sick**ness**, treat**ment**, beauti**ful**, care**less**

► In the starred word *awful*, the *e* was dropped from the base word *awe* before the suffix *-ful* was added.

Write each Spelling Word under its prefix or suffix.

Order of answers for each category may vary.

1. redo
2. treatment
3. rebuild
4. discolor
5. careless
6. dislike
7. sickness
8. beautiful
9. unlucky
10. awful*
11. reread
12. unsure
13. movement
14. peaceful
15. unpaid
16. distrust
17. kindness
18. useless
19. displease
20. powerful

re-

redo **(1 point)**

rebuild **(1)**

reread **(1)**

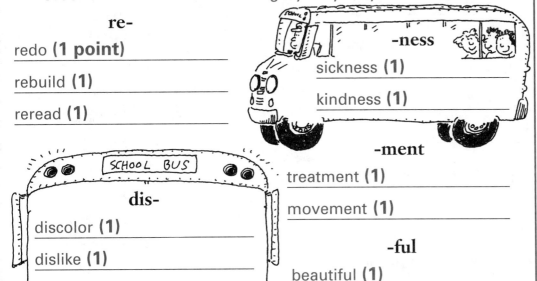

-ness

sickness **(1)**

kindness **(1)**

-ment

treatment **(1)**

movement **(1)**

dis-

discolor **(1)**

dislike **(1)**

distrust **(1)**

displease **(1)**

-ful

beautiful **(1)**

awful **(1)**

peaceful **(1)**

powerful **(1)**

un-

unlucky **(1)**

unsure **(1)**

unpaid **(1)**

-less

careless **(1)**

useless **(1)**

Theme 5: **Heroes** 295

Assessment Tip: Total **20** Points

Name _____

Spelling Spree

Finding Words Each word below is hidden in a Spelling Word. Write the Spelling Word.

Example: hop *hopeful*

1. ace _peaceful_ **(1 point)**
2. plea _displease_ **(1)**
3. eat _treatment_ **(1)**
4. rust _distrust_ **(1)**
5. are _careless_ **(1)**
6. owe _powerful_ **(1)**
7. red _redo_ **(1)**
8. disco _discolor_ **(1)**
9. aid _unpaid_ **(1)**
10. kin _kindness_ **(1)**

Questions Write the Spelling Word that best answers each question.

11. What is an antonym for *health*?
12. What kind of object serves no purpose?
13. What is a milder word for *hate*?
14. What might you do if your house burns down?
15. What is a synonym for *terrible*?
16. What is another word for "unfortunate"?

11. _sickness_ **(1)**   14. _rebuild_ **(1)**
12. _useless_ **(1)**   15. _awful_ **(1)**
13. _dislike_ **(1)**   16. _unlucky_ **(1)**

Spelling Words

1. redo
2. treatment
3. rebuild
4. discolor
5. careless
6. dislike
7. sickness
8. beautiful
9. unlucky
10. awful*
11. reread
12. unsure
13. movement
14. peaceful
15. unpaid
16. distrust
17. kindness
18. useless
19. displease
20. powerful

296   Theme 5: **Heroes**
Assessment Tip: Total **16** Points

Name _____

Proofreading and Writing

Proofreading Circle the four misspelled Spelling Words in this book review. Then write each word correctly.

Are you (unshure) why we honor Martin Luther King, Jr., with a holiday? If so, get hold of a copy of *Happy Birthday, Dr. King!* Jamal Wilson is the main character of this (beutiful) but powerful picture book. As Jamal learns about the civil rights (moovement,) readers do, too. Believe me, you won't read this book only once. You'll (rerread) it many times!

1. redo
2. treatment
3. rebuild
4. discolor
5. careless
6. dislike
7. sickness
8. beautiful
9. unlucky
10. awful*
11. reread
12. unsure
13. movement
14. peaceful
15. unpaid
16. distrust
17. kindness
18. useless
19. displease
20. powerful

1. unsure **(1 point)**   3. movement **(1)**

2. beautiful **(1)**   4. reread **(1)**

✏️➤ **Write Copy for a Book Jacket** Many books have jackets, paper covers that protect the hard covers. Book jacket copy tells some details about the book. However, it doesn't tell enough to spoil the book for readers.

On a separate sheet of paper, write copy for a book jacket for your favorite book. Tell only enough to make readers want to read the book. Use Spelling Words from the list. Responses will vary. **(6 points)**

Name _____

Happy Birthday, Dr. King!

Vocabulary Skill Dictionary:
Prefixes *re-, un-, dis-*

Crossword Prefixes

**Use the base words and prefixes in the box to make new words that match the clues. Enter the new words where they belong in the crossword puzzle.
(1 point each)**

Box:
un- dis- re-
appear important
changed like
common pay
cover respect
done write

Crossword answers:
2 across: undone
4 across: uncommon
5 across: disrespect
6 across: repay
7 across: disappear
1 down: unimportant
3 down: unchanged
4 down: uncover
7 down: dislike
8 down: rewrite

Across

2. The job isn't finished, so it is
   _____.

4. Something very different
   may be _____.

5. If you act rudely, you show
   _____.

6. When you give money back
   to people, you _____ them.

7. Something you lose may just
   seem to _____.

Down

1. If something doesn't matter much, it's
   _____.

3. It's no different than before, so it's
   _____.

4. Take your cap off and _____ your head.

7. If you don't care much for something
   you _____ it.

8. When you do your lesson over, you
   _____ it.

   Assessment Tip: Total **10** Points

Name _____

Replacing Nouns with Pronouns

For each sentence below, write a subject pronoun to replace the word or words given in parentheses. Write your sentence on the lines provided.

1. (Jamal's mother) looks at the pink slip.

   She looks at the pink slip. **(1 point)**

2. (Jamal) was in trouble now.

   He was in trouble now. **(1)**

3. His mother asked Jamal, "Did (Jamal) get in trouble today?"

   His mother asked Jamal, "Did you get in trouble today?" **(1)**

4. (Alisha) was not home yet.

   She was not home yet. **(1)**

5. (Jamal's classmates) are planning a celebration for Dr. King.

   They are planning a celebration for Dr. King. **(1)**

6. (Grandpa Joe) was angry with Jamal for fighting.

   He was angry with Jamal for fighting. **(1)**

7. (Jamal) listened to Grandpa Joe's story about the boycott.

   He listened to Grandpa Joe's story about the boycott. **(1)**

8. (Grandpa Joe and his wife) boycotted the buses.

   They boycotted the buses. **(1)**

Assessment Tip: Total **8** Points

In Search of a Subject Pronoun

Jamal's teacher, Mrs. Gordon, and the class are having a discussion about what to do for the Martin Luther King, Jr., celebration. Write a subject pronoun to replace the word or words in parentheses.

Mrs. Gordon: Jamal says that (Jamal) <u>he **(1 point)**</u> thinks a skit would be a good idea.

Jamal: Yes, that way (the rest of the class and I) <u>we **(1)**</u> could all have a part.

Albert: How about the subject of the skit? What will (the subject) <u>it **(1)**</u> be?

Mrs. Gordon: Jamal says that (Jamal) <u>he **(1)**</u> has an idea.

Jamal: Well, (Jamal) <u>I **(1)**</u> thought that we could do a skit about two boys on a bus. (The two boys) <u>They **(1)**</u> are arguing over an empty seat at the back of the bus.

Frieda: That skit sounds like a good idea. (The skit) <u>It **(1)**</u> is about Mrs. Parks's fight for civil rights.

Margie: Mrs. Gordon, would (Mrs. Gordon) <u>you **(1)**</u> direct the skit?

Mrs. Gordon: Yes, (Mrs. Gordon) <u>I **(1)**</u> would be happy to do that.

Billy: Aminta should have a part. (Aminta) <u>She **(1)**</u> can play the part of the bus driver.

Name _____

Sentence Combining with Subject Pronouns

When two sentences have different subjects but the same predicate, you can combine them into one sentence with a compound subject.

Read the sentences below. Then rewrite them, combining each pair of sentences into one sentence with a compound subject. Use the joining word in parentheses to write the new sentences.

1. She gave the bus driver money for a ticket. I gave the bus driver money for a ticket. (and)

   She and I gave the bus driver money for a ticket. **(2 points)**

2. You were there to hear the entire speech. They were there to hear the entire speech. (and)

   You and they were there to hear the entire speech. **(2)**

3. She will recite part of the speech from memory. You will recite part of the speech from memory. (or)

   She or you will recite part of the speech from memory. **(2)**

4. They listened to the words carefully. I listened to the words carefully. (and)

   They and I listened to the words carefully. **(2)**

5. She will prepare a report about Martin Luther King, Jr. I will prepare a report about Martin Luther King, Jr. (or)

   She or I will prepare a report about Martin Luther King, Jr. **(2)**

Assessment Tip: Total **10** Points

Name _____

Writing an Information Paragraph

Use this graphic organizer to help you plan your information paragraph about a leader you admire. Tell why you admire this person, and what he or she did that is admirable, and why you chose this leader.

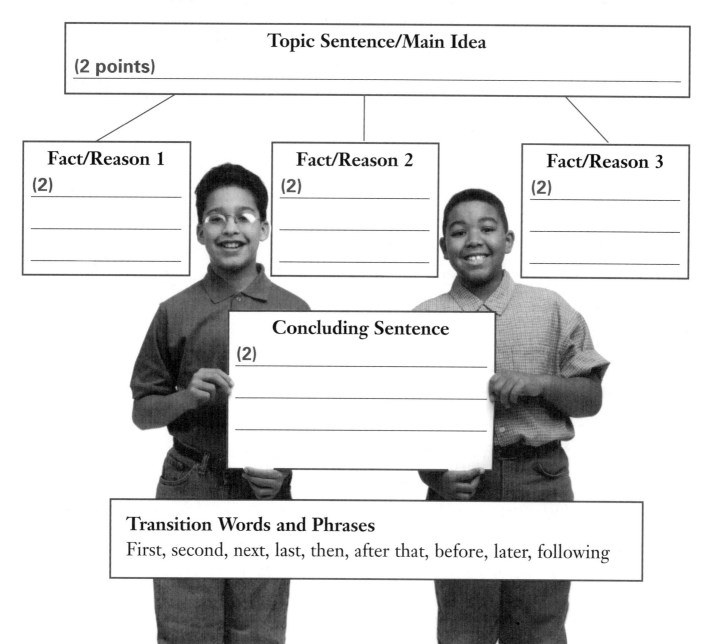

Topic Sentence/Main Idea

(2 points) _____

Fact/Reason 1

(2) _____

_____

_____

Fact/Reason 2

(2) _____

_____

_____

Fact/Reason 3

(2) _____

_____

_____

Concluding Sentence

(2) _____

_____

_____

Transition Words and Phrases

First, second, next, last, then, after that, before, later, following

Assessment Tip: Total **10** Points

Name _____

Using Facts

Good writers use facts to support the main idea of an information paragraph. To do so, they organize them in different ways.

► Writers use chronological order to put events in the order in which they happen.

► Writers use spatial order to describe how things look.

► Writers use the order of importance to organize facts from least to most important or from most to least important.

Read the following clusters of facts. Then decide on a main idea and use the facts to write a paragraph of information. Identify the kind of order you used. Sample answers shown.

1. On Tuesday, the math teacher gives us a mini-test.
   We have a history test on Wednesday.
   Monday afternoon, we have a special art class.
   Every Friday, there's a spelling quiz.

   The days at school are very busy. Monday afternoon we have a

   special art class. On Tuesday, the math teacher always gives us a

   mini-test. We have a history test on Wednesday. Every Friday,

   there's a spelling quiz. Chronological order. **(4 points)**

2. The third graders sang a medley of civil rights songs.
   Jamal's skit was the hit of the Dr. Martin Luther King, Jr., assembly.
   Everyone talked about it for weeks.
   The first graders recited Dr. King's "I Have a Dream" speech.

   Our school assembly celebrating Martin Luther King Day was a

   great success. The first graders recited Dr. King's "I Have a Dream"

   speech. The third graders sang a medley of civil rights songs.

   Jamal's skit was the hit of the program. Everyone talked about it

   for weeks. Order of importance. **(4)**

Name _____

Evaluating Your Personal Essay

Reread your personal essay. What do you need to make it better? Use this page to help you decide. Put a checkmark in the box for each sentence that describes your personal essay.

Rings the Bell!

☐ My essay has a beginning that will get my readers' attention.

☐ Each paragraph has a main idea, supported by details.

☐ It reads as if I were saying it to someone.

☐ I have a good conclusion that sums up my point.

☐ There are almost no mistakes.

Getting Stronger

☐ I could make the beginning more attention grabbing.

☐ My main ideas are there, but I need to add more details.

☐ It still could sound more like me.

☐ I need to add a stronger conclusion.

☐ There are a few mistakes.

Try Harder

☐ I need a better beginning.

☐ My main ideas aren't clear, and I need to add details.

☐ There is no conclusion.

☐ There are a lot of mistakes.

Pronoun Reference

Pronouns are words that replace nouns. Write the word or words that the underlined pronoun refers to in each exercise.

1. I would love to start my own magazine. <u>It</u> would be called *Cartoon*.

2. This magazine would be all cartoons. <u>They</u> would be on every page.

3. I would write all the articles for the magazine. My friend Jimmy would edit <u>them</u>.

4. "You write the articles," Jimmy says. "Let me edit <u>them</u>."

5. Jimmy and I love those old Bugs Bunny cartoons. We have made tapes of <u>them</u>.

6. We also love newspaper cartoons. Jimmy collects <u>them</u>.

7. We both really like *Peanuts* by Charles Schultz. <u>He</u> had his characters say such funny things.

8. My sister would like to interview Matt Groening. <u>She</u> thinks he is the best cartoonist of all.

9. Do you know who Matt Groening is? <u>He</u> is the creator of *The Simpsons*.

10. The characters on the show are based on real people. <u>They</u> have the same names as people in Groening's family.

1. magazine **(1 point)**

2. cartoons **(1)**

3. articles **(1)**

4. Jimmy **(1)**

5. Jimmy and I **(1)**

6. newspaper cartoons **(1)**

7. Charles Schultz **(1)**

8. My sister **(1)**

9. Matt Groening **(1)**

10. characters **(1)**

Theme 5: **Heroes**   305
Assessment Tip: Total **10** Points

Name _____

Spelling Words

Words Often Misspelled Look for familiar spelling patterns to help you remember how to spell the Spelling Words on this page. Think carefully about the parts that you find hard to spell in each word.

Write the missing letters in the Spelling Words below.

1. br o u g h t **(1)**
2. en o u g h **(1)**
3. b u y **(1)**
4. g u ess **(1)**
5. Sat u r day **(1)**
6. Jan u a r y **(1)**
7. Feb r u a r y **(1)**
8. favor i t e **(1)**

9. l y ing **(1)**
10. t y ing **(1)**
11. a round **(1)**
12. swim m ing **(1)**
13. h e a rd **(1)**
14. a l s o **(1)**
15. tr i e d **(1)**

Study List On a separate piece of paper, write each Spelling Word. Check your spelling against the words on the list. Order of words may vary. **(5 points)**

Assessment Tip: Total **20** Points

Name _____

Spelling Spree

Opposites Write a Spelling Word that means the opposite of the underlined words.

Spelling Words

1. brought
2. enough
3. buy
4. guess
5. Saturday
6. January
7. February
8. favorite
9. lying
10. tying
11. around
12. swimming
13. heard
14. also
15. tried

1. I was <u>telling the truth</u> when I said that I knew how to fly a plane. <u>lying **(1 point)**</u>

2. We went to the store to <u>sell</u> some groceries to get ready for the big storm. <u>buy **(1)**</u>

3. She <u>didn't attempt</u> to call you to let you know what the homework was. <u>tried **(1)**</u>

4. Isn't your <u>most disliked</u> singer playing a concert next month? <u>favorite **(1)**</u>

5. It was <u>nowhere near</u> ten o'clock when we finished watching the movie. <u>around **(1)**</u>

Crack the Code Some Spelling Words have been written in the code below. Use the code to figure out each word. Then write the words correctly.

CODE: u d m r s i q o b a c e f z v t y n p h
LETTER: a b c d e f g h i j l m n o r s t u w y

6. Aufnuvh   9. osuvr   12. sfznqo   15. qnstt

7. dvznqoy   10. yhbfq   13. uctz

8. tpbeebfq   11. Isdvnuvh   14. Tuynvruh

6. <u>January **(1)**</u>   10. <u>tying **(1)**</u>   14. <u>Saturday **(1)**</u>

7. <u>brought **(1)**</u>   11. <u>February **(1)**</u>   15. <u>guess **(1)**</u>

8. <u>swimming **(1)**</u>   12. <u>enough **(1)**</u>

9. <u>heard **(1)**</u>   13. <u>also **(1)**</u>

Name _____

Proofreading and Writing

Proofreading Circle the four misspelled Spelling Words in this inscription on a statue. Then write each word correctly.

This statue is in honor of the accomplishment of Elmer Fitzgerald on (Saterday,) February 21, 1920. On that day, he single-handedly caught (enouf) fish to feed his entire village for three months. Unfortunately, before the fish could be (brot) back to shore, they were all eaten by sharks. Elmer (treid) to drive the sharks off with his fishing pole, but there were just too many of them. At least, that's what Elmer told us.

1. brought
2. enough
3. buy
4. guess
5. Saturday
6. January
7. February
8. favorite
9. lying
10. tying
11. around
12. swimming
13. heard
14. also
15. tried

1. Saturday **(1 point)**

2. enough **(1)**

3. brought **(1)**

4. tried **(1)**

✏️ **Write a Round-Robin Story** Get together in a small group with other students. Then write a story about a hero, with each of you writing one sentence at a time. Use a Spelling Word from the list in each sentence.

Responses will vary. **(6 points)**

Assessment Tip: Total **10** Points

Name _____

Be a Recording Star!

**Complete the sentences in this ad for a recording company.
Use each vocabulary word once.**

> ## Vocabulary
>
> career   contract   demonstrated   eventually
> specializes   tireless   worldwide

Have you ever wanted a <u>career **(2 points)**</u> in music? Whiz Recordings can make your dream come true! Our company <u>specializes **(2)**</u> in making stars out of today's young hopefuls.

We have consistently <u>demonstrated **(2)**</u> our ability to get performers on the charts. Just last year we had forty-five performers get a top ten hit. Our constant, <u>tireless **(2)**</u> efforts pay off.

Join us and sign a <u>contract **(2)**</u> today! <u>Eventually **(2)**</u>, you just might make it on your own. And all our big stars are guaranteed a <u>worldwide **(2)**</u> tour within six months.

Name _____

Judgments Chart

Why Might Someone Call Gloria Estefan a "Hero"?

Chapter One: Escaping with Music

She quickly learns English, and is always at the head of her class.

She takes care of the family at age eleven.

She teaches herself how to play an instrument. **(4 points)**

Chapter Two: Making Music with Emilio and Chapter Three: Changes

She puts school first when offered a singing job.

Her band becomes one of the most popular groups in Latin America.

Her band starts becoming popular all over the world. **(4)**

Chapter Four: World Fame—and Tragedy

The band sells millions of records.

She is honored by President Bush for her drug prevention work.

She recovers from a terrible bus accident. **(4)**

Chapter Five: "Here for Each Other"

She is given a Congressional Medal of Honor.

She helps hurricane victims and abused children.

She declines movie offers to be with her family. **(4)**

Name _____

Music World

Help the reporter from *Music World* write an article on Gloria Estefan by answering his questions about the star. Use complete sentences.

I hear you have read a lot about Gloria Fajardo Estefan. Tell me something about her childhood, up to age 16.

She was born in Cuba but came with her family to the U.S. in 1959.

She had a lot of family responsibilities. Music was Gloria's escape.

She learned to sing and play the guitar. **(2 points)**

Tell me the story of how Gloria became a member of Emilio Estefan's band—and how they fell in love.

Estefan gave advice to a band Gloria sang with. Later he asked Gloria

to join his band. Gloria and Emilio had a lot in common and they fell

in love. **(2)**

In your opinion, what were Gloria's most important achievements before her accident in 1990? What are the most important things she has done since then?

Before the accident: Gloria recorded a string of worldwide hits with

the Miami Sound Machine. She received many musical honors—as

well as recognition for her drug prevention work with teens. **(2)**

Since the accident: Gloria made a complete recovery through

bravery, hard work, and determination. She continued to produce hit

albums with the Miami Sound Machine. **(2)**

What can a young person learn from Gloria Estefan?

Answers will vary. Possible answers: Hard work pays off. Happiness

comes from helping others in whatever way you can. **(2)**

Name _____

The Singing Cubs

Read the story. Then complete the following page.

My friends and I have a band that we call The Singing Cubs, and we're planning on entering the school talent show this year. I'm Bobby, the group's lead guitar player and singer. My friend Megan also plays the guitar, and Ralphie is our drummer.

The day before the talent show, the principal announced that all assignments had to be turned in first thing in the morning for those students participating in the show. We knew it would be a busy night.

Ralphie's parents decided they couldn't stand his messy room any longer. They said he needed to clean it up or no show. Then to make matters worse, my mother got sick and I had to help with dinnertime. I was so busy. I washed, carried, served, and washed again. Finally, dinner was over and I could begin my homework.

After dinner, I finished most of my homework. Then I called Megan because I needed help on my book report. She was also hard at work on her report. She needed help on it too. We talked a few things over and were soon ready to finish the reports on our own.

Then Ralphie called. He said, "There's no way I can get my room clean tonight. It's too messy." Both Megan and I went to Ralphie's house and worked hard on his room until it was spotless. Nothing could stand in our way now!

When it came time to perform the next day, we were exhausted but proud of ourselves. Mr. Major introduced us as "The Hard-Working Singing Cubs" and looked pleased with all that we had accomplished. Our parents were sitting in the front row, beaming with pride.

Name _____

The Singing Cubs continued

Complete this Judgments Chart for the story "The Singing Cubs."

Event	Response	Judgment
All talent show performers must hand in their homework early.	Bobby works hard to complete his homework. **(1 point)**	Bobby is a responsible student who hands in his assignments on time. **(1)**
Bobby's mom gets sick.	Bobby helps his mom with dinnertime. **(1)**	Bobby is a helpful and loving son. **(1)**
Ralphie cannot participate unless he cleans his room.	Bobby and Megan help Ralphie clean his room. **(1)**	Ralphie has good friends he can call on for help. **(1)**
Bobby and Megan need some help on their book reports.	Bobby and Megan discuss their book reports before completing them. **(1)**	Bobby and Megan are hard-working students. **(1)**
The principal realizes how hard the children have been working to be in the talent show.	The principal acknowledges the children's efforts and accomplishments. **(1)**	The principal is a good leader who respects the efforts of his students. **(1)**

Name _____

Musical Changes

**Make music of your own by joining the words and endings. Write
only one letter on each line. Remember, when a base word ends
with *y*, change the *y* to *i* before adding *-es*, *-er*, *-ed*, or *-est*.**

1. noisy + er

__n__ __o__ __i__ __s__ __i__ __e__ __r__ **(1 point)**
          7

2. marry + ed

__m__ __a__ __r__ __r__ __i__ __e__ __d__ **(1)**
         8

3. story + es

__s__ __t__ __o__ __r__ __i__ __e__ __s__ **(1)**
       4

4. hungry + er

__h__ __u__ __n__ __g__ __r__ __i__ __e__ __r__ **(1)**
     6

5. country + es

__c__ __o__ __u__ __n__ __t__ __r__ __i__ __e__ __s__ **(1)**
   9

6. early + est

__e__ __a__ __r__ __l__ __i__ __e__ __s__ __t__ **(1)**
       3   1

7. family + es

__f__ __a__ __m__ __i__ __l__ __i__ __e__ __s__ **(1)**
       5

8. worry + ed

__w__ __o__ __r__ __r__ __i__ __e__ __d__ **(1)**
     2

**Solve the riddle by writing each numbered letter on the line
with the matching number. (2)**

Riddle: What kind of music do shoes like to listen to?

__s__ __o__ __l__ __e__ __m__ __u__ __s__ __i__ __c__
1 2 3 4   5 6 7 8 9

Assessment Tip: Total **10** Points

Name _____

Changing Final *y* to *i*

If a word ends with a consonant and *y*, change the *y* to *i* when adding *-es*, *-ed*, *-er*, or *-est*.

city + es = cit**ies**   study + ed = stud**ied**
sunny + er = sunn**ier**   heavy + est = heav**iest**

Write each Spelling Word under its ending.
Order of answers for each category may vary.

Spelling Words

1. sunnier
2. cloudier
3. windier
4. cities
5. heaviest
6. prettiest
7. studied
8. easier
9. noisier
10. families
11. ferries
12. crazier
13. funnier
14. earlier
15. copied
16. hobbies
17. angriest
18. emptied
19. worried
20. happiest

-es or -ed

cities **(1 point)**

studied **(1)**

families **(1)**

ferries **(1)**

copied **(1)**

hobbies **(1)**

emptied **(1)**

worried **(1)**

-er or -est

sunnier **(1)**

cloudier **(1)**

windier **(1)**

heaviest **(1)**

prettiest **(1)**

easier **(1)**

noisier **(1)**

crazier **(1)**

funnier **(1)**

earlier **(1)**

angriest **(1)**

happiest **(1)**

Assessment Tip: Total **20** Points

Name _____

Spelling Spree

Meaning Match Write a Spelling Word that has each meaning and ending below.

1. do like + ed
2. making a lot of sound + er
3. having strong air movement + er
4. needing little effort + er
5. having great weight + est
6. full of sunshine + er
7. causing laughter + er

1. copied **(1)**
2. noisier **(1)**
3. windier **(1)**
4. easier **(1)**

5. heaviest **(1)**
6. sunnier **(1)**
7. funnier **(1)**

Code Breaker Some Spelling Words are written in the code below. Figure out each word, and write it correctly.

8. 6-5-15-15-9-5-16
9. 19-13-15-15-9-5-4
10. 3-10-13-18-4-9-5-15
11. 8-13-2-2-9-5-16

12. 5-11-14-17-9-5-4
13. 1-12-7-15-9-5-16-17
14. 16-17-18-4-9-5-4
15. 3-15-1-20-9-5-15

8. ferries **(1 point)**
9. worried **(1)**
10. cloudier **(1)**
11. hobbies **(1)**

12. emptied **(1)**
13. angriest **(1)**
14. studied **(1)**
15. crazier **(1)**

CODE:	1	2	3	4	5	6	7	8	9	10	11	12	13	14	15	16	17	18	19	20
LETTER:	a	b	c	d	e	f	g	h	i	l	m	n	o	p	r	s	t	u	w	z

Assessment Tip: Total **15** Points

Name _____

Proofreading and Writing

Proofreading Circle the five misspelled Spelling Words in this poster ad. Then write each word correctly.

ONE SHOW ONLY

COMING SOON!

SUNDAY 8 PM

Are you worried about what to do Sunday night? Well, make up your mind (earlyer) rather than later. These tickets are going FAST! At 8 P.M., Gloria Estefan and the Miami Sound Machine will be here at the Music Hall. Imagine that! Of all the (citties) the group could have visited, they chose ours! Come hear some of the (prittiest) music you've ever heard. Bring your (famlies,) too! You'll be the (hapiest) fans around!

DON'T MISS IT!

1. earlier **(1 point)**	4. families **(1)**
2. cities **(1)**	5. happiest **(1)**
3. prettiest **(1)**	

Spelling Words

1. sunnier
2. cloudier
3. windier
4. cities
5. heaviest
6. prettiest
7. studied
8. easier
9. noisier
10. families
11. ferries
12. crazier
13. funnier
14. earlier
15. copied
16. hobbies
17. angriest
18. emptied
19. worried
20. happiest

Write Interview Questions If you could interview Gloria Estefan, what questions would you ask her? Would you want to know more about her childhood? Would you ask why she chose to be a musician?

On a separate piece of paper, write a list of interview questions to ask Gloria Estefan. Use Spelling Words from the list.

Responses will vary. **(5 points)**

Name _____

Sounds Like

Have you ever used a spelling checker on a computer? Then you know that it cannot tell the difference between two homophones.

Help Rosa by proofreading her letter to her aunt. Write the correct word from each pair on the line. The first one has been done for you.

Dear Tía Lara,

(Your You're) __You're__ not going to believe this, but I finally (won one)

__won (1 point)__ something! You (no know) __know (1)__ that I
  1   2

like to play basketball. Well, (there they're) __there (1)__ was a
                                                                                3

contest to see who could get the most baskets in three minutes.

I (threw through) __threw (1)__ more than anyone. I (new knew)
                                          4

__knew (1)__ I had a good chance of winning. I practiced for
      5

(hours ours) __hours (1)__ the week before. The (whole hole)
                                  6

__whole (1)__ fourth grade took part, even the teachers. Our
      7

teacher, Mr. Barnes, (beet beat) __beat (1)__ all the others.
                                                        8

The coach asked if (weed we'd) __we'd (1)__ like to do it again,
                                                    9

and everyone said yes. So just (weight wait) __wait (1)__
                                                                          10

until next month!

                                          Love,
                                          Rosa

318   Theme 5: **Heroes**
       Assessment Tip: Total **10** Points

Name _____

Writing with Object Pronouns

Complete the following paragraph by writing the correct pronoun to replace the noun in parentheses. Be careful! Some of the pronouns are subjects. Use the lines provided.

When Gloria's father went to Cuba, (her father) <u>he **(1 point)**</u> was away for two years. Gloria and her mother did not know that (Gloria and her mother) <u>they **(1)**</u> would be alone so long. Although Gloria did not speak English, she learned (English) <u>it **(1)**</u> quickly. After her father came back from Cuba, (her father) <u>he **(1)**</u> joined the U.S. army. Her father became ill, and Gloria took care of (her father) <u>him **(1)**</u>. She listened to many songs and learned to sing (the songs) <u>them **(1)**</u>. Gloria wanted to be a professional singer but wasn't sure that (Gloria) <u>she **(1)**</u> could sing well enough. At first, singing with a band was a weekend job for (Gloria) <u>her **(1)**</u>. Gloria was singing but still made time for her school courses. She did not want to neglect (the courses) <u>them **(1)**</u>. Gloria and Emilio decided that (Gloria and Emilio) <u>they **(1)**</u> wanted to make music a full-time career.

Name _____

Object Pronouns

Emilio hired five workers to help him get ready for recording sessions at a studio. You are one of them! Fill in the schedule by writing your name on the line next to every *. Then use the schedule to answer each question with a complete sentence.

Answers will vary. Sample answers shown.

	Monday	Tuesday	Friday
6:00 A.M. Set up instruments	*_____ Enrique	Helene *_____	*_____ Teisha
8:00 A.M. Tune guitars	*_____ Enrique	Helene Teisha	*_____ Helene
5:00 P.M. Pack up audio	Helene Teisha	*_____ Helene	*_____ Enrique
7:00 P.M. Pack instruments	*_____ Lynn	Enrique Helene	Lynn Teisha

1. If no one arrives Monday at 6:00 A.M., whom should Emilio call?

   Emilio should call Enrique and me. **(2 points)**

2. Who is supposed to pack up instruments on Monday?

   Lynn and I are supposed to pack up instruments. **(2)**

3. Who is supposed to pack up the audio at 5:00 on Tuesday evening?

   Helene and I are supposed to pack up the audio. **(2)**

4. Emilio gives a key to the workers who set the instruments up. To whom should he give the key Friday morning?

   He should give the key to Teisha and me. **(2)**

5. E-mail messages are always sent to the workers who tune the guitars. To whom will they be sent on Friday?

   The e-mail messages will be sent to Helene and me.

Name _____

Using Correct Pronouns

Letty and her friends belong to a music club at school. One day they were having a discussion about their favorite Latin CDs. Read the paragraph to find out which of Gloria Estefan's albums they like best. You will have to choose and write in the correct pronouns in the sentences, so read carefully.

Letty said that (her, she) _she **(1 point)**_ likes Gloria Estefan's songs and knows (they, them) _them **(1)**_ all by heart. Ricardo thinks the Miami Sound Machine is one of the best bands that (he, him) _he **(1)**_ has ever heard. Alicia says that even the group's earliest hits are favorites with (she, her) _her **(1)**_. Alicia likes "Dr. Beat" because (they, it) _it **(1)**_ has a Latin style but is in English. Letty has two favorite songs, and (they, them) _they **(1)**_ are in English too. Letty says that *Eyes of Innocence* is special for (she, her) _her **(1)**_. (We, Us) _We **(1)**_ all like Jonathan's collection because (he, him) _he **(1)**_ has a lot of Latin albums. Jonathan met Gloria at a concert and told (we, us) _us **(1)**_ about the performance.

Gloria Estefan

Name _____

Problem/Solution Paragraph

Use this graphic organizer to plan your problem-solution paragraph. Write about a problem you faced at school or at home, or about a problem you might face in the future. Tell about the pros and cons of possible solutions. Then tell what solution you decided on.

Topic Sentence/Problem Statement:
(1 point) _____
_____

Possible Solution 1:	**Possible Solution 1:**
(1) _____	**(1)** _____
_____	_____
_____	_____
Pros: _____	**Pros:** _____
(1) _____	**(1)** _____
_____	_____
Cons: _____	**Cons:** _____
(1) _____	**(1)** _____
_____	_____

Concluding Sentence/Problem Solution Statement:
(1) _____
_____

Assessment Tip: Total **8** Points

Name _____

Combining with Pronouns

Writers avoid repeating the same noun over and over by replacing it with a pronoun.

Two sentences: The name of Emilio's band was **the Miami Latin Boys.**
The Miami Latin Boys soon changed the name.

One sentence: The name of Emilio's band was **the Miami Latin Boys,** but **they** soon changed the name.

Read each pair of sentences. Combine them by replacing a noun with a pronoun in the second sentence. You may need to add or delete some words from the sentences when you combine them.

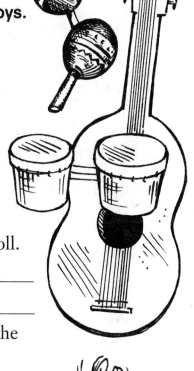

1. Gloria got good grades in school. Gloria made the honor roll.

   Gloria got good grades in school, and she made the honor roll.

   (2 points)

2. The band played gigs on weekends. School vacations gave the band a chance to play too.

   The band played gigs on weekends, and school vacations gave

   them a chance to play, too. **(2)**

3. Mrs. Fajardo was a kindergarten teacher in Cuba. Mrs. Fajardo had to go back to school to get her American teaching degree.

   Mrs. Fajardo was a kindergarten teacher in Cuba, but she had to

   go back to school to get her American teaching degree. **(2)**

4. Gloria's father had multiple sclerosis. Gloria had to give Gloria's father constant care.

   Gloria's father had multiple sclerosis, and Gloria had to give him

   constant care. **(2)**

5. Gloria loved singing. Singing became her profession.

   Gloria loved singing, and it became her profession. **(2)**

Name _____

Baseball Scramble

Unscramble the vocabulary words. Then unscramble the circled letters to solve the riddle.

SUTINECCOVE

c o n s (e) c u (t) i v e **(1 point)**

Hint: means "following one right after the other"

ROHON (h) o n o r **(1)**

Hint: means "to show special respect for"

SPOSTRANPIMSH

s p o r (t) s m a n s h i p **(1)**

Hint: means "quality of someone who acts with dignity in difficult situations"

NEDILFIG f i e (l) d i n g **(1)**

Hint: means "to catch, stop, or pick up a baseball in play and throw it to the correct player"

SMOEDT m o d (e) s t **(1)**

Hint: means "having a quiet, humble view of oneself"

FRITS SEMBANA

f i r s t (b) (a) s e m a n **(1)**

Hint: means "the person who plays the position around first base"

SPOTTROSH s (h) o (r) t s t o p **(1)**

Hint: means "the position in baseball between second and third bases"

What did the pitcher do? **(1)**

t h r e w t h e b a l l

Assessment Tip: Total **8** Points

Name _____

Fact and Opinion Chart

Statement Sample answers provided.	Fact or Opinion	How Can You Tell? Explain. Sample answers provided.
page 585 The first World Series was played in 1903. **(1 point)**	Fact	I can look this up in an encyclopedia. **(1)**
page 586 Through eight years of school Lou didn't miss a single day. **(1)**	Fact	I can check the school's records. **(1)**
page 589 Those were the first two games in what would become an amazing record. **(1)**	Opinion	No one can prove what is "amazing." **(1)**
page 590 He was selected again as the league's MVP in 1936. **(1)**	Fact	I can check this in a baseball record book. **(1)**
page 594 The 1927 Yankees were perhaps the best team ever. **(1)**	Opinion	What is "best" can't be proven. **(1)**
page 597 It was a courageous speech. **(1)**	Opinion	What is "courageous" can be different from person to person. **(1)**
page 598 The more than sixty thousand fans in Yankee Stadium stood to honor Lou Gehrig. **(1)**	Fact	I can talk to someone who was there and check the team records. **(1)**

Assessment Tip: Total **14** Points

Name _____

Lou Hits a Home Run

Start at home plate and round the bases. Add words to complete each sentence that tells about an important event in Lou Gehrig's life.

3. Lou played 2,130 consecutive games for the <u>New York Yankees **(1 point)**</u>.

4. Lou had to stop playing baseball because <u>he</u> <u>suffered from a</u> <u>serious disease</u> <u>that affects the</u> <u>central nervous</u> <u>system **(1)**</u>.

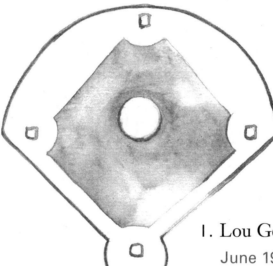

2. He was a star on his high school's <u>baseball team **(1)**</u> _____.

1. Lou Gehrig was born on <u>June 19, 1903 **(1)**</u>.

5. Lou was inducted into the <u>Baseball</u> <u>Hall of Fame **(1)**</u> in December 1939 and is remembered for his <u>courage, modesty and good</u> <u>sportsmanship **(1)**</u>.

Name _____

Check Your Facts

Read the story. Then complete the chart on the following page.

A Hero for All Seasons

Roberto Clemente is the greatest baseball player of all time. He had an incredible batting average—above .300 twelve out of the eighteen seasons he played. Having won four batting titles, twelve Gold Glove awards, and a Most Valuable Player award, he is certainly the best that ever played.

Besides being the best baseball player, Roberto Clemente was also a great man and a hero. In 1972, there was an earthquake in Nicaragua. On December 31 of that year, Clemente flew to Nicaragua to take supplies to the people. Almost immediately after takeoff, the plane crashed into the Caribbean Sea.

The best honors for Clemente came after he died. He was the first Latino voted into the Baseball Hall of Fame. In 1999, the city of Pittsburgh, where he played baseball, renamed a bridge after him—a bridge that leads to the city's beautiful new stadium.

No one summed up the life of Roberto Clemente as well as the baseball commissioner when, at Clemente's Hall of Fame award ceremony, he said, "He was so very great a man, as a leader and humanitarian, so very great an inspiration to the young and to all in baseball, especially to the proud people of his homeland, Puerto Rico." The commissioner further honored Clemente by creating a sportsmanship award in his name.

Name _____

Check Your Facts continued

Complete the chart below with facts and opinions from the story "A Hero for All Seasons."

Facts	Opinions
He hit above .300 twelve out of eighteen seasons.	Roberto Clemente is the greatest baseball player of all time.
He won four batting titles.	Hitting above .300 is incredible.
He won twelve Gold Glove awards.	He was a great man and a hero.
He won the Most Valuable Player award.	The best honors came after his death.
There was an earthquake in Nicaragua in 1972.	Pittsburgh's new stadium is beautiful.
His plane crashed on December 31, 1972.	No one summed up his life as well as the commissioner.
He was the first Latino in the Baseball Hall of Fame.	He is an inspiration.
There was a bridge named after him.	**(7)**
He played baseball in Pittsburgh.	
There is an award named after him. **(7 points)**	

   Assessment Tip: Total **14** Points

Name _____

Syllable Scores

As you read each sentence, pay careful attention to the underlined words. If the first vowel in a word has a long sound, circle the word. If the first vowel has a short sound, put a box around the word.

1. Lou Gehrig was a baseball player with amazing ⬚talent.⬚ **(1 point)**

2. He was twice ⭕chosen⭕ as the American League's MVP. **(1)**

3. Gehrig was a real ⭕hero⭕ because of the way he acted. **(1)**

4. No matter how great he was, he was always a ⬚modest⬚ person. **(1)**

5. When Gehrig stopped playing baseball, many people wanted to ⬚honor⬚ him. **(1)**

6. It was only ⬚proper⬚ that Lou Gehrig know how people cared about him. **(1)**

7. Thousands of fans wanted to say their ⭕final⭕ good-byes to Lou Gehrig. **(1)**

8. No Yankee will ever again wear the number 4 on his ⭕uniform.⭕ **(1)**

9. Lou Gehrig was ⬚visibly⬚ moved by the way the fans acted. **(1)**

10. There will ⬚never⬚ be another baseball player quite like Lou Gehrig. **(1)**

Count the number of words in boxes and enter the number in the box. Count the number of words in circles and enter the number in the circle below. Which team won? Home Team

	Hits	Runs
Home Team	10	⬚6⬚
Visitors	7	⭕4⭕

Assessment Tip: Total **10** Points

Name _____

VCV Pattern

Divide a VCV word into syllables before the consonant if the first vowel sound is long or if the first syllable ends with a vowel sound. Divide a VCV word into syllables after the consonant if the first syllable has a short vowel sound followed by a consonant sound.

Copyright © Houghton Mifflin Company. All rights reserved.

Spelling Words

1. pilot
2. depend
3. visit
4. human
5. seven
6. chosen
7. paper
8. reason
9. become
10. parent
11. never
12. modern
13. tiny
14. tuna
15. event
16. fever
17. moment
18. prison
19. basic
20. open

V|CV: **pi | lot**   VC|V: **vis | it**

Write each Spelling Word under the heading that tells where its syllables are divided.

Order of answers for each category may vary.

V|CV

pilot **(1 point)**	tiny **(1)**
depend **(1)**	tuna **(1)**
human **(1)**	event **(1)**
chosen **(1)**	fever **(1)**
paper **(1)**	moment **(1)**
reason **(1)**	basic **(1)**
become **(1)**	open **(1)**

VC|V

visit **(1)**	never **(1)**
seven **(1)**	modern **(1)**
parent **(1)**	prison **(1)**

Assessment Tip: Total **20** Points

Name _____

Spelling Spree

Hidden Words Write the Spelling Word that you find in each row of letters. Don't let the other words fool you!

Example: s k i o r a n g e p   *orange*

1. e a t u n a b i   tuna **(1 point)**

2. o r p r i s o n e t   prison **(1)**

3. s t o p v i s i t r n   visit **(1)**

4. p o s h u m a n d   human **(1)**

5. w o n e v e n t h   event **(1)**

6. i r k r e a s o n e   reason **(1)**

7. b u s e v e n c e   seven **(1)**

8. r i p a r e n t i c   parent **(1)**

9. t o p e n i t h   open **(1)**

10. t i n e v e r e s   never **(1)**

1. pilot
2. depend
3. visit
4. human
5. seven
6. chosen
7. paper
8. reason
9. become
10. parent
11. never
12. modern
13. tiny
14. tuna
15. event
16. fever
17. moment
18. prison
19. basic
20. open

Syllable Match Match the syllables at the top with the numbered syllables to write Spelling Words.

 mod   lot   ti   ver   pa

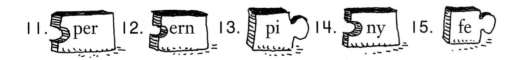

11. per   12. ern   13. pi   14. ny   15. fe

11. paper **(1)**   14. tiny **(1)**

12. modern **(1)**   15. fever **(1)**

13. pilot **(1)**

Theme 5: **Heroes**   331

Assessment Tip: Total **15** Points

Name _____

Proofreading and Writing

Proofreading Circle the five misspelled Spelling Words in these rules. Then write each word correctly.

You, too, can (bicome) one of baseball's finest hitters! The trick is to learn a few (basick) rules:

▶ Make sure that you have (chozen) a bat that's the right size for you.

▶ Be sure that you never stand too close to the plate.

▶ Keep your eye on the ball from the (momment) it leaves the pitcher's hand.

▶ Do not (depenned) on getting a perfect pitch.

1. become **(1 point)**

2. basic **(1)**

3. chosen **(1)**

4. moment **(1)**

5. depend **(1)**

Spelling Words

1. pilot
2. depend
3. visit
4. human
5. seven
6. chosen
7. paper
8. reason
9. become
10. parent
11. never
12. modern
13. tiny
14. tuna
15. event
16. fever
17. moment
18. prison
19. basic
20. open

✏️ **Write an Opinion** An **opinion** tells how you think or feel about something. For example, you might think that baseball is an exciting sport. On the other hand, you might feel that baseball is a slow, dull game.

On a separate piece of paper, write your opinion about a popular sport or game. Give reasons to back up your opinion. Use Spelling Words from the list. Responses will vary. **(5 points)**

332 Theme 5: **Heroes**
   Assessment Tip: Total **10** Points

Name _____

History of Base and Ball

Baseball is made up of two words, *base* and *ball*.

Read the sentences below. Write the number of the definition that shares the same word history as the underlined word or words.

base¹ *noun* **1.** The lowest part; bottom. **2.** A part used for support. **3.** The main part of something. **4.** One of the four corners of a baseball diamond. [Middle English, from Old French, from Latin *basis*, from Greek]

base² *adjective* **1.** Not honorable; shameful. **2.** Not of great value. [Middle English *bas*, low, from Old French, from Medieval Latin *bassus*]

ball¹ *noun* **1.** Something that is round. **2.** A round object used in a game or sport. **3.** A game, especially baseball, that is played with a ball. **4.** A baseball pitch that is not swung at by the batter and not thrown over home plate between the batter's knees and shoulders. [Middle English *bal*, probably from Old English *beall*]

ball² *noun* A formal social dance. [French *bal*, from Old French, from *baller*, to dance, from Late Latin *ballāre*, from Greek *ballizein*]

1. Our <u>basement</u> flooded during the storm.
   base¹, def. 1 or 2 **(2 points)**

2. The <u>base</u> word of hitter is hit. base¹, def. 3 **(2)**

3. She goes to <u>ballet</u> class every Saturday.
   ball² **(2)**

4. The <u>wedding</u> was held in a large ballroom.
   ball² **(2)**

5. Everyone in the <u>ballpark</u> cheered after the home run.
   ball¹, def. 3 **(2)**

Assessment Tip: Total **10** Points

Name _____

Announcements with Possessives

Finish the baseball stadium announcer's greeting by completing the sentences with possessive pronouns.

Good afternoon, ladies and gentlemen. The Centerville Bombers are playing <u>their **(1 point)**</u> fiftieth game of the season today. The players and the management hope you will enjoy <u>your **(1)**</u> afternoon at the ballpark. We in the booth will do <u>our **(1)**</u> best to make sure you do. Brenda Jones, the manager, has <u>her **(1)**</u> work cut out for her. Larraine Gillespie at first base has hurt <u>her **(1)**</u> foot. The center fielder and right fielder have misplaced <u>their **(1)**</u> sunglasses. We hope they catch the fly balls out there. The pitcher thinks that the mitt she is using may not be <u>hers **(1)**</u>. Carl Staub, the catcher, is now pulling on <u>his **(1)**</u> face mask. We hope you have <u>your **(1)**</u> scorecards ready. We have <u>ours **(1)**</u>.

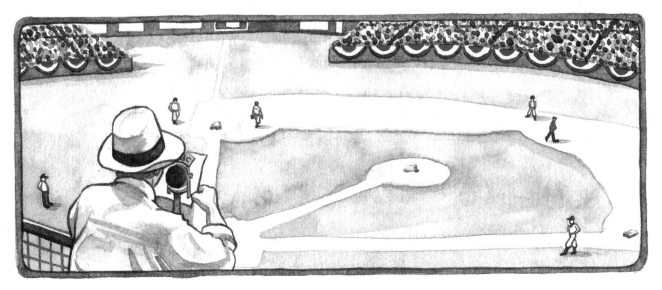

Assessment Tip: Total **10** Points

Name _____

Play Ball!

Here is a baseball game you can play. Fill in the missing possessive pronouns for the players in their positions on the field.

The center fielder knows the next job at bat will be
<u>hers</u> **(1)** _____ .

The left fielder is checking
<u>his</u> **(1)** _____ mitt.

The second-base player moves to <u>her</u> **(1)** _____
left.

The third-base player says the error was
<u>his</u> **(1)** _____ .

The first-base player looks at the pitcher and tosses the ball to
<u>his</u> **(1)** _____ right.

The pitcher thinks, "<u>My</u> **(1)** _____ arm is still good."

The manager tells a player, "You will get
<u>your</u> **(1)** _____ time to bat."

The catcher and pitcher almost get <u>their</u> **(1)** _____
signals mixed.

Theme 5: **Heroes**   335
Assessment Tip: Total **8** Points

Name _____

Watching Your *its* and *it's*

Good writers are careful to use the possessive pronoun *its* and the contraction *it's* correctly in sentences.

Read the paragraph below. On the blank lines, write either *its* or *it's*, depending on which is correct. Then rewrite the paragraph correctly on the lines provided.

<u>It's</u> no secret that Lou Gehrig was one of the Yankees' best players. The team moved <u>its</u> home from Baltimore to New York in 1903. Some people say of 1903, "<u>It's</u> a fateful year." <u>It's</u> the same year in which Lou Gehrig was born. Even when he was younger, Lou was a talented player. <u>It's</u> significant that playing on his high school baseball team, he was one of <u>its</u> stars. At Columbia University, Lou was a good player on <u>its</u> baseball team, too. In one of the games there, a Yankee scout saw him play. <u>It's</u> a fact of history that the Yankees signed him soon afterward.

It's **(1)** no secret that Lou Gehrig was one of the Yankees' best players. The team moved its **(1)** home from Baltimore to New York in 1903. Some people say of 1903, "It's **(1)** a fateful year." It's **(1)** the same year in which Lou Gehrig was born. Even when he was younger, Lou was a talented player. It's **(1)** significant that playing on his high school baseball team, he was one of its **(1)** stars. At Columbia University, Lou was a good player on its **(1)** baseball team, too. In one of the games there, a Yankee scout saw him play. It's **(1)** a fact of history that the Yankees signed him soon afterward.

Assessment Tip: Total **8** Points

Name _____

Planning a Magazine Article

Use this organizer to plan a magazine article about a sports hero or other person you admire.

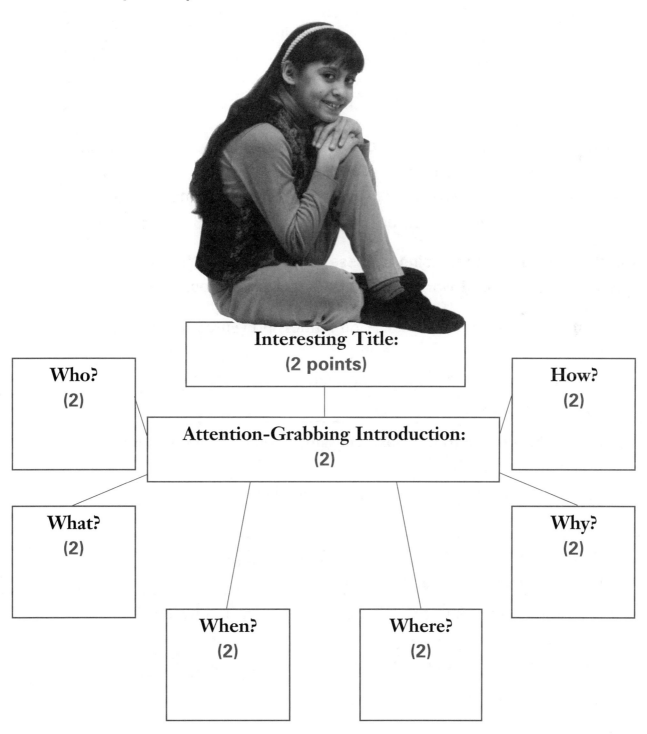

Interesting Title:
(2 points)

Who?
(2)

How?
(2)

Attention-Grabbing Introduction:
(2)

What?
(2)

Why?
(2)

When?
(2)

Where?
(2)

Assessment Tip: Total **16** Points

Name _____

Using Possessive Pronouns

Good writers combine sentences using possessive pronouns to improve their sentence.

► Writers use possessive pronouns to show ownership.

Singular Possessives: my, your, his, her, its

Plural Possessives: our, your, their

► Writers combine sentences using possessive pronouns to avoid repetition.

Two sentences: Doctors wanted to examine **Lou Gehrig**.
                   They ran tests on **Lou Gehrig's** condition.

One Sentence: Doctors wanted to examine **Lou Gehrig**, and they ran tests on **his** condition.

Combine the sentences using a possessive pronoun. You may need to delete or add words to combine the sentences.

1. Lou stayed with the Yankees. Lou's illness prevented him from playing.

   Lou stayed with the Yankees, but his illness prevented him from playing. **(2 points)**

2. Lou Gehrig spoke to the fans. He said, "Lou Gehrig's wife is a tower of strength."

   Lou Gehrig spoke to the fans and said, "My wife is a tower of strength." **(2)**

3. Lou was losing weight. Lou's hair was turning gray.

   Lou was losing weight, and his hair was turning gray. **(2)**

4. Sixty thousand fans were in the stadium. Lou would never forget the fans' cheers.

   Sixty thousand fans were in the stadium, and Lou would never forget their cheers. **(2)**

338   Theme 5: **Heroes**
        Assessment Tip: Total **8** Points

Name _____

Writing an Answer to a Question

Use what you have learned about taking tests to help you write answers to questions about something you have read. This practice will help you when you take this kind of test.

Read these paragraphs from the selection *Happy Birthday, Dr. King!*

Grandpa Joe took a deep breath and began . . .

"A long time ago I was raising my family in Montgomery, Alabama. This is what used to happen when African Americans wanted to ride the city buses.

"First, we'd get on at the front of the bus, pay our fare, and get off. Then we'd get back on again at the rear of the bus. We didn't like it, but that's how things were. It was the law. Then one day, in 1955, a lady named Rosa Parks . . . "

"Rosa Parks," Jamal interrupted, "we read about her. She sat in the front of the bus and wouldn't give her seat to a white man, and she got arrested."

"But, Jamal, there is more to the story. When African Americans heard about her arrest, many of us stopped riding the buses. We wanted to protest her arrest and get the same rights that white people had. That was the Montgomery Bus Boycott. And the boycott worked. We finally won — without fighting."

Name _____

Writing an Answer to a Question continued

Now write your answer to each question.

1. Why was Rosa Parks arrested in 1955? *(cause and effect)*

   Sample answer: Rosa Parks was arrested because she sat in the

   front of the bus and wouldn't give her seat to a white man.

   (5 points)

   _____

   _____

2. Why did many African Americans stop riding the city buses
   when they heard that Rosa Parks had been arrested? *(cause and effect)*

   Sample answer: They were protesting her arrest, and they wanted

   to have the same rights as white people. **(5)**

   _____

   _____

   _____

3. What happened as a result of the Montgomery Bus Boycott? *(cause and effect)*

   Sample answer: African Americans won the same rights as

   white people. **(5)**

   _____

   _____

   _____

Theme 5: **Heroes**   341
Assessment Tip: Total **15** Points

Name _____

Spelling Review

Write Spelling Words from the list on this page to answer the questions.

Order of answers in each category may vary.

1–10. Which ten words have prefixes (*re-*, *dis-*, or *un-*) or suffixes (*-ment*, *-ful*, or *-less*)?

1. unsure **(1 point)**
2. displease **(1)**
3. redo **(1)**
4. dislike **(1)**
5. reread **(1)**

6. powerful **(1)**
7. kindness **(1)**
8. movement **(1)**
9. peaceful **(1)**
10. useless **(1)**

11–20. Which ten words have a base word that changes the final *y* to *i* when an ending is added?

11. angriest **(1)**
12. families **(1)**
13. crazier **(1)**
14. cities **(1)**
15. easier **(1)**

16. happiest **(1)**
17. studied **(1)**
18. copied **(1)**
19. earlier **(1)**
20. worried **(1)**

21–30. Write the ten words with the VCV pattern that do not have prefixes, suffixes, or endings. Then draw a line between each syllable.

21. par | ent **(2)**
22. fe | ver **(2)**
23. vis | it **(2)**
24. sev | en **(2)**
25. tu | na **(2)**

26. nev | er **(2)**
27. pa | per **(2)**
28. pris | on **(2)**
29. be | come **(2)**
30. rea | son **(2)**

Assessment Tip: Total **40** Points

Spelling Words

1. parent
2. angriest
3. fever
4. powerful
5. visit
6. unsure
7. families
8. seven
9. crazier
10. displease
11. tuna
12. redo
13. kindness
14. cities
15. dislike
16. easier
17. never
18. paper
19. movement
20. reread
21. happiest
22. prison
23. become
24. peaceful
25. studied
26. reason
27. copied
28. earlier
29. useless
30. worried

Name _____

Spelling Spree

Crossword Puzzle Write a Spelling Word in the puzzle that means the same as each clue. **(1 point each)**

Across

1. not *warlike* but _____
3. I study now. You _____ yesterday.
5. one, three, five, _____, nine
7. happy, happier, _____

Down

1. pencil and _____
2. towns and _____
4. the opposite of *like*
6. not *later* but _____

Context Clues Use a Spelling Word to finish each phrase.

9. not free but in prison **(1)**
10. not carefree but worried **(1)**
11. not the happiest but the angriest **(1)**
12. not weak but powerful **(1)**

13. not the child but the parent **(1)**
14. not a salmon but a tuna **(1)**
15. not motionless but showing movement **(1)**

Theme 5: **Heroes**   343

Assessment Tip: Total **15** Points

Name _____

Proofreading and Writing

Proofreading Circle the six misspelled Spelling Words in this essay. Then write each word correctly.

When we (rereed) stories about heroes, we find that they almost (nevur) attempt (useles) tasks. They often come from (familys) where honesty is important. Sometimes they are shown much (kindnes) by others. Sometimes they are (unshur) of themselves.

1. reread **(1 point)**

2. never **(1)**

3. useless **(1)**

4. families **(1)**

5. kindness **(1)**

6. unsure **(1)**

Spelling Words

1. redo
2. reread
3. unsure
4. useless
5. displease
6. kindness
7. easier
8. families
9. copied
10. crazier
11. visit
12. reason
13. become
14. never
15. fever

Description of a Hero Write Spelling Words to complete this description.

Every day Mrs. Mendez goes to 7. visit *a family nearby. The* 8. reason *she does this is to help them. One day their baby had a high* 9. fever. *The parents kept getting* 10. crazier *with worry, but they didn't have a car. Mrs. Mendez took them to the doctor in her car, which was much* 11. easier *and faster than riding the bus. Some neighbors have* 12. copied *Mrs. Mendez's idea and are helping others. I hope to* 13. become *a neighborhood hero like Mrs. Mendez! Her actions never* 14. displease *anyone. First I will help my sister* 15. redo *her homework.*

✏️➤ **Write a Letter** On a separate sheet of paper, write a letter to a friend about a hero you admire. Use the Spelling Review Words. Responses will vary.

Assessment Tip: Total **15** Points

Name _____

Talking About Tales

Compare and contrast two of the pourquoi tales you just read by completing the chart below.

	Story #1 _____ (title)	Story #2 _____ (title)
How are the characters the same and different?		
How is the problem and solution the same and different?		
How is the language the same and different?		

Answers will vary. (**6 points** for each story)

Now tell which pourquoi tale is your favorite and why.

_____

_____

_____

_____

Answers will vary. (**2**)

Name _____

Believe It or Not!

You are a news reporter for a local television station. Your program is called "Believe It or Not!" You have just found a very large turtle sleeping in the mud during winter. How will you explain it to your viewers? Tell them a pourquoi tale.

Write your notes below. Also, write questions you could ask the people — and animals — on the scene. (Answers will vary.)

(8 points)

Name _____

Nature: Friend and Foe

How can nature be a friend? How can it be a foe?

Complete the word webs with words and phrases that describe spiders and thunderstorms, both as friends and as foes.

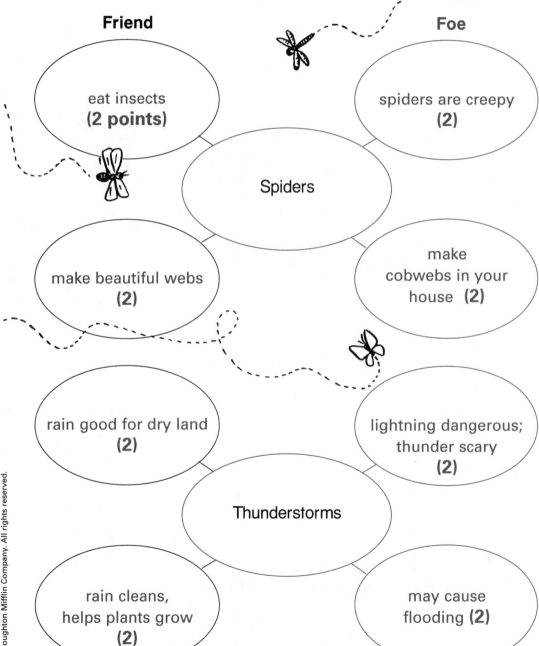

Friend

Foe

eat insects
(2 points)

spiders are creepy
(2)

Spiders

make beautiful webs
(2)

make
cobwebs in your
house **(2)**

rain good for dry land
(2)

lightning dangerous;
thunder scary
(2)

Thunderstorms

rain cleans,
helps plants grow
(2)

may cause
flooding **(2)**

Name _____

Nature: Friend and Foe

	Is nature shown as a friend or a foe? Explain.	What do you think this selection says about people's relationship with nature?
Salmon Summer	Friend; Alex and his family take only what they need from nature; nature gives them food, beauty, and fun. **(3 points)**	It demonstrates the importance of using natural resources wisely; shows people enjoying the outdoors. **(3)**
Wildfires	Both; many forest fires help renew the forest, and people try to be friends with nature by managing the fires. However, some forest fires cause great damage. **(3)**	*Wildfires* shows that many ecosystems have cycles that take care of themselves naturally; questions human interference, even in fighting a forest fire. **(3)**
Skylark	Foe; although nature has given many things to the family in the past, the drought is shown as a cruel enemy. **(3)**	This story shows people trying—and failing—to conquer nature. People need to adapt to what nature gives them. **(3)**

Tell how one selection changed the way you think of nature.

Answers will vary. **(4)**

_____

_____

_____

Name _____

Word Riddle

Write a word from the box that answers the riddle.

1. What do you call relatives from whom you have
descended? <u>ancestors</u> **(1 point)**

2. What do you call it when fish lay eggs and reproduce
in a river? <u>spawn</u> **(1)**

3. What do you call a plentiful supply
of something?
<u>abundance</u> **(1)**

4. I am the fake bait that
fishermen use to attract fish.
What am I?
<u>lure</u> **(1)**

5. I'm the name for animals
that feed on dead plants
and animals. What am I?
<u>scavengers</u> **(1)**

Write a sentence using two words from the box.

(1) _____

_____

Name _____

Directions Flow Chart

	Catching and Preparing Salmon to Eat	Hooking Halibut and Making Tamuuq
Materials Needed	net, gloves, knife, salmon, rope, smokehouse **(3 points)**	line, hook, salmon bait, halibut, knife, rope **(3)**
Steps	set a gill net **(1)** ▼ pull the net the next day **(1)** ▼ put on gloves **(1)** ▼ separate fish ▼ cut off the head **(1)** ▼ pull out the guts **(1)** ▼ leave the skin and tail on **(1)** ▼ hang outside ▼ leave scraps for scavengers **(1)** ▼ put cleaned fish in the smokehouse **(1)** ▼ hang fish outside to cure **(1)** ▼ The salmon is ready to eat.	bait the hook with salmon **(1)** ▼ attach heavy sinker to hook **(1)** ▼ hang line overboard ▼ wait and feel for a tug on the line **(1)** ▼ give line a hard tug when fish nibble **(1)** ▼ hold on and pull line in ▼ slice halibut into strips **(1)** ▼ hang up to dry **(1)** ▼ wait ten days **(1)** ▼ The tamuuq is ready to eat.

Assessment Tip: Total **22** Points

Name _____

Nothing But the Truth

Mark T if the statement is true and F if it is false. If the statement is false, rewrite it on a separate sheet of paper to make a true statement.

Statement	True or False?
1. Alex's favorite snack is smoked salmon.	1. __F__ **(1 point)**
2. When he cleans fish for the smokehouse, Alex leaves the tails and skin on.	2. __T__ **(1)**
3. Magpies and gulls are scavengers that eat fish scraps.	3. __T__ **(1)**
4. Alex hangs smoked salmon in a closet to cure.	4. __F__ **(1)**
5. Alex baits lobster traps with small salmon.	5. __F__ **(1)**
6. When a crab is too big to keep, Alex throws it back.	6. __F__ **(1)**
7. Alex fishes with a line and a silver lure.	7. __T__ **(1)**
8. The fish head downstream to mate.	8. __F__ **(1)**
9. To catch a halibut, Alex baits his hook with a salmon.	9. __T__ **(1)**
10. To make tamuuq takes about ten hours.	10. __F__ **(1)**

Assessment Tip: Total **10** Points

Name _____

Following Tradition

Read the story below and then answer the questions on the following page.

Thanksgiving with the Muslovs

It was the night before Thanksgiving and in the Muslov family that meant it was time to prepare the salmon. It was the way they had always celebrated, and this year was special for Leonin — he was finally old enough to help prepare the fish.

"Leo," his father called from the kitchen. "Go get the recipe box, will you?" Leonin got up from the living room floor where he was reading and quickly brought the recipe box into the kitchen. "Thank you, Leo. You ready? Okay. Read me the instructions, please."

"It says we need two to three pounds of salmon filets," Leo said carefully. "We need to place the salmon in a mixture of water, salt, sugar, garlic, and dill. The filets need to be coated with the mixture and then covered with plastic wrap. Then it says to leave them in the refrigerator overnight." Leo paused for a moment. "But Dad, we don't have any filets."

"You're right, but we do have whole salmon in the refrigerator. Your job is to cut off their heads and tails and pull out their insides. Then you have to carefully remove their bones so you're left with the biggest, most tender piece of meat. That's the filet."

It was at that moment that Leonin began to wonder why he had been so excited to help.

Name _____

Following Tradition continued

Complete the chart below and answer the questions based on "Thanksgiving with the Muslovs."

What ingredients and materials do you need?

salmon filets, water, salt, sugar, garlic, dill, a bowl, a
spoon, a knife, a cutting board **(5 points)**

What are the step-by-step directions for preparing the salmon?

Cut off the heads and tails of the salmon.

Pull out the insides of the fish.

Remove the bones.

Mix together the salt, sugar, garlic, and dill in a bowl.

Place the filets in the mixture.

Coat the salmon with the mixture.

Cover the salmon with plastic wrap.

Place salmon in the refrigerator overnight. **(5)**

Why do you think the salmon is supposed to be left in the mixture overnight? What do you think would happen if it wasn't?
(Accept reasonably varied answers.)

I think the salmon is left overnight in the mixture so it can absorb

the flavor of those ingredients. If this step was left out, the

salmon probably wouldn't taste very good. **(5)**

Name _____

Seaworthy Syllables

Read this description of a well-known sea animal. Write the number below each underlined word next to the word's definition. Use a dictionary if you need help. Then use the clues in the description to identify the sea animal. (1 point for each word)

     This animal may <u>inhabit</u> shallow parts of the ocean or live in deep
             1
waters. It got its name because of the eight long arms sticking out of its
head. The <u>underside</u> of each arm has <u>powerful</u> sucker. These suckers
         2   3
can provide <u>enormous</u> suction to help the animal attach itself to rocks.
            4
This sea creature has two eyes, one on each side of its head. These
eyes are <u>similar</u> to the eyes of human beings. This animal has many
          5
enemies, including whales, seals, and even certain fish. To protect
itself against these <u>predators</u>, this animal hides itself by <u>discharging</u>
              6   7
a cloud of inky fluid. It may also escape by <u>rapidly</u> changing its
                                8
color to scare an enemy or blend with its surroundings.

4 _____ very large

7 _____ releasing

1 _____ live in

6 _____ enemies

8 _____ quickly

5 _____ like

3 _____ having great strength

2 _____ surface underneath

The name of this sea animal is: <u>octopus **(2)**</u>.

Assessment Tip: Total **10** Points

Name _____

Three-Syllable Words

To spell a three-syllable word, divide the word into syllables. Remember to look for familiar spelling patterns. Pay attention to the spelling of the unstressed syllables. Spell the word by syllables.

yes | ter | day   /yĕsʹ tər dā/   **de | liv | er**   /dĭ lĭvʹ ər/

Write each Spelling Word under the heading that tells which syllable is stressed. Order of answers for each category may vary.

Spelling Words

1. deliver
2. favorite
3. camera
4. yesterday
5. tomorrow
6. important
7. together
8. victory
9. remember
10. library
11. enemy
12. animal
13. another
14. however
15. banana
16. alphabet
17. hospital
18. hamburger
19. carpenter
20. several

First Syllable Stressed

favorite **(1 point)**

camera **(1)**

yesterday **(1)**

victory **(1)**

library **(1)**

enemy **(1)**

animal **(1)**

alphabet **(1)**

hospital **(1)**

hamburger **(1)**

carpenter **(1)**

several **(1)**

Second Syllable Stressed

deliver **(1)**

tomorrow **(1)**

important **(1)**

together **(1)**

remember **(1)**

another **(1)**

however **(1)**

banana **(1)**

Name _____

Spelling Spree

Questions **Write a Spelling Word to answer each question.**

1. Which word names a fruit?
2. Who builds things?
3. What do you call a living organism that is not a plant?
4. What word names more than one?
5. What tastes great with ketchup?
6. Where do you go when you need an operation?
7. Where is the quietest place in town?
8. What do you need to make any word?
9. What day came just before today?
10. What word is the opposite of *friend*?

1. banana **(1 point)**
2. carpenter **(1)**
3. animal **(1)**
4. several **(1)**
5. hamburger **(1)**

6. hospital **(1)**
7. library **(1)**
8. alphabet **(1)**
9. yesterday **(1)**
10. enemy **(1)**

Word Search **Write the Spelling Word that is hidden in each sentence.**

Example: The troop leaders always r<u>un happ</u>y meetings. *unhappy*

11. Are membership forms available for the Girl Scouts?
12. I'd like to show everyone this video.
13. My mother made liver and bacon for dinner.
14. Which team was the victor yesterday?
15. The fire truck came racing down the street.

11. remember **(1)**
12. however **(1)**
13. deliver **(1)**
14. victory **(1)**
15. camera **(1)**

356   Theme 6: **Nature: Friend and Foe**

Assessment Tip: Total **15** Points

Name _____

Proofreading and Writing

Proofreading Circle the five misspelled Spelling Words in this part of an e-mail message. Then write each word correctly.

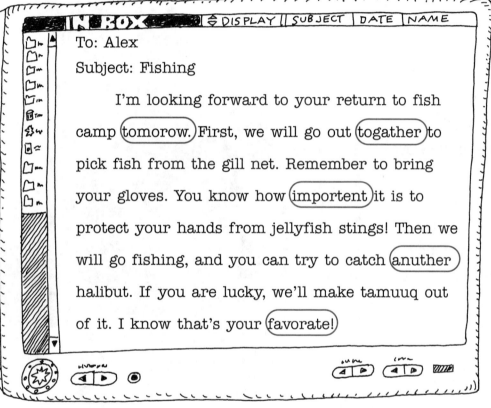

Spelling Words

1. deliver
2. favorite
3. camera
4. yesterday
5. tomorrow
6. important
7. together
8. victory
9. remember
10. library
11. enemy
12. animal
13. another
14. however
15. banana
16. alphabet
17. hospital
18. hamburger
19. carpenter
20. several

1. tomorrow **(1 point)**
2. together **(1)**
3. important **(1)**
4. another **(1)**
5. favorite **(1)**

✏️ **Write Animal Facts** Alex knew a lot about salmon. He could recognize the different kinds, and he knew about the life cycle of the salmon. What animal do you know facts about?

On a separate sheet of paper, write a paragraph of information about an animal that you find interesting. Make sure to tell why you find this animal interesting. Use Spelling Words from the list. Responses will vary. **(5 points)**

Name _____

Sensible Meanings

As you read each sentence, think about the meaning of the underlined word. Then find the numbered meaning in the box. Print that number on the line by the sentence.

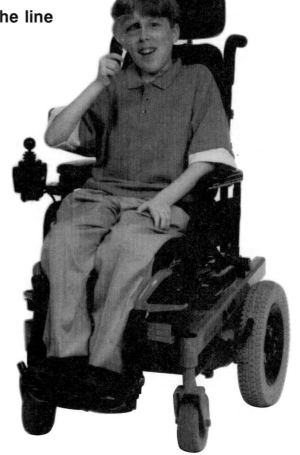

1. Water mammal
2. To close tightly
3. To go separate ways
4. A role
5. To be in flight
6. Two-winged insect
7. To pay out money
8. To pass time

1. The family will <u>fly</u> from California to Alaska. __5__ **(1 point)**

2. The <u>seal</u> dove into the water and caught a fish. __1__ **(1)**

3. We always <u>spend</u> the summer at the beach. __8__ **(1)**

4. Henry and Lou were such good friends that they hated to <u>part</u>. __3__ **(1)**

5. Toby licked the envelope to <u>seal</u> it. __2__ **(1)**

6. He got the <u>part</u> of the detective because of his fine acting. __4__ **(1)**

7. Every time we open the door, another <u>fly</u> comes in. __6__ **(1)**

8. Don't <u>spend</u> all your allowance at once. __7__ **(1)**

Name _____

Riddles with Adverbs

Read these riddles about the animals on Kodiak Island.
Underline the adverb in each riddle. On the line, write the
animal that the riddle is about.

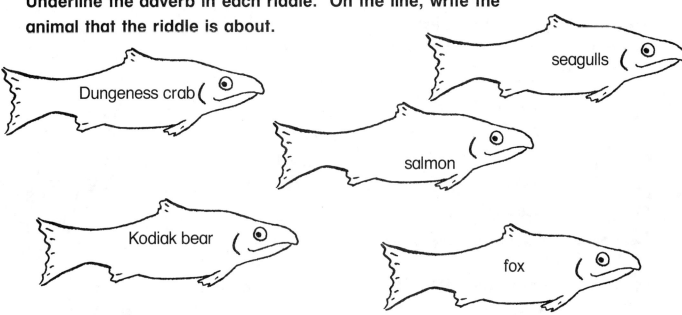

1. These animals swim <u>alone</u> into the river to catch their fish.
   Kodiak bears **(2 points)**
   _____

2. These fish swim <u>upstream</u> to spawn and die.
   salmon **(2)**
   _____

3. These birds swoop <u>down</u> to catch fish scraps.
   seagulls **(2)**
   _____

4. This animal looks <u>watchfully</u> for food for her young pups.
   fox **(2)**
   _____

5. This animal crawls <u>backward</u> on the sea bottom.
   Dungeness crab **(2)**
   _____

On a separate sheet of paper, write two riddles of your own
about other things in the story. Use an adverb in each and
underline it. Draw a clue for each riddle. (5 points)

Name _____

Adverbs and Kodiak Island

The Fremson family members are taking a trip to Kodiak Island. Complete the sentences by writing adverbs that tell how, when, or where. The word in parentheses tells you what kind of adverb to use. Answers may vary. Sample answers are shown.

cheerfully	early
close	happily
curiously	quickly
outside	slowly
suddenly	soon

1. We leave _early **(1 point)**_ in the morning. (when)

2. Mother and Father put their coats on _quickly **(1)**_. (how)

3. _Suddenly **(1)**_, a taxi arrives. (how)

4. The family goes _outside **(1)**_. (where)

5. The Fremsons _cheerfully **(1)**_ wave goodbye to their neighbors. (how)

6. The taxi moves _slowly **(1)**_ down the street. (how)

7. Brenda _happily **(1)**_ sings a song. (how)

8. Marcus studies the map _curiously **(1)**_. (how)

9. _Soon **(1)**_ the taxi arrives at the airport. (when)

10. The taxi stops _close **(1)**_ to the entrance. (where)

Assessment Tip: Total **10** Points

Name _____

Writing with Adverbs

Adverbs add specific details to your sentences and make them more interesting.

Read the sentences, and then choose an adverb from the list below to expand each sentence. Write your sentences on the lines.

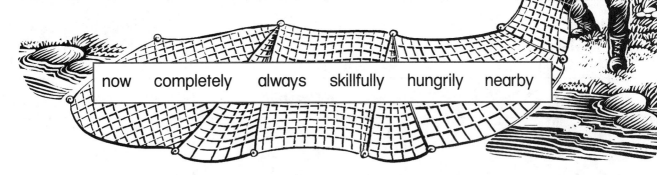

| now | completely | always | skillfully | hungrily | nearby |

1. Alex and his father fish in the neighborhood stream. (where)

   Alex and his father fish in the neighborhood stream nearby. **(1 point)**

2. At age nine, the boy can help his father fish with a net. (when)

   At age nine, the boy can now help his father fish with a net. **(1)**

3. The boy picks fish from the net. (how)

   Skillfully, the boy picks fish from the net. **(1)**

4. Alex wears gloves to protect his hands. (when)

   Alex always wears gloves to protect his hands. **(1)**

5. Alex cuts the fish and hangs them up to dry. (how)

   Alex cuts the fish and hangs them up to dry completely. **(1)**

6. Alex and his brother Larry eat the smoked salmon. (how)

   Alex and his brother Larry eat the smoked salmon hungrily. **(1)**

On another sheet of paper, write two of your own sentences about Alex. Use at least one adverb in each sentence. Underline the adverb.

Answers will vary. **(4 points)**

Salmon Summer

Writing Skill A How-to Paragraph

Name ______________________

How-to Paragraph Planner

You can use this graphic organizer to help plan your how-to paragraph. Then write an interesting topic sentence and a closer that sums up the directions.

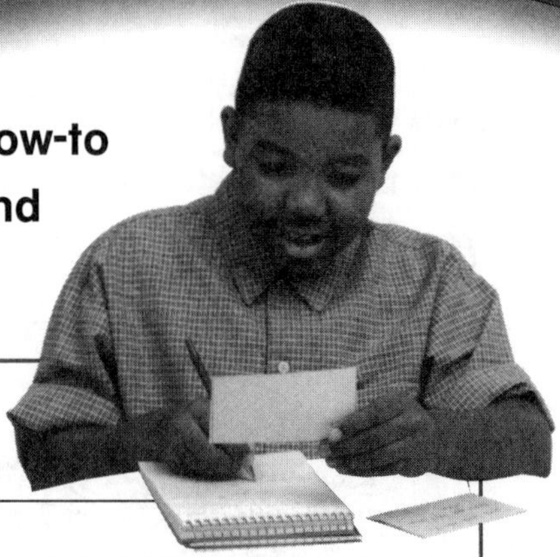

Topic: How to

(1 point) ______________________

Steps	Materials	Details
(1)	(1)	(1)
(1)	(1)	(1)
(1)	(1)	(1)

Topic Sentence:

(2) ______________________

____

Closing Sentence:

(2) ______________________

____

Assessment Tip: Total **14** Points

Name _____

Order Words and Phrases

Good writers use order words and phrases to tell the
sequence of steps and make instructions easy to follow.

Order words and phrases include **first, second, next, during,
while, now, then, later, after that, the next step,** and **finally.**

**Read each how-to paragraph. Rewrite the paragraph,
adding order words or phrases.** Sample answers are shown.

1. Making an apple and peanut butter sandwich is easy. All you
   need is an apple, a knife, and a jar of peanut butter. You slice the
   apple into thin wedges. You spread every other apple slice with
   peanut butter. You put one clean slice and one peanut butter slice
   together to make a sandwich.

Making an apple and peanut butter sandwich is easy. All you need

is an apple, a knife, and a jar of peanut butter. First, you slice the

apple into thin wedges. Second, you spread every other slice with

peanut butter. Finally, you put one clean slice and one peanut butter

slice together to make a sandwich. **(5 points)**

2. Eli makes his own trail mix. He needs a large plastic container,
   raisins, peanuts, chocolate chips, and half a dried apple. He puts
   the raisins, peanuts, and chocolate chips into the container. He
   cuts up the dried apple into small pieces. He adds the apple pieces
   to the mix. He puts the lid on the container and shakes it up.

Eli makes his own trail mix. He needs a large plastic container, raisins,

peanuts, chocolate chips, and half a dried apple. First, he puts raisins,

peanuts, and chocolate chips into the container. Next, he cuts up the

dried apple into small pieces. After that he adds the apple pieces to

the mix. Finally, he puts the lid on the container and shakes it up. **(5)**

_____

Name _____

Evaluating Your Report

Reread your research report. How can you make it better? Use this page to help you decide. Put a checkmark in the box for each sentence that describes your research report.

Rings the Bell!

☐ I chose an interesting topic to research.

☐ I used an outline to help plan my report.

☐ I used reliable sources to find information on the topic.

☐ I took careful notes and used them to write my report.

☐ My paragraphs contain topic sentences and supporting facts.

☐ I used adverbs correctly.

☐ There are very few mistakes.

Getting Stronger

☐ I could make the topic sound more interesting to the reader.

☐ More sources might help me make sure I have the facts right.

☐ I need to follow my notes more closely.

☐ Some of my pronoun references are unclear.

☐ There are quite a few errors that need to be fixed.

Try Harder

☐ My topic isn't very interesting.

☐ I didn't use enough sources to find my facts.

☐ I didn't take careful notes on what I found out.

☐ Too many mistakes make the report hard to read.

Name _____

Using Adverbs Correctly

Underline the adverb that correctly completes each sentence.

1. I love watching (quiet/<u>quietly</u>) as rain comes down outside. **(1 point)**

2. I like to hear the thunder boom (loud/<u>loudly</u>). **(1)**

3. My cat, Molly, moves (careful/<u>carefully</u>) across the room. **(1)**

4. The thunder is (real/<u>really</u>) loud. **(1)**

5. Molly slinks (slow/<u>slowly</u>) under the couch. **(1)**

6. The lightning flashes (bright/<u>brightly</u>) in the sky. **(1)**

7. The room lights up (total/<u>totally</u>). **(1)**

8. Molly meows (sad/<u>sadly</u>) from under the couch. **(1)**

9. I reach under the couch to pet her (gentle/<u>gently</u>). **(1)**

10. She hisses (anger, <u>angrily</u>), thinking I'm the thunder coming to get her. **(1)**

Theme 6: **Nature: Friend and Foe**   365
Assessment Tip: Total **10** Points

Name _____

Spelling Words

Most of the Spelling Words on the list are homophones. Homophones are words that sound alike but have different meanings and spellings. When you write a homophone, be sure to spell the word that has the meaning you want.

Write the missing letters and apostrophes in the Spelling Words below.

Spelling Words

1. their
2. there
3. they're
4. your
5. you're
6. its
7. it's
8. to
9. too
10. two
11. they
12. than
13. then
14. right
15. write

1. th __e__ __i__ r **(1 point)**

2. th __e__ r __e__ **(1)**

3. th __e__ __y__ ' __r__ __e__ **(1)**

4. y __o__ __u__ __r__ **(1)**

5. you __'__ __r__ __e__ **(1)**

6. it __s__ **(1)**

7. it __'__ __s__ **(1)**

8. t __o__ **(1)**

9. t __o__ __o__ **(1)**

10. t __w__ __o__ **(1)**

11. th __e__ __y__ **(1)**

12. th __a__ n **(1)**

13. th __e__ n **(1)**

14. r __i__ __g__ __h__ __t__ **(1)**

15. __w__ rite **(1)**

Study List On a separate sheet of paper, write each Spelling Word. Check your spelling against the words on the list. Order of words may vary. **(5)**

Assessment Tip: Total **20** Points

Name _____

Spelling Spree

Homophone Blanks The blanks in each of the following sentences can be filled with homophones from the Spelling Word list. Write the words in the correct order.

1–3. It's <u>two</u> o'clock now, so it's probably
　　　　　　 1

　　　<u>too</u> late <u>to **(3 points)**</u> go out for lunch.
　　　 2　　　　　 3

4–5. So <u>you're</u> telling me that's not <u>your **(2)**</u> car?
　　　　 4　　　　　　　　　　 5

6–7. I heard <u>it's</u> unusual to see a snake during the
　　　　　　 6

　　　time it sheds <u>its **(2)**</u> skin.
　　　　　　　 7

8–9. When you address the letter, be sure to <u>write</u>
　　　　　　　　　　　　　　　　　　　　　 8

　　　the <u>right **(2)**</u> zip code.
　　　　 9

Th- Clues Use the clues to write these *th-* Spelling Words.

10. If someone asks you the question "where?" you can use this word to answer.

11. This word is used to compare (more ____, less ____).

12. This contraction can be used to tell what others are doing.

13. This is a word for something that belongs to others.

14. This is a word you can use to talk about a group of people.

15. This word can be used to put a story in the right order.

10. <u>there **(1)**</u>

11. <u>than **(1)**</u>

12. <u>they're **(1)**</u>

13. <u>their **(1)**</u>

14. <u>they **(1)**</u>

15. <u>then **(1)**</u>

Spelling Words

1. their
2. there
3. they're
4. your
5. you're
6. its
7. it's
8. to
9. too
10. two
11. they
12. than
13. then
14. right
15. write

Name _____

Proofreading and Writing

Proofreading Circle the five misspelled words in this storm warning. Then write each word correctly.

The National Weather Service has issued a tornado warning for our viewing area. So far, (too) tornadoes have already touched down, and they're saying that more could hit before this storm passes. If you are out in (you're) car, try to find shelter as quickly as you can. Get off the road right now even if the sky looks okay to you—better to be safe (then) sorry. Do the (rite) thing and go somewhere safe. We'll keep you posted on this storm until (its) over.

1. their
2. there
3. they're
4. your
5. you're
6. its
7. it's
8. to
9. too
10. two
11. they
12. than
13. then
14. right
15. write

two **(1 point)** _____

your **(1)** _____

than **(1)** _____

right **(1)** _____

it's **(1)** _____

✏️ **Write a Poem On a separate piece of paper, write a short poem about nature in its role of friend, foe, or both. Use Spelling Words from the list.**

Responses will vary. **(5)**

Assessment Tip: Total **10** Points

Name _____

Fire Words

**Choose the meaning that best fits the underlined
vocabulary word as it is used in the sentence.
Write the letter of your answer on the line.** (1 point each)

1. Forest fires seem to occur in cycles. C _____
   A. hilly areas   C. repeating periods of time
   B. circles   D. dry areas

2. If that liquid is flammable, keep it away from the fire. A _____
   A. able to be set on fire   C. hot
   B. excitable   D. oily and thick

3. The burning ember perhaps caused the fire. B _____
   A. yellow rock   C. red rock
      found on a beach
   B. piece of glowing   D. fountain
      wood or coal

4. The firefighters fought the blaze aggressively and bravely. B _____
   A. from the air   C. in great fear
   B. forcefully   D. with axes and knives

5. The fire consumed almost all the trees and bushes in the area. D _____
   A. blew down   C. protected
   B. held in   D. burned up

6. Some of the trees were charred but not burned completely. A _____
   A. burned slightly   C. reduced to ashes
   B. scratched   D. dry

7. Eventually the tops of the trees were ablaze. B _____
   A. bright green and in bloom   C. falling to earth
   B. in flames   D. saved from fire

8. After a fire, plant life will soon renew itself. C _____
   A. relax   C. bring new life to
   B destroy   D. take away some of

Theme 6: **Nature: Friend and Foe**   369
Assessment Tip: Total **8** Points

Main Idea and Details Chart

Topic: Wildfires **(2 points)** _____

---

page 662   Main Idea

Wildfires are frightening.

(2)

Supporting Details

Living trees burn as fast as cardboard.

Flames can move faster than a

running person.

Wildfires can destroy homes and kill

people. **(3)**

---

page 664   Main Idea

Plants and animals have adjusted to

wildfires. **(2)**

Supporting Details

Many trees need cycles of fire to grow.

Other trees grow back quickly.

Most animals flee from fires.

Plants that grow quickly give animals

food. **(3)**

---

page 662   Main Idea

Wildfires are good for bugs and
animals.

Supporting Details

Fire beetles lay eggs on charred logs.

Hawks and owls hunt in the open

spaces.

Dead trees make good nesting sites.

New grasses and flowers attract

animals. **(3)**

---

page 664   Main Idea

Wildfires don't hurt every animal and

actually help some. **(2)**

Supporting Details

Nests are not usually threatened

because fires don't start in the wet

season. Mature birds fly away.

Small animals run away or hide.

Scavengers feed on the animals that

are killed. **(3)**

Assessment Tip: Total **18** Points

Name _____

A Fire Gone Wild

Complete each sentence with information from the selection _Wildfires_.

1. The selection mainly deals with the hot, dry summer of <u>1988 **(1 point)**</u>.

2. On June 23, a <u>flash of lightning **(1)**</u> started a fire in Yellowstone National Park.

3. Officials previously had allowed such fires to burn themselves out unless <u>they threatened structures built by people **(1)**</u>.

4. Officials changed their mind when more fires <u>drove tourists from the park **(1)**</u>.

5. Hundreds of <u>firefighters **(1)**</u> were sent to battle and stop the fires.

6. On August 19, the wind blew <u>embers **(1)**</u> a mile away and started new fires.

7. August 20, known as <u>Black Saturday **(1)**</u>, saw an area more than twice the size of Chicago burning.

8. <u>Weather **(1)**</u>, not humans, saved the day and finally ended the fires.

9. Yellowstone could now start the process of <u>renewal **(1)**</u>.

10. New <u>plants and animals **(1)**</u> began to appear and thrive in the charred woods.

Name _____

What's the Big Idea?

Read the story. Then complete the chart about the topic, main idea, and supporting details on the following page.

Bye-Bye Beaches?

Along both coasts of America, land is being eroded away by the nonstop crashing of ocean waves. During big storms, especially hurricanes, there are pictures on newscasts and in newspapers showing large chunks of earth falling and sliding into the sea. Houses are seen collapsing into the ocean. It's a frightening sight, yet people continue to build homes on the water's edge.

What should these people do about the problem of erosion? Should they build walls to keep the water away? Should they pile up sand into huge mounds that look like dunes? Should they build their homes up high on stilts?

Of course, a problem is who should pay to help keep the water from damaging the land. Many people who own homes on the water believe that the government should pay since it owns much of the coastline. Others believe it is the homeowners' problem, so they should fix it. Some people even want nothing done, believing the beaches should not have houses on them in the first place. They would be happy if all the houses were washed away.

Whatever side you stand on, our beaches need to be protected before they disappear.

Name _____

What's the Big Idea? continued

Complete the chart below about topic, main idea, and supporting details based on "Bye-Bye Beaches?" from the previous page.

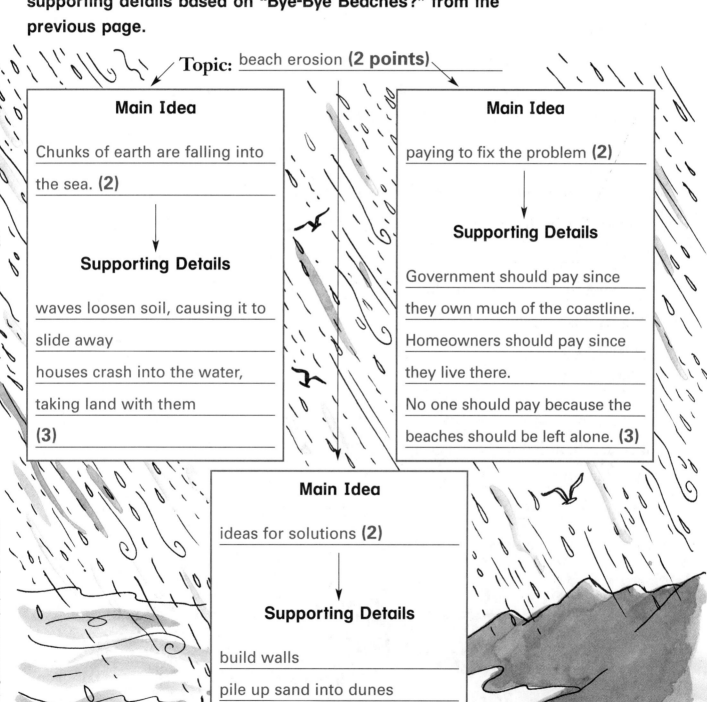

Topic: beach erosion **(2 points)**

Main Idea

Chunks of earth are falling into the sea. **(2)**

↓

Supporting Details

waves loosen soil, causing it to slide away

houses crash into the water, taking land with them

(3)

Main Idea

paying to fix the problem **(2)**

↓

Supporting Details

Government should pay since they own much of the coastline.

Homeowners should pay since they live there.

No one should pay because the beaches should be left alone. **(3)**

Main Idea

ideas for solutions **(2)**

↓

Supporting Details

build walls

pile up sand into dunes

build homes on stilts **(3)**

Theme 6: **Nature: Friend and Foe**   373
Assessment Tip: Total **15** Points

Name _____

Sleepy Suffixes

Use what you know about suffixes to help you complete this TV advertisement with words from the box. If you need help, use a dictionary.

hopeless	invention	loveliness	decision	sleepless
restless	action	happiness	darkness	solution

Are you tired of <u>restless **(1 point)**</u> nights spent tossing and turning in the <u>darkness **(1)**</u>? If so, we've got the <u>solution **(1)**</u> to your problem. With the Sleep-o-matic you'll never have another <u>sleepless **(1)**</u> night again! Plug in this marvelous <u>invention **(1)**</u> and end the <u>hopeless **(1)**</u> struggle to fall asleep. The <u>loveliness **(1)**</u> of a new morning will amaze you after a good night's rest. Instead of feeling tired all the time, your days will be filled with energy and <u>happiness **(1)**</u>! The <u>decision **(1)**</u> is easy. Take <u>action **(1)**</u> now! Call 1-800-555-REST and order your new Sleep-o-matic today!

Name _____

Unusual Spellings

Some words have sounds with unusual spelling patterns. The spellings of these words have to be remembered.

Write the Spelling Words. Underline the unusual spelling patterns. Order of answers may vary.

h<u>ea</u>lth **(1 point)**	g<u>ui</u>de **(1)**
bl<u>oo</u>d **(1)**	st<u>y</u>le **(1)**
t<u>y</u>pe **(1)**	w<u>ea</u>lth **(1)**
ag<u>ai</u>nst **(1)**	g<u>ui</u>lt **(1)**
rec<u>ei</u>ve **(1)**	sa<u>ys</u> **(1)**
f<u>oo</u>d **(1)**	g<u>u</u>ard **(1)**
m<u>o</u>nth **(1)**	w<u>o</u>nder **(1)**
maga<u>zine</u> **(1)**	g<u>u</u>est **(1)**
g<u>u</u>ess **(1)**	gasol<u>ine</u> **(1)**
w<u>o</u>m<u>e</u>n **(1)**	n<u>ei</u>ther **(1)**

Spelling Words

1. health
2. blood
3. type
4. against
5. receive
6. flood
7. month
8. magazine
9. guess
10. women
11. guide
12. style
13. wealth
14. guilt
15. says
16. guard
17. wonder
18. guest
19. gasoline
20. neither

Name _____

Spelling Spree

Sentence Fillers Write the Spelling Word that best completes each sentence.

Example: The naughty puppy chewed my left _____!
shoe

1. Be my _____ and help yourself to the food.
2. If you can't find a book, read a _____.
3. The thief admitted his _____.
4. First came the rain, then came the _____.
5. I _____ what I'll be when I grow up.
6. The millionaire accumulated his _____ through hard work.
7. I _____ a letter from my pen pal every month.

1. guest **(1 point)**
2. magazine **(1)**
3. guilt **(1)**
4. flood **(1)**
5. wonder **(1)**
6. wealth **(1)**
7. receive **(1)**

Words in Words Write the Spelling Word in each word below.

Example: forehead   *head*

8. lifeguard   guard **(1)**
9. bloodshed   blood **(1)**
10. essays   says **(1)**
11. bimonthly   month **(1)**
12. guesswork   guess **(1)**
13. typewriter   type **(1)**
14. freestyle   style **(1)**

376   Theme 6: **Nature: Friend and Foe**
Assessment Tip: Total **14** Points

Name _____

Proofreading and Writing

Proofreading Circle the six misspelled Spelling Words in this notice. Then write each word correctly.

Spelling Words

1. health
2. blood
3. type
4. against
5. receive
6. flood
7. month
8. magazine
9. guess
10. women
11. guide
12. style
13. wealth
14. guilt
15. says
16. guard
17. wonder
18. guest
19. gasoline
20. neither

State Forestry Service Warning!

To (gard) against wildfires, tend your campfires carefully. Put out cooking fires completely, and bury the ashes. Remember, (niether) matches nor pocket lighters should be used carelessly. Never bring (gasaline) to a campsite! All men, (wemen,) and children must follow the rules of safe camping. Your (helth) and safety depend on it. Pick up our (guid) on the use of fire in the state forest at the nearest ranger station.

1. guard **(1 point)**
2. neither **(1)**
3. gasoline **(1)**
4. women **(1)**
5. health **(1)**
6. guide **(1)**

✏️ **Write a Safety Poster** Everyone must be careful in the woods, for one's own safety and for the protection of the forest. Think of some safety rules or tips for hikers and campers.

On a separate piece of paper, write and decorate a poster about safety in the woods. Use Spelling Words from the list.

Responses will vary. **(6 points)**

Name _____

How Are They Related?

Think about the relationship between the first two items in the analogies below. Write the word that best completes the analogy.

1. **Ankle** is to **wrist** as **knee** is to _elbow **(1 point)**_____.
   toe   calf   elbow

2. **Right** is to **correct** as **wrong** is to _incorrect **(1)**_____.
   grade   incorrect   friend

3. **Seed** is to **sprout** as **child** is to _grow **(1)**_____ .
   grow   play   eat

4. **Ash** is to **burning** as **water** is to _melting **(1)**_____.
   flame   melting   cold

5. **Pine** is to **tree** as daisy is to _flower **(1)**_____.
   flower   elm   rose

6. **Writer** is to **poem** as **painter** is to _picture **(1)**_____.
   paint   sculpture   picture

7. **Softball** is to **sports** as **jazz** is to _music **(1)**_____.
   saxophone   music   country

8. **Hard** is to **soft** as **cruel** is to _kind **(1)**_____.
   friend   enemy   kind

9. **Baby** is to **adult** as **fawn** is to _deer **(1)**_____.
   deer   lion   pack

10. **Egg** is to **dozen** as **milk** is to _gallon **(1)**_____.
    chocolate   gallon   cow

Assessment Tip: Total **10** Points

Name _____

Writing with Adverbs

Write the correct form of the adverb given in parentheses to complete each statement.

1. After a forest fire, young plants grow
   <u>most quickly **(1 point)**</u> of all. (quickly)

2. The Yellowstone National Park fire of 1988 burned some areas
   <u>more completely **(1)**</u> than others. (completely)

3. Animals die in a forest fire <u>more rarely **(1)**</u>
   than you might think. (rarely)

4. Some blazes spread <u>faster **(1)**</u> than a
   person can run. (fast)

5. Matches are the cause of fires <u>more frequently **(1)**</u>
   than some other things. (frequently)

6. The <u>sooner **(1)**</u> firefighters get to a fire,
   the sooner it can be controlled. (soon)

7. Fire spreads through the treetops
   <u>more easily **(1)**</u> than it does on the ground.
   (easily)

8. In a fire, energy is released <u>instantly **(1)**</u> as
   heat and light. (instantly)

9. Fires start from natural causes <u>more often **(1)**</u>
   than from other causes. (often)

10. Big wildfires burn <u>most intensely **(1)**</u> of all when
    small fires are not allowed to burn. (intensely)

Theme 6: **Nature: Friend and Foe** 379
Assessment Tip: Total **10** Points

Name _____

Writing with Adverbs

**Write the correct form of the adverb in parentheses to complete
each statement.**

1. After a fire, the owl finds food
   <u>more easily **(1 point)**</u> in open areas. (easily)

2. The bison gets to eat new grass
   <u>more often **(1)**</u>. (often)

3. The woodpecker finds insects <u>most quickly **(1)**</u>
   of all in dead bark. (quickly)

4. The tree swallow can build a nest <u>more rapidly **(1)**</u>
   in a dead tree than in a live one. (rapidly)

5. The deer walks away from a burnout
   <u>sooner **(1)**</u> than other animals. (soon)

6. The elk finds grass <u>closer **(1)**</u> to a fire
   than deer do. (close)

7. The fire beetle lays eggs <u>most successfully **(1)**</u> of all
   in burnt logs. (successfully)

8. The hawk can see food <u>most clearly **(1)**</u> of all
   after a fire. (clearly)

Name _____

Writing with Comparisons

Using *good* and *well* Good writers are careful to use
good and *well* correctly in their sentences.

**Fill in the blanks with either *good* or *well*. Then rewrite
each sentence correctly on the line below it.**

1. I hope everyone learns the lessons of wildfires _well_____.
   I hope everyone learns the lessons of wildfires well. **(1 point)**

2. Fire can sometimes be a _good_____ thing.
   Fire can sometimes be a good thing. **(1)**

3. Scavengers eat _well_____ after a fire.
   Scavengers eat well after a fire. **(1)**

4. Birds eat many _good_____ meals of insects.
   Birds eat many good meals of insects. **(1)**

5. Rodents find _good_____ hiding places under rocks.
   Rodents find good hiding places under rocks. **(1)**

6. Other small animals do _well_____ in burrows.
   Other small animals do well in burrows. **(1)**

7. Some pine cones open only as a result of a _good_____, hot fire.
   Some pine cones open only as a result of a good, hot fire. **(1)**

8. It is _good_____ for them when fire burns away the resin.
   It is good for them when fire burns away the resin. **(1)**

9. Plants without diseases look _good_____ when checked.
   Plants without diseases look good when checked. **(1)**

10. Some of these photos of the fire of 1988 are very _good_____.
    Some of these photos of the fire of 1988 are very good. **(1)**

Name _____

Learning Log Entry

Select three examples of your own writing. Write a paragraph commenting on your writing. Then fill in the Learning Log entry.

Learning Log

What I Learned:

(5 points) _____

_____

_____

_____

_____

_____

_____

_____

_____

_____

_____

_____

_____

My Goals:

(5) _____

_____

_____

_____

_____

Assessment Tip: Total **10** Points

Name _____

Elaborating with Adverbs

Good writers improve their sentences by using **adverbs**
to tell more. Adverbs can describe verbs, by telling *how* or *when*
an action occurs.

How	When
rapidly	always
quietly	sometimes
quickly	once
noisily	anytime
slowly	now
happily	then
dangerously	again

**Complete the sentences by filling each blank with an adverb
that answers the question in parentheses.**

Answers will vary. Sample answers shown.

1. Wet wood burns _slowly **(1 point)**_____ because

   water keeps air from reaching the fire. (how?)

2. _Once **(1)**_____, in 1988, fire and smoke in

   Yellowstone Park drove thousands of tourists away. (when?)

3. Gale-force winds can _dangerously **(1)**_____ drive

   burning embers to start new fires. (how?)

4. Nature adjusts _quickly **(1)**_____ to changes,

   finding new life in a burnt forest. (how?)

5. New meadows grow _again **(1)**_____ where

   once there was scorched earth. (when?)

Name _____

Prairie Scene

Choose the word from the vocabulary list that makes the most sense in the sentence. Write the word on the line provided.

Vocabulary

corral
coyote
drought
phonograph
prairie
slump

1. Among the animals on the Great Plains, the <u>prairie **(1 point)**</u> dog protects itself by burrowing in the ground.

2. When no rain falls for a long time, the land suffers from a <u>drought **(1)**</u>.

3. Sometimes people get so hot in the summer they faint and <u>slump **(1)**</u> to the ground.

4. Horses on a farm often are kept from wandering by enclosing them in a <u>corral **(1)**</u>.

5. At one time, the only way people could hear music that wasn't live was to play records on a <u>phonograph **(1)**</u>.

6. A <u>coyote **(1)**</u> is a kind of wolf that lives on the prairie.

Inferences Chart

Answers will vary.

Page 690

Details About Anna	Anna asks Sarah if she remembers the wildflowers, the roses, and singing. **(2 points)**
	+
What I Know	If someone is asking me if I remember things that make me happy, that person is probably feeling sad. **(2)**
	=
Inference	Anna feels sad and wishes things were better. **(2)**

Page 692

Details About Papa's Feelings Toward Sarah	Papa puts his arm around Sarah as she cries and tells her that everything will be okay. **(2)**
	+
What I Know	I would feel cared for and loved if someone comforted me like this. **(2)**
	=
Inference	Papa cares deeply for Sarah. **(2)**

Page 700

Details About Sarah and Papa and the Fire	Sarah and Papa are shouting at each other and the kids. They try hard to put out the fire, but they cannot. **(2)**
	+
What I Know	People shout when they are scared or angry. If I tried hard but couldn't do something, I'd feel angry or sad. **(2)**
	=
Inference	Sarah and Papa are angry and sad **(2)**

Theme 6: **Nature: Friend and Foes**   385
Assessment Tip: Total **18** Points

Name _____

The Reasons for Their Actions

Complete the chart below. Fill in the empty boxes to show who does what in *Skylark*, and why. Some boxes have been filled in for you.

Who	What They Do	Why?
page 690: Papa	gets his rifle	to shoot a coyote that is drinking from a bucket at the farm
page 692: Sarah **(2 points)**	stops Papa from shooting	she feels sorry for the coyote, who only wants water, as the family does
pages 693 – 695: Papa, Anna, and Caleb	give a party for Sarah **(2)**	because it is her birthday, and they hope it will cheer her up
page 699: Matthew, Maggie, and their children	leave their farm	because their well dries up **(2)**
page 699: Anna **(2)**	has a dream about her family playing in lots of water	because she is wishing very hard that the drought will end
page 700: Caleb	runs to get Moonbeam	because there is a fire **(2)**
page 703: Sarah	shakes her head, no, twice	she is having a discussion with Papa about leaving the farm **(2)**
page 703: Papa **(2)**	plans to stay on the farm while the rest of the family goes to Maine	someone needs to take care of the animals and rebuild the farm.

Name _____

Reading Between the Lines

Read the story below. Then answer the questions about the story on the following page.

The Long Wait

Lucy came into the cottage in only her stocking feet. She had left her boots and coat on the porch. She began to warm her hands and feet by the fire when she noticed her brother, Seth, sitting at the kitchen table with a wool blanket wrapped around him, peeling small potatoes for supper.

Seth turned toward Lucy and asked, "How are Starlight and the cows? Did they get enough food?"

"They're doing as well as can be expected," Lucy said. "Starlight's having a bit of trouble breathing again, but she'll be fine."

"You worried about Mama and Pa yet?" Seth asked.

"Nah, not really. They'll be home soon. They only went into town for a few supplies and the wagon ought to be working okay. The snow isn't falling as hard anymore."

"I just hope they will be here soon," Seth said. "I don't like it when our family is apart."

"I know what you mean, Seth. I know what you mean."

Name _____

Reading Between the Lines continued

Answer the following questions based on your reading of "The Long Wait." (Accept reasonably varied answers.)

How would you describe Lucy?

Details		**What You Know**
She was outside in the cold feeding the animals. She says that she isn't worried about her parents. She doesn't like it when the family is apart. **(3 points)**	+	It takes a love of animals to go outside in the cold to feed them. I would be trying to comfort that person. I miss my mom and dad when they travel. **(3)**

Inference

Lucy cares very much for her brother and her family and their safety. **(2)**

How would you describe Seth?

Details		**What You Know**
He is peeling potatoes for dinner. He asks how the animals are. He asks Lucy if she is worrying about Mama and Pa. He hopes his parents return soon. **(3)**	+	I help with dinner when I want to be near my family. I'd ask these questions if I were worried. I'd wish for my parents to be home soon if I missed them. **(3)**

Inference

Seth feels really close to his family and loves them very much. **(2)**

Name _____

Root Out the Roots

graph means "to write, draw, or record"
tract means "to draw or pull"

**Write the root *graph* or *tract* to complete each word.
Then write the word to complete each sentence.**

1. something that draws attention away:
   dis <u>tract **(1 point)**</u> ion
   The birthday party was a wonderful <u>distraction **(1)**</u>
   from the troubles caused by the drought.

2. pleasing, drawing attention: at <u>tract **(1)**</u> ive
   Papa looked <u>attractive **(1)**</u> in his clean shirt and vest.

3. a written story of a person's life: bio <u>graph **(1)**</u> y
   Anna's gift was a <u>biography **(1)**</u> about Sarah's life.

4. a division of writing that contains sentences on a single idea:
   para <u>graph **(1)**</u>
   Sarah read the first <u>paragraph **(1)**</u> aloud.

5. an image recorded by a camera: photo <u>graph **(1)**</u>
   Anna wished she had a <u>photograph **(1)**</u> of the party.

**Now write two sentences of your own. In one sentence,
use a word with the root *graph*. In the other, use a word
with the root *tract*.**

Answers will vary. (**2 points** per sentence)
_____

_____

_____

Name _____

Silent Consonants

Some words have consonants that are not pronounced. These consonants are called "silent" consonants. The spellings of words with silent consonants have to be remembered.

<table>
<tr><td>**k**neel</td><td>clim**b**</td><td>ca**l**f</td><td>**w**rinkle</td><td>**h**onest</td></tr>
</table>

Write each Spelling Word under the heading that shows its silent consonant. Order of answers for each category may vary.

1. knight
2. soften
3. honor
4. kneel
5. climb
6. wrinkle
7. limb
8. handsome
9. answer
10. calf
11. listen
12. calm
13. knit
14. often
15. palm
16. thumb
17. wrist
18. lamb
19. knob
20. honest

/n/ Spelled *kn*

knight **(1 point)**

kneel **(1)**

knit **(1)**

knob **(1)**

/m/ Spelled *mb*

climb **(1)**

limb **(1)**

thumb **(1)**

lamb **(1)**

/r/ Spelled *wr*

wrinkle **(1)**

wrist **(1)**

/ŏ/ Spelled *ho*

honor **(1)**

honest **(1)**

Silent *l*

calf **(1)**

calm **(1)**

palm **(1)**

Silent *t*

soften **(1)**

listen **(1)**

often **(1)**

Silent *d*

handsome **(1)**

Silent *w*

answer **(1)**

Assessment Tip: Total **20** Points

Name _____

Spelling Spree

Opposites Write a Spelling Word that means the opposite of each word or group of words below.

Example: right *wrong*

1. question   answer **(1)**
2. excited   calm **(1)**
3. harden   soften **(1)**
4. rarely   often **(1)**
5. descend   climb **(1)**
6. back of the hand palm **(1)**
7. ugly   handsome **(1)**

Word Addition Write a Spelling Word by adding the beginning of the first word to the middle and end of the second word.

Example: top + walk   *talk*

8. know + slob
9. hope + finest
10. write + twinkle
11. knee + light
12. they + crumb
13. wrap + mist
14. list + comb
15. knot + wheel

8. knob **(1)**
9. honest **(1)**
10. wrinkle **(1)**
11. knight **(1)**
12. thumb **(1)**
13. wrist **(1)**
14. limb **(1)**
15. kneel **(1)**

Spelling Words

1. knight
2. soften
3. honor
4. kneel
5. climb
6. wrinkle
7. limb
8. handsome
9. answer
10. calf
11. listen
12. calm
13. knit
14. often
15. palm
16. thumb
17. wrist
18. lamb
19. knob
20. honest

Theme 6: **Nature: Friend and Foe**   391
Assessment Tip: Total **15** Points

Name _____

Proofreading and Writing

Proofreading Circle the five misspelled Spelling Words in this journal entry. Then write each word correctly.

May 9 — I love to (lisen) to the birds at dawn. Their songs are so happy. They make me hopeful that rain is on the way. As I lay in bed I thought about the new (caff) born last night. It's strong like its mother. I have the (honer) of owning not one but three baby animals! This spring a tiny (lame) was born to my sheep, and Star's colt gets friskier every day. He will be a handsome horse. I have to go now. Before I do my chores, Sarah wants me to help her (nit) a sweater for Maggie's baby.

	Spelling Words
1.	knight
2.	soften
3.	honor
4.	kneel
5.	climb
6.	wrinkle
7.	limb
8.	handsome
9.	answer
10.	calf
11.	listen
12.	calm
13.	knit
14.	often
15.	palm
16.	thumb
17.	wrist
18.	lamb
19.	knob
20.	honest

1. listen **(1 point)**
2. calf **(1)**
3. honor **(1)**
4. lamb **(1)**
5. knit **(1)**

✏️➤ **Write a Weather Report** Prairie families were dependent on the weather for their livelihood. Too little rain would cause the crops to die, but too much rain could result in flash floods. Blizzards and tornadoes were also common on the prairies.

On a separate sheet of paper, write a weather report for a family living on the prairie in the 1800s. Be sure to include details that you think would be useful for a family back then to know. Use Spelling Words from the list.

Responses will vary. **(5)**

Name _____

Nouns, Verbs, and Adjectives

Use each word below in a sentence. Make sure to use the word as the part of speech given.

Answers will vary.

1. stream (v.) **(1 point)** _____

   _____

2. post (v.) **(1)** _____

   _____

3. post (n.) **(1)** _____

   _____

4. catch (n.) **(1)** _____

   _____

5. fire (v.) **(1)** _____

   _____

Read the sentences below. Tell the part of speech for the underlined word.

6. Sarah walked to the <u>window</u> to look out too. noun **(1)** _____

7. Caleb's hair was brushed <u>smooth</u>. adjective **(1)** _____

8. We will <u>write</u> letters. verb **(1)** _____

9. Sometimes it was hard to <u>adapt</u> to prairie life. verb **(1)** _____

10. A thin <u>coyote</u> was drinking water out of the pail. noun **(1)** _____

Name _____

Prepositions and Prepositional Phrases

Complete Papa's directions by using prepositions from the list.
You will use some words more than once. Answers may vary.

Sample answers shown.

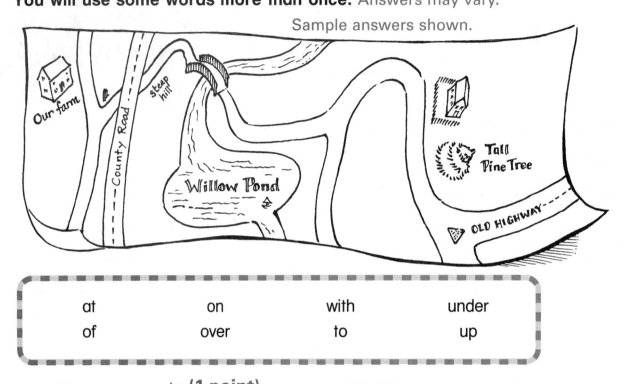

at	on	with	under
of	over	to	up

When you get <u>to **(1 point)**</u> the Old Highway, turn right.

Soon you will see <u>on **(1)**</u> your right a tree we call the Tall

Pine Tree. Next, you will see a house <u>with **(1)**</u> a picket

fence. Then drive carefully <u>on **(1)**</u> the curvy road until

you turn right again. When the road straightens, you will have a

lovely view <u>of **(1)**</u> Willow Pond. The road turns right

and passes <u>over **(1)**</u> a bridge and <u>up **(1)**</u> a steep

hill. Next you will drive <u>under **(1)**</u> the County Road. Turn

right immediately <u>at **(1)**</u> the stop sign, and you will be

<u>at **(1)**</u> our farm.

Assessment Tip: Total **10** Points

Completing with Prepositions

**Read the sentences. Underline the prepositions in each
sentence. Then list each prepositional phrase on the lines
provided under each sentence.**

1. The horse paddock is <u>across</u> the driveway <u>from</u> the barn.

   across the driveway; from the barn **(2 points)**

2. The chicken coop is <u>near</u> the vegetable garden.

   near the vegetable garden **(2)**

3. The farmhouse is <u>at</u> the end <u>of</u> the driveway.

   at the end; of the driveway **(2)**

4. The barn is <u>between</u> the farmhouse and the horse paddock.

   between the farmhouse and the horse paddock **(2)**

5. The vegetable garden is <u>beside</u> the farmhouse.

   beside the farmhouse **(2)**

Theme 6: **Nature: Friend and Foe**   395
Assessment Tip: Total **10** Points

Name _____

Using Prepositions

Good writers use prepositional phrases to add specific details to their writing.

Read the paragraph below. Then rewrite it, adding prepositional phrases to the sentences on the lines provided. Use phrases from the list. Answers will vary.

> on the phonograph
> to the music
> down the stairs
> in the yard
> of food and drinks
>
> on the porch
> out her window
> to her
> with a cloth

Wagons were pulling up <u>in the yard **(1 point)**</u>. Sarah heard the noise outside and looked <u>out her window **(1)**</u>. Papa saw her running <u>down the stairs **(1)**</u>. A table had been set <u>in the yard **(1)**</u>. It was full <u>of food and drinks **(1)**</u>. Papa carried a large object covered <u>with a cloth **(1)**</u>. Sarah appeared <u>on the porch **(1)**</u>. Everyone turned <u>to her **(1)**</u> and sang "Happy Birthday." Papa uncovered the large object. It was a phonograph! Then Anna handed Papa a record. He put a needle <u>on the phonograph **(1)**</u>, and soon everyone was dancing <u>to the music **(1)**</u>.

Assessment Tip: Total **10** Points

Name _____

Planning a Speech

Use this graphic organizer to help you plan your speech. Write notes for a speech about something that happened to you or something you feel strongly about. Then write your speech on another sheet of paper.

Title: _____ **(1 point)** _____

Opening sentence: _____

_____ **(1)**

Event 1: _____ **(1)**

  details: _____ **(2)**

_____

_____

Event 2: _____ **(1)**

  details: _____ **(2)**

_____

_____

_____

Event 3: _____ **(1)**

  details: _____ **(2)**

_____

_____

_____

Concluding sentence: _____ **(1)**

Name _____

Prepositional Phrases

Good writers combine sentences to make their writing smoother. Sometimes combining sentences with prepositions helps avoid repetition.

Two sentences: Papa looked **up the stairs.**
                Papa looked **at Sarah.**
One sentence: Papa looked **up the stairs at Sarah.**
Two sentences: Maggie liked the pink roses.
                The roses were **on the dress.**
One sentence: Maggie liked the pink roses **on the dress.**

Combine each set of sentences. You may need to add, delete, or change words to combine the sentences.

1. Sarah and Papa danced. They danced on the lawn.
   Sarah and Papa danced on the lawn. **(2 points)**

2. They could not live without water. The water was in the well.
   They could not live without water in the well. **(2)**

3. Anna fell asleep. The time was about midnight.
   Anna fell asleep about midnight. **(2)**

4. Sarah wiped the tears. The tears were from her eyes.
   Sarah wiped the tears from her eyes. **(2)**

5. The party was a great success. The party was for Sarah's birthday.
   The party for Sarah's birthday was a great success. **(2)**

Assessment Tip: Total **10** Points

Name _____

Writing an Opinion Essay

Use what you have learned about taking tests to help you write an essay that tells your opinion about a topic. This practice will help you when you take this kind of test.

Fires can happen in all forests. In *Wildfires*, you read about the ways wildfires help the forest. Write an essay explaining why you think fire helps or hurts the forest.

Answers will vary. **(15 points)**

_____

_____

_____

_____

_____

_____

_____

_____

_____

_____

_____

_____

_____

_____

_____

_____

_____

_____

Name _____

Writing an Opinion Essay continued

Read your essay. Check to be sure that

➤ the opening introduces your topic in an interesting way

➤ each paragraph has a topic sentence that tells the main idea

➤ your reasons are strong and are supported with details

➤ your conclusion sums up the important points

➤ there are few mistakes in capitalization, punctuation, grammar, and spelling

Now pick one way to improve your essay. Make your changes below.

Answers will vary. **(5 points)**

_____

_____

_____

_____

_____

_____

_____

_____

_____

_____

_____

_____

_____

_____

Name _____

Spelling Review

Write Spelling Words from the list on this page to answer the questions.

Order of answers in each category may vary.

1–11. Which eleven words have three syllables?

1. favorite **(1 point)**

2. library **(1)**

3. deliver **(1)**

4. gasoline **(1)**

5. alphabet **(1)**

6. however **(1)**

7. another **(1)**

8. banana **(1)**

9. remember **(1)**

10. camera **(1)**

11. animal **(1)**

12–21. Which ten words have silent consonants?

12. listen **(1)**

13. honor **(1)**

14. knight **(1)**

15. calf **(1)**

16. climb **(1)**

17. handsome **(1)**

18. kneel **(1)**

19. soften **(1)**

20. thumb **(1)**

21. wrist **(1)**

22–30. Which nine remaining words have an unusual spelling of a short or long vowel sound or the consonant sound /g/?

22. style **(1)**

23. women **(1)**

24. guard **(1)**

25. neither **(1)**

26. against **(1)**

27. says **(1)**

28. blood **(1)**

29. health **(1)**

30. wonder **(1)**

Spelling Words

1. listen
2. favorite
3. style
4. library
5. honor
6. deliver
7. knight
8. gasoline
9. alphabet
10. calf
11. however
12. climb
13. handsome
14. another
15. women
16. guard
17. banana
18. neither
19. kneel
20. soften
21. against
22. says
23. remember
24. blood
25. thumb
26. wrist
27. camera
28. health
29. animal
30. wonder

Name _____

Spelling Spree

Analogies Write a Spelling Word that completes each analogy.

1. **Dog** is to **puppy** as **cow** is to ___calf **(1 point)**___.

2. **Taste** is to **apple** as ___listen **(1)**___ is to **music**.

3. **Stand** is to **feet** as ___kneel **(1)**___ is to **knees**.

4. **Electricity** is to **refrigerator** as ___gasoline **(1)**___ is to **automobile**.

5. **Pump** is to **water** as **heart** is to ___blood **(1)**___.

6. **Go** is to **come** as **forget** is to ___remember **(1)**___.

7. **Heard** is to **hears** as **said** is to ___says **(1)**___.

8. **Wade** is to **stream** as ___climb **(1)**___ is to **mountain**.

Spelling Words
1. wonder
2. favorite
3. another
4. blood
5. remember
6. camera
7. says
8. calf
9. animal
10. listen
11. climb
12. gasoline
13. library
14. style
15. kneel

Phrase Filler Complete each phrase by writing a Spelling Word.

9. a furry little ___animal **(1)**___

10. my ___favorite **(1)**___ color

11. to ___wonder **(1)**___ why

12. an attractive hair ___style **(1)**___

13. a ___library **(1)**___ full of books

14. a ___camera **(1)**___ and film

15. ___another **(1)**___ day of rain

Assessment Tip: Total **15** Points

Name _____

Proofreading and Writing

Proofreading Circle the six misspelled Spelling Words in this scientist's log. Then write each word correctly.

September 12 Today Julia fell, sprained her (rist,) and hurt her (thum.) Then we saw three monkeys share a (bannana.) Nature can be both friend and foe. At night one of us is always on (gard.) When I keep watch, I lean (agianst) a tree. Luckily, (niether) wild nor tame beasts have bothered us.

1. honor
2. deliver
3. knight
4. alphabet
5. however
6. handsome
7. women
8. guard
9. banana
10. neither
11. soften
12. against
13. thumb
14. wrist
15. health

1. wrist **(1 point)**
2. thumb **(1)**
3. banana **(1)**
4. guard **(1)**
5. against **(1)**
6. neither **(1)**

Help the Announcer Write Spelling Words in the blanks to complete this TV commercial.

Attention men and 7. _____! Do us the 8. _____ of watching *Nature Knows*. See a wild and 9. _____ lion play and a huge elephant eat. Watch a baboon 10. _____ a gift to his girlfriend. Study an entire 11. _____ of animals from ape to zebra. Seeing cuddly tiger cubs will 12. _____ your views about fierce cats. All animals are important; 13. _____, many are in trouble. Their 14. _____ is endangered. Be a 15. _____ in shining armor and help save these animals. Watch our show to find out how.

7. women **(1)**
8. honor **(1)**
9. handsome **(1)**
10. deliver **(1)**
11. alphabet **(1)**
12. soften **(1)**
13. however **(1)**
14. health **(1)**
15. knight **(1)**

✏️ **Write a Description** **On a separate sheet of paper, describe a scientific trip you would like to take. Use Spelling Review Words.** Responses will vary. **(5)**

Student Handbook

Contents

How to Study a Word

1. LOOK at the word.
➤ What does the word mean?

➤ What letters are in the word?

➤ Name and touch each letter.

2. SAY the word.
➤ Listen for the consonant sounds.

➤ Listen for the vowel sounds.

3. THINK about the word.
➤ How is each sound spelled?

➤ Close your eyes and picture the word.

➤ What familiar spelling patterns do you see?

➤ Did you see any prefixes, suffixes, or other word parts?

4. WRITE the word.
➤ Think about the sounds and the letters.

➤ Form the letters correctly.

5. CHECK the spelling.
➤ Did you spell the word the same way it is spelled in your word list?

➤ If you did not spell the word correctly, write the word again.

again	eighth	January		
all right	enough			
a lot	every	knew		
also	everybody	know	really	two
always	everyone		received	tying
another	excite	let's	right	
anyone		letter		until
anything	family	little	said	usually
anyway	favorite	loose	Saturday	
around	February	lose	school	very
	finally	lying	someone	
beautiful	first		stopped	weird
because	friend	might	stretch	we're
before		millimeter	suppose	where
believe	getting	minute	sure	while
brought	girl	morning	swimming	whole
build	goes	myself		won't
buy	going		than	world
	guess	ninety	that's	would
cannot			their	wouldn't
can't	happened	o'clock	then	write
caught	haven't	off	there	writing
choose	heard	once	there's	
chose	height	other	they	your
clothes	here	our	they're	you're
coming			thought	
could	I'd	people	through	
cousin	I'll	pretty	to	
	I'm	probably	tongue	
didn't	instead		tonight	
different	into	quit	too	
divide	its	quite	tried	
don't	it's		truly	

Grandfather's Journey

The /ĭ/, /ī/, /ŏ/, /ō/ Sounds

/ĭ/ ➡ st**i**ll
/ī/ ➡ cr**i**me, fl**igh**t, gr**i**nd
/ŏ/ ➡ sh**o**ck
/ō/ ➡ wr**o**te, c**oa**st, sn**ow**, g**o**ld

Spelling Words

1. snow
2. grind
3. still
4. coast
5. odd
6. crime
7. gold
8. wrote
9. flight
10. build
11. broke
12. blind
13. folk
14. grown
15. shock
16. ripe
17. coal
18. inch
19. sigh
20. built

Challenge Words

1. remind
2. approach
3. rigid
4. recognize
5. continent

My Study List

Add your own spelling words on the back. ➡

Journeys
Reading-Writing Workshop

Look for familiar spelling patterns in these words to help you remember their spellings.

Spelling Words

1. cannot
2. can't
3. don't
4. haven't
5. won't
6. wouldn't
7. I'd
8. I'll
9. let's
10. we're
11. I'm
12. didn't
13. o'clock
14. that's
15. there's

Challenge Words

1. minute
2. stretch
3. instead
4. ninety
5. divide

My Study List

Add your own spelling words on the back. ➡

Akiak

The /ă/, /ā/, /ĕ/, and /ē/ Sounds

/ă/ ➡ p**a**st
/ā/ ➡ s**a**fe, g**ai**n, gr**ay**
/ĕ/ ➡ k**e**pt
/ē/ ➡ r**ea**ch, sw**ee**t

Spelling Words

1. gain
2. cream
3. sweet
4. safe
5. past
6. reach
7. kept
8. gray
9. field
10. break
11. east
12. shape
13. steep
14. pray
15. pain
16. glass
17. west
18. cheap
19. steak
20. chief

Challenge Words

1. graceful
2. descent
3. athletic
4. knead
5. activity

My Study List

Add your own spelling words on the back. ➡

Name _____

 My Study List

1. _____
2. _____
3. _____
4. _____
5. _____
6. _____
7. _____
8. _____
9. _____
10. _____

Review Words

1. need
2. last
3. stage
4. left
5. paint

How to Study a Word

Look at the word.
Say the word.
Think about the word.
Write the word.
Check the spelling.

Name _____

 My Study List

1. _____
2. _____
3. _____
4. _____
5. _____
6. _____
7. _____
8. _____
9. _____
10. _____

How to Study a Word

Look at the word.
Say the word.
Think about the word.
Write the word.
Check the spelling.

Name _____

My Study List

1. _____
2. _____
3. _____
4. _____
5. _____
6. _____
7. _____
8. _____
9. _____
10. _____

Review Words

1. drop
2. mix
3. smoke
4. sight
5. know

How to Study a Word

Look at the word.
Say the word.
Think about the word.
Write the word.
Check the spelling.

Journeys
Spelling Review

Spelling Words

1. safe	16. few
2. kept	17. trunk
3. gray	18. steal
4. grown	19. weight
5. wrote	20. meat
6. blind	21. past
7. suit	22. reach
8. crumb	23. coast
9. wait	24. odd
10. creak	25. sigh
11. steep	26. true
12. gain	27. tube
13. still	28. steel
14. gold	29. creek
15. crime	30. meet

See the back for Challenge Words.

My Study List
Add your own spelling words on the back. ➡

By the Shores of Silver Lake

> **Homophones**
> **Homophones** are words that sound alike but have different spellings and meanings.

Spelling Words

1. steel	11. beet
2. steal	12. beat
3. lead	13. meet
4. led	14. meat
5. wait	15. peek
6. weight	16. peak
7. wear	17. deer
8. ware	18. dear
9. creak	19. ring
10. creek	20. wring

Challenge Words

1. pour
2. pore
3. vain
4. vein
5. vane

My Study List
Add your own spelling words on the back. ➡

Finding the *Titanic*

> **The /ŭ/, /yo͞o/, and /o͞o/ Sounds**
> /ŭ/ ➡ brush
> /yo͞o/ ➡ **tube, few,**
> and /o͞o/ **true, juice**

Spelling Words

1. brush	11. suit
2. juice	12. pump
3. fruit	13. due
4. tube	14. dull
5. lunch	15. tune
6. crumb	16. blew
7. few	17. trunk
8. true	18. sum
9. truth	19. glue
10. done	20. threw

Challenge Words

1. newscast
2. commute
3. continue
4. attitude
5. slumber

My Study List
Add your own spelling words on the back. ➡

Name _____

 My Study List

1. _____
2. _____
3. _____
4. _____
5. _____
6. _____
7. _____
8. _____
9. _____
10. _____

Review Words

1. chew
2. blue
3. rub
4. shut
5. June

How to Study a Word

Look at the word.
Say the word.
Think about the word.
Write the word.
Check the spelling.

Name _____

 My Study List

1. _____
2. _____
3. _____
4. _____
5. _____
6. _____
7. _____
8. _____
9. _____
10. _____

Review Words

1. its
2. it's
3. there
4. their
5. they're

How to Study a Word

Look at the word.
Say the word.
Think about the word.
Write the word.
Check the spelling.

Name _____

 My Study List

1. _____
2. _____
3. _____
4. _____
5. _____
6. _____
7. _____
8. _____
9. _____
10. _____

Challenge Words

1. descent
2. graceful
3. rigid
4. newscast
5. knead
6. remind
7. continue
8. pour
9. slumber
10. pore

How to Study a Word

Look at the word.
Say the word.
Think about the word.
Write the word.
Check the spelling.

Tanya's Reunion

The /o͞o/ and /o͝o/ Sounds

/o͞o/ ➡ t**oo**l
/o͝o/ ➡ w**oo**d, p**u**t

Spelling Words

1. wood
2. brook
3. tool
4. put
5. wool
6. push
7. full
8. roof
9. group
10. prove
11. stood
12. stool
13. hook
14. smooth
15. shoot
16. bush
17. fool
18. pull
19. soup
20. move

Challenge Words

1. soot
2. marooned
3. pudding
4. cocoon
5. superb

My Study List
Add your own spelling words on the back. ➡

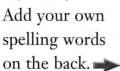

American Stories
Reading-Writing Workshop

Look for familiar spelling patterns in these words to help you remember their spellings.

Spelling Words

1. a lot
2. other
3. another
4. anyone
5. every
6. someone
7. myself
8. family
9. friend
10. people
11. again
12. anything
13. anyway
14. everyone
15. first

Challenge Words

1. beautiful
2. clothes
3. cousin
4. everybody
5. weird

My Study List
Add your own spelling words on the back. ➡

Tomás and the Library Lady

The /ou/ and /ô/ Sounds

/ou/ ➡ h**ow**l, p**ou**nd
/ô/ ➡ j**aw**, c**au**se, **a**lways

Spelling Words

1. pound
2. howl
3. jaw
4. bounce
5. cause
6. always
7. shout
8. aloud
9. south
10. couple
11. drawn
12. scout
13. false
14. proud
15. frown
16. sauce
17. gown
18. couch
19. dawn
20. mount

Challenge Words

1. gnaw
2. prowl
3. pounce
4. doubt
5. scrawny

My Study List
Add your own spelling words on the back. ➡

Take-Home Word List

Name _____

 My Study List

1. _____
2. _____
3. _____
4. _____
5. _____
6. _____
7. _____
8. _____
9. _____
10. _____

Review Words

1. walk
2. lawn
3. loud
4. sound
5. clown

How to Study a Word

Look at the word.
Say the word.
Think about the word.
Write the word.
Check the spelling.

Take-Home Word List

Name _____

 My Study List

1. _____
2. _____
3. _____
4. _____
5. _____
6. _____
7. _____
8. _____
9. _____
10. _____

How to Study a Word

Look at the word.
Say the word.
Think about the word.
Write the word.
Check the spelling.

Take-Home Word List

Name _____

My Study List

1. _____
2. _____
3. _____
4. _____
5. _____
6. _____
7. _____
8. _____
9. _____
10. _____

Review Words

1. cook
2. spoon
3. shook
4. school
5. tooth

How to Study a Word

Look at the word.
Say the word.
Think about the word.
Write the word.
Check the spelling.

American Stories
Spelling Review

Spelling Words

1. howl	16. year
2. false	17. alarm
3. sauce	18. horse
4. put	19. curl
5. roof	20. return
6. hardly	21. jaw
7. dairy	22. dawn
8. charge	23. tool
9. dirty	24. full
10. world	25. gear
11. bounce	26. spare
12. couch	27. cheer
13. wood	28. chore
14. push	29. heard
15. pull	30. search

**See the back for
Challenge Words.**

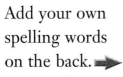

My Study List
Add your own
spelling words
on the back. ➡

415

A Very Important Day

> **The /ôr/, /ûr/, and /yŏor/ Sounds**
> /ôr/ ➡ h**or**se, ch**ore**
> /ûr/ ➡ f**ir**m, c**ur**ve,
> l**ear**n, w**or**m
> /yŏor/ ➡ p**ure**

Spelling Words

1. horse	11. heard
2. chore	12. return
3. firm	13. cure
4. learn	14. score
5. dirty	15. worm
6. curve	16. thirteen
7. world	17. worn
8. pure	18. curl
9. board	19. shirt
10. course	20. search

Challenge Words
1. thoroughbred
2. fortunate
3. hurdle
4. foreign
5. earnest

My Study List
Add your own
spelling words
on the back. ➡

415

Boss of the Plains

> **The /îr/, /är/, and /âr/ Sounds**
> /îr/ ➡ g**ear**, ch**eer**
> /är/ ➡ sh**ar**p
> /âr/ ➡ st**are**, h**air**y

Spelling Words

1. gear	11. starve
2. spear	12. charm
3. sharp	13. beard
4. stare	14. hardly
5. alarm	15. spare
6. cheer	16. stairs
7. square	17. year
8. hairy	18. charge
9. heart	19. dairy
10. weird	20. scarce

Challenge Words
1. pioneer
2. awareness
3. startle
4. marvel
5. weary

My Study List
Add your own
spelling words
on the back. ➡

415

Take-Home Word List

Name _____

 My Study List

1. _____
2. _____
3. _____
4. _____
5. _____
6. _____
7. _____
8. _____
9. _____
10. _____

Review Words

1. air
2. near
3. large
4. scare
5. chair

How to Study a Word

Look at the word.
Say the word.
Think about the word.
Write the word.
Check the spelling.

Take-Home Word List

Name _____

 My Study List

1. _____
2. _____
3. _____
4. _____
5. _____
6. _____
7. _____
8. _____
9. _____
10. _____

Review Words

1. first
2. hurt
3. work
4. third
5. storm

How to Study a Word

Look at the word.
Say the word.
Think about the word.
Write the word.
Check the spelling.

Take-Home Word List

Name _____

My Study List

1. _____
2. _____
3. _____
4. _____
5. _____
6. _____
7. _____
8. _____
9. _____
10. _____

Challenge Words

1. pounce
2. pudding
3. cocoon
4. awareness
5. fortunate
6. scrawny
7. marooned
8. pioneer
9. marvel
10. earnest

How to Study a Word

Look at the word.
Say the word.
Think about the word.
Write the word.
Check the spelling.

Cendrillon

Final /ər/, /l/, or /əl/

/ər/ → weath**er**, harb**or**, sug**ar**

/l/ → mod**el**, fin**al**, or /əl/ midd**le**

Spelling Words

1. harbor
2. final
3. middle
4. weather
5. labor
6. model
7. chapter
8. special
9. sugar
10. bottle
11. medal
12. collar
13. proper
14. towel
15. beggar
16. battle
17. trouble
18. shower
19. uncle
20. doctor

Challenge Words

1. shoulder
2. decimal
3. trifle
4. solar
5. cancel

My Study List
Add your own spelling words on the back. ➡

417

That's Amazing!
Reading-Writing Workshop

Look for familiar spelling patterns in these words to help you remember their spellings.

Spelling Words

1. tonight
2. whole
3. while
4. could
5. world
6. writing
7. build
8. school
9. finished
10. morning
11. coming
12. stopped
13. getting
14. goes
15. going

Challenge Words

1. happened
2. received
3. believe
4. quit
5. quite

My Study List
Add your own spelling words on the back. ➡

417

The Stranger

Compound Words
A compound word may be written as one word, as two words joined by a hyphen, or as two separate words.

Spelling Words

1. railroad
2. airport
3. seat belt
4. everywhere
5. homesick
6. understand
7. background
8. anything
9. ninety-nine
10. already
11. fireplace
12. ourselves
13. all right
14. forever
15. breakfast
16. whenever
17. everything
18. meanwhile
19. afternoon
20. make-believe

Challenge Words

1. landmark
2. nationwide
3. postscript
4. motorcycle
5. handkerchief

My Study List
Add your own spelling words on the back. ➡

417

Take-Home Word List

Name _____

 My Study List

1. _____
2. _____
3. _____
4. _____
5. _____
6. _____
7. _____
8. _____
9. _____
10. _____

Review Words

1. inside
2. outside
3. birthday
4. baseball
5. sometimes

How to Study a Word

Look at the word.
Say the word.
Think about the word.
Write the word.
Check the spelling.

Take-Home Word List

Name _____

My Study List

1. _____
2. _____
3. _____
4. _____
5. _____
6. _____
7. _____
8. _____
9. _____
10. _____

How to Study a Word

Look at the word.
Say the word.
Think about the word.
Write the word.
Check the spelling.

Take-Home Word List

Name _____

 My Study List

1. _____
2. _____
3. _____
4. _____
5. _____
6. _____
7. _____
8. _____
9. _____
10. _____

Review Words

1. neighbor
2. little
3. dollar
4. daughter
5. circle

How to Study a Word

Look at the word.
Say the word.
Think about the word.
Write the word.
Check the spelling.

My Name Is María Isabel

The /k/, /ng/, and /kw/ Sounds
/k/ ➡ shar**k**, atta**ck**, publi**c**
/ng/ ➡ si**n**k
/kw/ ➡ **qu**estion

Spelling Words

1. shark
2. attack
3. risk
4. public
5. sink
6. question
7. electric
8. jacket
9. blank
10. ache
11. crooked
12. drink
13. topic
14. track
15. blanket
16. struck
17. mistake
18. junk
19. squirrel
20. stomach

Challenge Words

1. aquatic
2. comic
3. tropical
4. speckled
5. peculiar

My Study List
Add your own spelling words on the back. ➡

That's Amazing!
Spelling Review

Spelling Words

1. railroad
2. homesick
3. anything
4. seat belt
5. battle
6. beggar
7. doctor
8. smelling
9. pleasing
10. dimmed
11. airport
12. understand
13. ninety-nine
14. final
15. trouble
16. towel
17. medal
18. striped
19. skipped
20. checking
21. all right
22. make-believe
23. whenever
24. proper
25. uncle
26. weather
27. raced
28. snapping
29. hiking
30. fainted

See the back for Challenge Words.

My Study List
Add your own spelling words on the back. ➡

Heat Wave!

Words with -ed or -ing
race + **ed** = rac**ed**
land + **ed** = land**ed**
snap + **ing** = sna**pping**

Spelling Words

1. dancing
2. skipped
3. hiking
4. flipped
5. snapping
6. raced
7. landed
8. pleasing
9. checking
10. dared
11. dimmed
12. rubbing
13. striped
14. wasting
15. traced
16. stripped
17. tanning
18. smelling
19. phoning
20. fainted

Challenge Words

1. breathing
2. tiring
3. urged
4. scrubbed
5. striving

My Study List
Add your own spelling words on the back. ➡

Name _____

 My Study List

1. _____
2. _____
3. _____
4. _____
5. _____
6. _____
7. _____
8. _____
9. _____
10. _____

Review Words

1. cared
2. joking
3. tapping
4. wrapped
5. fixing

How to Study a Word

Look at the word.
Say the word.
Think about the word.
Write the word.
Check the spelling.

Name _____

 My Study List

1. _____
2. _____
3. _____
4. _____
5. _____
6. _____
7. _____
8. _____
9. _____
10. _____

Challenge Words

1. handkerchief   6. postscript
2. motorcycle   7. shoulder
3. decimal   8. cancel
4. scrubbed   9. breathing
5. striving   10. urged

How to Study a Word

Look at the word.
Say the word.
Think about the word.
Write the word.
Check the spelling.

Name _____

 My Study List

1. _____
2. _____
3. _____
4. _____
5. _____
6. _____
7. _____
8. _____
9. _____
10. _____

Review Words

1. quick
2. luck
3. picnic
4. basket
5. sock

How to Study a Word

Look at the word.
Say the word.
Think about the word.
Write the word.
Check the spelling.

The Last Dragon

Final /j/ and /s/
/j/ ➡ bri**dge**, stran**ge**
/ĭj/ ➡ villa**ge**
/s/ ➡ fen**ce**

Spelling Words

1. village
2. cottage
3. bridge
4. fence
5. strange
6. chance
7. twice
8. cage
9. change
10. carriage
11. glance
12. ridge
13. manage
14. damage
15. since
16. marriage
17. edge
18. lodge
19. cabbage
20. dodge

Challenge Words

1. fleece
2. fragrance
3. homage
4. fringe
5. excellence

My Study List
Add your own
spelling words
on the back. ➡

421

Marven of the Great North Woods

Final /ē/
Final /ē/ ➡ beauty, honey

Spelling Words

1. beauty
2. ugly
3. lazy
4. marry
5. ready
6. sorry
7. empty
8. honey
9. valley
10. movie
11. duty
12. hungry
13. lonely
14. alley
15. body
16. twenty
17. turkey
18. hockey
19. fifty
20. monkey

Challenge Words

1. fiery
2. envy
3. mercy
4. chimney
5. imaginary

My Study List
Add your own
spelling words
on the back. ➡

421

Problem Solvers

Reading-Writing Workshop

Look for familiar spelling patterns in these words to help you remember their spellings.

Spelling Words

1. sure
2. here
3. knew
4. might
5. pretty
6. really
7. very
8. where
9. little
10. until
11. into
12. off
13. said
14. our
15. letter

Challenge Words

1. finally
2. different
3. excite
4. truly
5. suppose

My Study List
Add your own
spelling words
on the back. ➡

421

Name _____

 My Study List

1. _____
2. _____
3. _____
4. _____
5. _____
6. _____
7. _____
8. _____
9. _____
10. _____

How to Study a Word

Look at the word.
Say the word.
Think about the word.
Write the word.
Check the spelling.

Name _____

 My Study List

1. _____
2. _____
3. _____
4. _____
5. _____
6. _____
7. _____
8. _____
9. _____
10. _____

Review Words

1. pretty
2. sadly
3. friendly
4. city
5. slowly

How to Study a Word

Look at the word.
Say the word.
Think about the word.
Write the word.
Check the spelling.

Name _____

My Study List

1. _____
2. _____
3. _____
4. _____
5. _____
6. _____
7. _____
8. _____
9. _____
10. _____

Review Words

1. nice
2. place
3. huge
4. judge
5. page

How to Study a Word

Look at the word.
Say the word.
Think about the word.
Write the word.
Check the spelling.

Happy Birthday, Dr. King!

Words with a Prefix or a Suffix

re + paint	= **re**paint
dis + like	= **dis**like
un + lucky	= **un**lucky
un + pack	= **un**pack

sick**ness**   treat**ment**

beauti**ful**   care**less**

Spelling Words

1. redo
2. treatment
3. rebuild
4. discolor
5. careless
6. dislike
7. sickness
8. beautiful
9. unlucky
10. awful
11. reread
12. unsure
13. movement
14. peaceful
15. unpaid
16. distrust
17. kindness
18. useless
19. displease
20. powerful

Challenge Words

1. unusual
2. rearrange
3. appointment
4. discontinue
5. resourceful

My Study List
Add your own spelling words on the back. ➡

Problem Solvers
Spelling Review

Spelling Words

1. sink
2. squirrel
3. question
4. twenty
5. alley
6. twice
7. chance
8. glance
9. thirty
10. afraid
11. blanket
12. crooked
13. honey
14. monkey
15. ready
16. cottage
17. since
18. other
19. corner
20. office
21. mistake
22. attack
23. lonely
24. beauty
25. strange
26. ridge
27. village
28. suppose
29. degree
30. whether

See the back for Challenge Words.

My Study List
Add your own spelling words on the back. ➡

Sing to the Stars

VCCV Pattern

VC | CV :	**dan|ger,**
	at|tend,
	din|ner
V | CCV :	**a|fraid**
VCC | V :	**rock|et**

Spelling Words

1. bottom
2. picture
3. other
4. attend
5. capture
6. common
7. danger
8. afraid
9. borrow
10. office
11. arrow
12. suppose
13. escape
14. whether
15. pillow
16. dinner
17. thirty
18. degree
19. allow
20. corner

Challenge Words

1. method
2. concert
3. narrate
4. abrupt
5. challenge

My Study List
Add your own spelling words on the back. ➡

Name _____

 My Study List

1. _____
2. _____
3. _____
4. _____
5. _____
6. _____
7. _____
8. _____
9. _____
10. _____

Review Words

1. between
2. lesson
3. enjoy
4. happen
5. teacher

How to Study a Word

Look at the word.
Say the word.
Think about the word.
Write the word.
Check the spelling.

Name _____

 My Study List

1. _____
2. _____
3. _____
4. _____
5. _____
6. _____
7. _____
8. _____
9. _____
10. _____

Challenge Words

1. comic
2. aquatic
3. imaginary
4. homage
5. concert
6. tropical
7. chimney
8. fiery
9. fleece
10. narrate

How to Study a Word

Look at the word.
Say the word.
Think about the word.
Write the word.
Check the spelling.

Name _____

 My Study List

1. _____
2. _____
3. _____
4. _____
5. _____
6. _____
7. _____
8. _____
9. _____
10. _____

Review Words

1. hopeful
2. remake
3. rewrite
4. useful
5. unfair

How to Study a Word

Look at the word.
Say the word.
Think about the word.
Write the word.
Check the spelling.

Lou Gehrig

VCV Pattern

V | CV :   **pi | lot,**
        mo | ment
VC | V :   **vis | it,**
        par | ent

Spelling Words

1. pilot
2. depend
3. visit
4. human
5. seven
6. chosen
7. paper
8. reason
9. become
10. parent
11. never
12. modern
13. tiny
14. tuna
15. event
16. fever
17. moment
18. prison
19. basic
20. open

Challenge Words

1. alert
2. license
3. select
4. radar
5. feature

My Study List
Add your own
spelling words
on the back. ➡

425

Gloria Estefan

Changing Final *y* to *i*

city   + es   = cit**ies**
study + ed   = stud**ied**
sunny + er   = sunn**ier**
heavy + est = heav**iest**

Spelling Words

1. sunnier
2. cloudier
3. windier
4. cities
5. heaviest
6. prettiest
7. studied
8. easier
9. noisier
10. families
11. ferries
12. crazier
13. funnier
14. earlier
15. copied
16. hobbies
17. angriest
18. emptied
19. worried
20. happiest

Challenge Words

1. iciest
2. hazier
3. breezier
4. companies
5. qualities

My Study List
Add your own
spelling words
on the back. ➡

425

Heroes
Reading-Writing Workshop

Look for familiar spelling patterns in these words to help you remember their spellings.

Spelling Words

1. brought
2. enough
3. buy
4. guess
5. Saturday
6. January
7. February
8. favorite
9. lying
10. tying
11. around
12. swimming
13. heard
14. also
15. tried

Challenge Words

1. choose
2. chose
3. loose
4. lose
5. millimeter

My Study List
Add your own
spelling words
on the back. ➡

425

Name _____

 My Study List

1. _____
2. _____
3. _____
4. _____
5. _____
6. _____
7. _____
8. _____
9. _____
10. _____

How to Study a Word

Look at the word.
Say the word.
Think about the word.
Write the word.
Check the spelling.

Name _____

 My Study List

1. _____
2. _____
3. _____
4. _____
5. _____
6. _____
7. _____
8. _____
9. _____
10. _____

Review Words

1. hurried
2. stories
3. carried
4. pennies
5. babies

How to Study a Word

Look at the word.
Say the word.
Think about the word.
Write the word.
Check the spelling.

Name _____

My Study List

1. _____
2. _____
3. _____
4. _____
5. _____
6. _____
7. _____
8. _____
9. _____
10. _____

Review Words

1. before
2. travel
3. orange
4. ever
5. begin

How to Study a Word

Look at the word.
Say the word.
Think about the word.
Write the word.
Check the spelling.

Nature: Friend and Foe
Reading-Writing
Workshop

Look for familiar spelling patterns in these words to help you remember their spellings.

Spelling Words

1. their
2. there
3. they're
4. your
5. you're
6. its
7. it's
8. to
9. too
10. two
11. they
12. than
13. then
14. right
15. write

Challenge Words

1. all right
2. usually
3. eighth
4. height
5. tongue

My Study List
Add your own spelling words on the back. ➡

Salmon Summer

> **Three-Syllable Words**
> yes | ter | day ➡
> /yĕs′ tər dā/
> de | liv | er ➡
> /dĭ lĭv′ ər/

Spelling Words

1. deliver
2. favorite
3. camera
4. yesterday
5. tomorrow
6. important
7. together
8. victory
9. remember
10. library
11. enemy
12. animal
13. another
14. however
15. banana
16. alphabet
17. hospital
18. hamburger
19. carpenter
20. several

Challenge Words

1. interview
2. article
3. halibut
4. edition
5. photograph

My Study List
Add your own spelling words on the back. ➡

Heroes
Spelling Review

Spelling Words

1. redo
2. unsure
3. useless
4. kindness
5. easier
6. copied
7. crazier
8. seven
9. become
10. fever
11. dislike
12. movement
13. displease
14. cities
15. families
16. worried
17. angriest
18. paper
19. parent
20. prison
21. reread
22. peaceful
23. powerful
24. studied
25. earlier
26. happiest
27. visit
28. reason
29. never
30. tuna

See the back for Challenge Words.

My Study List
Add your own spelling words on the back. ➡

Name _____

 My Study List

1. _____
2. _____
3. _____
4. _____
5. _____
6. _____
7. _____
8. _____
9. _____
10. _____

Challenge Words

1. unusual
2. resourceful
3. breezier
4. select
5. radar
6. discontinue
7. companies
8. iciest
9. alert
10. license

How to Study a Word

Look at the word.
Say the word.
Think about the word.
Write the word.
Check the spelling.

Name _____

My Study List

1. _____
2. _____
3. _____
4. _____
5. _____
6. _____
7. _____
8. _____
9. _____
10. _____

Review Words

1. grandmother
2. grandfather
3. October
4. November
5. unhappy

How to Study a Word

Look at the word.
Say the word.
Think about the word.
Write the word.
Check the spelling.

Name _____

My Study List

1. _____
2. _____
3. _____
4. _____
5. _____
6. _____
7. _____
8. _____
9. _____
10. _____

How to Study a Word

Look at the word.
Say the word.
Think about the word.
Write the word.
Check the spelling.

Nature: Friend and Foe
Spelling Review

Spelling Words

1. favorite
2. camera
3. banana
4. remember
5. neither
6. against
7. wonder
8. climb
9. thumb
10. calf
11. animal
12. however
13. alphabet
14. health
15. guard
16. blood
17. women
18. listen
19. honor
20. kneel
21. another
22. library
23. deliver
24. says
25. gasoline
26. style
27. soften
28. wrist
29. handsome
30. knight

See the back for Challenge Words.

Skylark

Silent Consonants
Some words have a consonant that is not pronounced.
kneel   clim**b**   cal**f**
wrinkle   **h**onest

Spelling Words

1. knight
2. soften
3. honor
4. kneel
5. climb
6. wrinkle
7. limb
8. handsome
9. answer
10. calf
11. listen
12. calm
13. knit
14. often
15. palm
16. thumb
17. wrist
18. lamb
19. knob
20. honest

Challenge Words

1. drought
2. knoll
3. heir
4. debt
5. wrestle

Wildfires

Unusual Spellings
/ĕ/ ➡ h**ea**lth, ag**ai**nst, s**ay**s
/ĭ/ ➡ w**o**men
/ŭ/ ➡ bl**oo**d, m**o**nth
/ē/ ➡ rec**ei**ve, maga**zine**
/ī/ ➡ t**y**pe
/g/ ➡ **gu**ess

Spelling Words

1. health
2. blood
3. type
4. against
5. receive
6. flood
7. month
8. magazine
9. guess
10. women
11. guide
12. style
13. wealth
14. guilt
15. says
16. guard
17. wonder
18. guest
19. gasoline
20. neither

Challenge Words

1. vaccine
2. quarantine
3. guarantee
4. threaten
5. rhyme

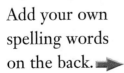

My Study List
Add your own spelling words on the back. ➡

My Study List
Add your own spelling words on the back. ➡

My Study List
Add your own spelling words on the back. ➡

Name _____

 My Study List

1. _____
2. _____
3. _____
4. _____
5. _____
6. _____
7. _____
8. _____
9. _____
10. _____

Review Words

1. front
2. head
3. does
4. shoe
5. gym

How to Study a Word

Look at the word.
Say the word.
Think about the word.
Write the word.
Check the spelling.

Name _____

My Study List

1. _____
2. _____
3. _____
4. _____
5. _____
6. _____
7. _____
8. _____
9. _____
10. _____

Review Words

1. talk
2. knife
3. wrong
4. knock
5. hour

How to Study a Word

Look at the word.
Say the word.
Think about the word.
Write the word.
Check the spelling.

Name _____

My Study List

1. _____
2. _____
3. _____
4. _____
5. _____
6. _____
7. _____
8. _____
9. _____
10. _____

Challenge Words

1. halibut
2. photograph
3. rhyme
4. drought
5. debt
6. edition
7. threaten
8. guarantee
9. heir
10. knoll

How to Study a Word

Look at the word.
Say the word.
Think about the word.
Write the word.
Check the spelling.

Problem Words

Words	Rules	Examples
are our	*Are* is a verb. *Our* is a possessive pronoun.	<u>Are</u> these gloves yours? This is <u>our</u> car.
doesn't don't	Use *doesn't* with singular nouns, *he*, *she*, and *it*. Use *don't* with plural nouns, *I*, *you*, *we*, and *they*.	Dad <u>doesn't</u> swim. We <u>don't</u> swim.
good well	Use the adjective *good* to describe nouns. Use the adverb *well* to describe verbs.	The weather looks <u>good</u>. She sings <u>well</u>.
its it's	*Its* is a possessive pronoun. *It's* is a contraction of *it is*.	The dog wagged <u>its</u> tail. <u>It's</u> cold today.
set sit	*Set* means "to put." *Sit* means "to rest or stay in one place."	<u>Set</u> the vase on the table. Please <u>sit</u> in this chair.
their there they're	*Their* means "belonging to them." *There* means "at or in that place." *They're* is a contraction of *they are*.	<u>Their</u> coats are on the bed. Is Carlos <u>there</u>? <u>They're</u> going to the store.
two to too	*Two* is a number *To* means "toward." *Too* means "also" or "more than enough."	I bought <u>two</u> shirts. A cat ran <u>to</u> the tree. Can we go <u>too</u>? I ate <u>too</u> many peas.
your you're	*Your* is a possessive pronoun. *You're* is a contraction of *you are*.	Are these <u>your</u> glasses? <u>You're</u> late again!

Read each question below. Then check your paper. Correct any mistakes you find. After you have corrected them, put a check mark in the box next to the question.

☐ 1. Did I indent each paragraph?

☐ 2. Does each sentence tell one complete thought?

☐ 3. Do I have any run-on sentences?

☐ 4. Did I spell all words correctly?

☐ 5. Did I use capital letters correctly?

☐ 6. Did I use punctuation marks correctly?

☐ 7. Did I use commas and apostrophes correctly?

☐ 8. Did I spell all the words the right way?

Is there anything else you should look for? Make your own proofreading checklist.

☐ _____

☐ _____

☐ _____

☐ _____

☐ _____

☐ _____

☐ _____

Proofreading Marks

Mark	Explanation	Examples
¶	Begin a new paragraph. Indent the paragraph.	¶We went to an air show last Saturday. Eight jets flew across the sky in the shape of V's, X's, and diamonds.
∧	Add letters, words, or sentences.	The leaves were red ^and^ orange.
⌀	Take out words, sentences, and punctuation marks. Correct spelling.	The sky is bright ~~blew~~ blue. Huge clouds, move quickly.
/	Change a capital letter to a small letter.	The Fireflies blinked in the dark.
≡	Change a small letter to a capital letter.	New York city is exciting.

My Notes